SIMPLY BRITISH

ALSO BY SYBIL KAPOOR

Modern British Food

Sybil Kapoor

SIMPLY
BRITISH

MICHAEL JOSEPH
LONDON

MICHAEL JOSEPH LTD
Published by the Penguin Group
27 Wrights Lane, London w8 5TZ
Viking Penguin Inc., 375 Hudson Street, New York, New York 10014, USA
Penguin Books Australia Ltd, Ringwood, Victoria, Australia
Penguin Books Canada Ltd, 10 Alcorn Avenue, Toronto, Ontario, Canada M4V 3B2
Penguin Books (NZ) Ltd, 182–190 Wairau Road, Auckland 10, New Zealand

Penguin Books Ltd, Registered Offices: Harmondsworth, Middlesex, England

First published in Great Britain 1998
Copyright © Sybil Kapoor 1998
Illustrations copyright © John Spencer 1998
1 3 5 7 9 10 8 6 4 2

Set in 10¾/13¾pt Monotype Sabon
Typeset by Rowland Phototypesetting Ltd, Bury St Edmunds, Suffolk
Printed in England by Clays Ltd, St Ives plc

A CIP catalogue record for this book is available from the British Library

ISBN 0 7181 4149 0

The moral right of the author has been asserted

For Raju, with love

CONTENTS

ACKNOWLEDGEMENTS

I would like to thank Louise Haines, my editor, whose sound editorial advice has made the writing of this book a pleasure. I would also like to thank Christabel Gairdner, Lindsey Jordan, Annie Lee, Nicola Stanley and John Hamilton for all their kind words and hard work. Of the many other people who have generously helped, I would particularly like to thank my parents, Helen and Frederick Polhill, and my brother and his wife, Julian and Claire Polhill, who between them have dug up vegetables and answered peculiar questions whenever I called. Nigel Slater, Lynda Brown, Joanna Blythman, Michael Raffael, Anne Dolamore, Clarissa Dickson Wright and Linda Tubby are among the many other people who have my whole-hearted thanks for answering questions on everything from green geese to mushy peas. I must also thank everyone at Books for Cooks, and Janet Clarke who lent me her own copy of *The Cultivated Fruits of Britain* by F. A. Roach when none could be had. Fleur Olby, John Spencer and Marks & Spencer (who supplied the rhubarb) also have my sincere thanks for making this a beautiful book. Lastly, but most importantly, I would like to thank my husband for all his love and support while I was writing this book.

I should also like to thank all the authors and publishers who have kindly given me permission to quote from their books and use their recipes. These include *Cold Comfort Farm* copyright © Stella Gibbons 1932, *Not That it Matters* copyright © A. A. Milne, 1919, both reproduced by permission of Curtis Brown, London; *The Collected Essays, Journalism and Letters of George Orwell*, published by Secker & Warburg, copyright © George Orwell 1945, reproduced with the kind permission of Mark Hamilton as the Literary Executor of the Estate of the late Sonia Brownell Orwell and Martin Secker & Warburg Ltd; *Very Good, Jeeves* by P. G. Wodehouse (Hutchinson); *Cider with Rosie* by Laurie Lee (Hogarth Press); *The Gentle Art of Cookery* by Mrs C. F. Leyel and Miss Olga Hartley (Chatto & Windus); *The Anatomy of Dessert* by Edward Bunyard (Chatto & Windus); *The Diary of Virginia Woolf* (Hogarth Press), reproduced by permission of the Executors of the Estate; *Food in England* by Dorothy Hartley (Little, Brown & Co (UK)); 'Bustopher Jones: The Cat about Town', *Old Possum's Book of Practical*

Cats by T. S. Eliot (Faber and Faber Ltd); *Spices, Salt and Aromatics in the English Kitchen* by Elizabeth David (Penguin Books, 1970) copyright © Elizabeth David, 1970; *The Constance Spry Cookery Book* by Constance Spry and Rosemary Hume (J. M. Dent); *Four Seasons Cookery Book* by Margaret Costa (Grub Street); *English Puddings Sweet & Savoury* by Mary Norwak (Grub Street); *Cassell's Dictionary of Cookery* (Cassell & Company Ltd, 1899).

Every effort has been made to trace copyright holders of material in this book. The publishers apologize if any material has been included without permission and would be glad to be told of anyone who has not been consulted.

INTRODUCTION

Every author who writes about cookery in the English language and for English readers is, by implication, writing about English cookery. If he is not, then he might as well write his book in Chinese or Armenian.

Spices, Salt and Aromatics in the English Kitchen by Elizabeth David, 1970

The publication of my first book, *Modern British Food*, forcefully revealed to me how very opinionated we all are about what constitutes British food. Friends took me aside to question how I could possibly include curry or pizza in a book on British cooking; surely, they argued, these are Indian or Italian dishes. In their minds Lancashire hot pot or roast beef were typically British, and other more obviously foreign dishes had no part in our national cuisine, modern or not. Yet even they could not give a clear definition as to what makes British food British. Others questioned the value of writing about British food at all, since in their opinion, our indigenous food is so intrinsically bad as to be unworthy of special attention. In my opinion there is only one thing that unifies and defines British cooking and that is its ingredients. This book is an attempt to try to place these in context. I hope it will bring as much pleasure to the reader as it has given me in the writing.

It seemed to me that the majority of people categorize their national food in a very simple way, not by dishes or culinary techniques, but by ingredients. Bacon, oats, raspberries and honey, for example, immediately suggest British food, just as basil, tomatoes, olive oil, Parmesan and pasta recall Italian dishes. This does not mean that we do not use pasta or that the Italians do not use honey, merely that such ingredients do not conform to our national sense of culinary identity. So important are many of these key ingredients that they live in our common imagination and references to them are scattered throughout our literature, from the symbolic Welsh leek to the Arcadian strawberry. As a nation we will crave crisp bacon when travelling abroad and long for a homely dish of blackberry crumble in times of stress. The key to understanding British food appears to lie in identifying these particular ingredients.

So I set about making lists of what I considered to be typically British foods. Not an easy task, for although there was no question that national oddities such as gooseberries, kippers and elderflowers should be included, many other foods raised serious questions as to why they were considered intrinsically British. Apples, for example, are eaten all over the world, yet we consider them our own. The first phrase that every British child learns at school is 'A is for Apple'. These are difficult questions, not easily answered in a simple cookbook, as they raise the issue of our relationship with food, both historically and symbolically. Our obsession with beef in the eighteenth century, for example, when it was adopted as a national symbol of independence, lives on despite the fact that our consumption of beef has been steadily falling for years, long before the arrival of BSE. I believe that in our increasingly urban society we impart to many of our favourite ingredients a wide variety of cultural myths and symbols. Dipping the spoon into a jar of thick honey, for instance, can evoke idyllic images of the countryside, just as biting into some deliciously buttery potted shrimp on hot toast can allow one momentarily to experience the sea. Such sensations are brief, almost unconscious, but together they create a separate secret image of Britain.

Naturally, any selection of ingredients will be a personal interpretation of British food. By default my beliefs will be shaped by my age and cultural background. Nevertheless, there are strong common strands or tastes that when woven together make up the British palate. The most obvious is our love of pure fresh flavours, such as strawberry, cucumber or watercress. These are foods that are perfect in their own right and need little attention from the cook. A bowl of strawberries, sprinkled with sugar and eaten with cream, is still considered food fit for the gods, just as is fresh watercress, dressed only with the buttery juices of roast quail. Prepared well these simple flavours are never dull. Yet we also adore piquant foods, from spicy pickles to salted and smoked ingredients like bacon, kippers or smoked haddock. Such flavours can be used to stimulate the appetite and enhance the sweet freshness of our plainer dishes. I suspect that such tastes were developed because we were a northern country heavily dependent on preserved foods during the winter months. Perhaps our susceptibility to the ever-changing weather also accounts for our predilection for fragrant foods. Few nations are so addicted to preserving the scent and flavour of spring, summer or autumn through their use of herbs, flowers and wild fruits. A delicate custard infused with elderflowers evokes early summer, while a hot scone, spread with blackberry jelly, tastes of autumn. We use our food to express the seasons in a subtle but truly sublime way.

As I researched each chosen ingredient I was fascinated to discover the links between the present and the past. The same combinations occur again and again over the centuries, subtly amended in favour of the latest fashion. Thus, in *The Accomplisht Cook* in 1685 Robert May recommends serving watercress in a salad of oranges, lemons, alexander buds, raisins and pears, whereas today it might be served as an accompaniment to pears roasted with Stilton or very simply with oranges and red onions. Our recipes are continually evolving to accommodate the demands of each age. New ingredients and methods are gradually integrated into our so-called *traditional* cooking. The modern British cook is as eager as his or her predecessor to cook greens, but instead of vigorously boiling mature curly kale leaves, he or she will stirfry its tender young leaves with chilli and fresh ginger. The latest introductions, such as succulent pak choi, may still accompany a roast joint, but they are also added to exciting new dishes such as lightly spiced creamy chicken.

Perhaps we have forgotten our rich culinary heritage in the many years of poor cooking, rationing and institutional food that followed two world wars. Surely it is time once more to appreciate the extraordinary sensitivity and imagination that every British cook displays when they set to in the kitchen. Rarely do we acknowledge the utter deliciousness of grilled salmon with mint mayonnaise, for example, or gooseberry tart, roast venison and home-made gingerbread. Nor do we often praise the consummate skill with which British chefs marry the old with the new; leek and lemon grass vichyssoise, sweet-tasting beetroot crisps, grilled prawns with spiced cucumber dressing and greengage yoghurt fool, to name but a few. Such dishes are redefining British cooking.

It is time to renounce our predilection for moaning about our food and to banish our tendency towards culinary self-abasement, for the simple reason that the majority of British cooking is very good indeed, and good because we are not hidebound by old-fashioned culinary traditions. As a nation we are blessed with an unusual open-mindedness to new ideas that allows us to experiment with new and interesting recipes, many of which are far better suited to our modern lives. We are fortunate that we are also able to retain a sense of our nationality by our unerring selection of typically British ingredients. If we continue along our current path, we may surprise ourselves and lead Europe into the next millennium with a new, elegant and very British style of cooking.

CONVERSION TABLES

Weights

7.5g	¼oz	85g	3oz	340g	12oz	1.1kg	2½lb
15g	½oz	90g	3½oz	370g	13oz	1.4kg	3lb
20g	¾oz	115g	4oz	400g	14oz	1.5kg	3½lb
30g	1oz	140g	5oz	425g	15oz	1.8kg	4lb
35g	1¼oz	170g	6oz	455g	1lb	2kg	4½lb
40g	1½oz	200g	7oz	565g	1¼lb	2.3kg	5lb
50g	1¾oz	225g	8oz	680g	1½lb	2.7kg	6lb
55g	2oz	255g	9oz	795g	1¾lb	3.1kg	7lb
65g	2¼oz	285g	10oz	905g	2lb	3.6kg	8lb
70g	2½oz	310g	11oz	1kg	2lb 3oz	4.5kg	10lb
80g	2¾oz						

Oven Temperatures

Very cool	110°C	225°F	Gas ¼
Very cool	130°C	250°F	Gas ½
Cool	140°C	275°F	Gas 1
Slow	150°C	300°F	Gas 2
Moderately slow	170°C	325°F	Gas 3
Moderate	180°C	350°F	Gas 4
Moderately hot	190°C	375°F	Gas 5
Hot	200°C	400°F	Gas 6
Very hot	220°C	425°F	Gas 7
Very hot	230°C	450°F	Gas 8
Hottest	240°C	475°F	Gas 9

Volume

5ml		1 teaspoon	120ml		
10ml		1 dessertspoon	130ml	4.5fl oz	
15ml	0.5fl oz	1 tablespoon	140ml	5fl oz	¼ pint
20ml			155ml	5.5fl oz	
25ml			170ml	6fl oz	
30ml	1fl oz		180ml		
35ml			185ml	6.5fl oz	
40ml	1.5fl oz		200ml	7fl oz	
45ml			215ml	7.5fl oz	
50ml			225ml	8fl oz	
55ml	2fl oz		240ml	8.5fl oz	
60ml			255ml	9fl oz	
70ml	2.5fl oz		270ml	9.5fl oz	
75ml			285ml	10fl oz	½ pint
80ml			400ml	14fl oz	
85ml	3fl oz		425ml	15fl oz	¾ pint
90ml	3.5fl oz		565ml	20fl oz	1 pint
95ml			710ml	25fl oz	1¼ pints
100ml			850ml	30fl oz	1½ pints
105ml			1 litre	35fl oz	1¾ pints
115ml	4fl oz				

APPLES

No fruit is more to our English taste than the Apple. Let the Frenchman have his Pear, the Italian his Fig, the Jamaican may retain his farinaceous Banana, and the Malay his Durian, but for us the Apple.

In a careful pomological study of my fellow-men I have met but one who really disliked apples, but as he was a Scotsman born in Bavaria, educated in England, domiciled in Italy, he is quite obviously ruled out.

The Anatomy of Dessert by Edward Bunyard, 1929

If there is one fruit that the British identify as their own, it is the apple. It is irrelevant to them that apples are grown around the world, and it would be fruitless to argue that foreign-grown varieties can taste as good as home-grown produce, because love is, after all, irrational. The apple has become an intrinsic part of British life and it is no more possible to escape its culinary past than it is to dismiss it as a symbol of knowledge.

Such a passion took root with our Celtic ancestors, who believed that their wild crab apples were imbued with magical powers pertaining to love, fertility and regeneration. Even today the simple act of bobbing for apples or binding them into kissing boughs of evergreen and mistletoe is a continuation of ancient pagan rites. However, the arrival of the domesticated apple, along with the Romans, ensured its establishment as the nation's favourite fruit. After all, which other fruit so perfectly combined those peculiarly British virtues of adaptability, tolerance, productivity and diversity? Who could not love this pretty fruit that thrived on our wet and windy island and suffered none of the suspiciously luscious qualities of Mediterranean fruit? It became a symbol for love, learning, temptation and utopia. Even the Puritans, not known for their culinary good taste, encouraged the tending of orchards for the benefit of body and soul. Embraced by all and sundry, apples were added to an extraordinary diversity of dishes.

Aside from the essential manufacture of cider and apple brandy, apples were pressed into verjuice, a sour liquid not unlike vinegar, which was widely used in medieval cooking. The rich enjoyed elegantly spiced apple-flavoured broths, soups and pies, while commoners relished the delights of baked apples from roving street sellers. By the late thirteenth century demand outstripped supply and large quantities began to be imported from France. The growers, not willing to miss out on a ready market, began to plant popular French varieties, Costards, Blandurels and Ricardons alongside their native Pearmains. It was the beginning of a long cycle of competition between grower and importer.

Countless varieties of apples have been grown in Britain ever since, many of which were developed to meet the demands of the latest culinary fashion, from the jewel-like apple cheeses of the sixteenth century to the smooth sharp apple sauces of the nineteenth century. In a frantic world favourite recipes are continually being updated. Quick-cooking sautés have replaced the old-fashioned French stews of apple and pork, and distilled rose water is added to delicate apple pies instead of layers of rose petals and home-made apple syrup. Even crisp apple charlottes no longer contain thick apple purée; instead they are filled with succulent cubes of apple mixed with cider, dried cherries, blueberries and cranberries.

Practical guide

In Britain apples are divided into three groups: cooking, dual-purpose and dessert. Cooking apples were developed in the nineteenth century as a result of the incredible popularity of apple puddings. A good cooker should be large, flavoursome and acidic. If it lacks acidity its flesh will not cook into the fluffy pulp so essential for apple sauce, apple snow, baked apples *et al.* Bramley's Seedling remains the dominant commercial cooking apple, although enthusiasts can seek out and plant such culinary delights as Golden Noble (considered the best cooking apple by many), Warner's King (ultra-fluffy), Dumelow's Seedling (acidic and perfect for northern gardens) and Keswick Codlin (also suitable for northern gardens).

Dual-purpose apples are mainly used as dessert apples, but because they tend to be very acidic early in the season they can initially be used as cookers. James Grieve and Charles Ross are classic examples.

There is an enormous range of dessert apples available to the modern shopper. Apple aficionados will compartmentalize them according to shape, colour and family, but this holds little charm for most cooks. Be guided by your instincts instead. Choose firm, unbruised apples. Apples with russeting or a rosy blush often indicate a better flavour, as the fruit has been exposed to warm days and cold nights. Experiment by buying different varieties, as they will change week by week during the peak season of September to December.

The supermarkets are reinstating many native varieties alongside an increasingly large range of imported apples. Much remains to be learnt about the optimum picking and storing time for each variety, but here are a few examples currently being sold. Sweet, fresh-flavoured Discovery (August to September) usually starts the British season, followed by Worcester Pearmain (September to October). This is an apple that needs to sit on the tree before picking so that its flavour is deliciously rounded. Nutty-flavoured and rough-skinned Egremont Russet (October to December) follows in time for

Christmas, with the essential Cox's Orange Pippin (October to January). No winter would be complete without the sweet woody taste of Chiver's Delight (November to January) and the aromatic fruit of D'Arcy Spice (January to April).

Gardeners will know that only certain varieties of apple keep well and these need to be carefully stored to last you through the winter months. Arrange them well spaced, on wooden slats or cardboard fruit trays, in a cool, dry place. Discard any that develop bruising and store only hand-picked apples. Windfalls should be cooked immediately – either freeze or make into jams, jellies, fruit cheese, chutneys or mincemeat.

It is important when preparing apples to toss them in some form of acid to prevent them from discolouring. Lemon, orange and lime juice are most favoured, but you can use a vinaigrette or even wine, depending on the recipe. Some writers advocate using water, but I think that this lessens their flavour. If using an apple corer, remember to remove the core before peeling the apple, otherwise your apple may break. If you simply need the apple flesh, peel first then slice down around the core so that you are left with four apple pieces and a square core. Apple parings make a tasty addition to ham stock.

Taste notes

◊ Eating a good dessert apple with cheese is a peculiarly British habit. Apples are regarded by their fans as being akin to wine – they have to be savoured and carefully matched with the right cheese. For example, Blenheim Orange and Chiver's Delight complement Stilton beautifully.

◊ With the exception of apple sauce, dessert apples are mainly used in savoury dishes as they hold their shape when cooked. Their subtle flavour works well with pheasant, guinea fowl and pork. Grated apples, of either denomination, make a lovely addition to stuffings, adding moisture and flavour.

◊ Use dessert apples for puddings where you need the apple to hold its shape, for example, apple fritters, stuffed apple pancakes or apple tarts. Cooking apples are excellent added to ice creams, apple purées, soufflés and the like.

◊ The combination of apples with vegetables is not widely eaten in Britain, although it does occur in a variety of soups and root vegetable purées, namely beetroot, carrot and parsnip. In each case the tart flavour of culinary apples works best. Spicy red cabbage dishes and crunchy salads tend to employ dessert apples for obvious reasons. Celery, cabbage and raw carrot all taste good with the sweeter strains of apple.

◊ Honey, anise, caraway, rose water, cinnamon, cloves and ginger have all been used with apples since medieval times. Dried fruits, including candied peel, have also always been a favourite addition, although latterly dried cranberries, sour cherries and blueberries are becoming increasingly popular.

Spiced parsnip soup

The delicate spicing of apples in soup may seem modern but dates back to the fourteenth century, when apples were cooked in broth with saffron, sugar and ginger. The flavours in this soup develop beautifully if made the day before you need it. It can be served hot or chilled. (Serves 4)

4 tablespoons vegetable oil	2 Bramley cooking apples
1 onion, diced	565ml/1 pint water
2 cloves garlic, diced	salt and freshly ground black
½ teaspoon ground turmeric	pepper
½ teaspoon ground cumin	285ml/½ pint double cream
½ teaspoon chilli powder	2 tablespoons finely sliced
½ teaspoon ground ginger	chives
400g/14oz parsnips	

Heat the oil in a heavy-bottomed saucepan and gently fry the onion and garlic until soft, but not coloured. Add the spices and continue to fry over a low heat for a further minute.

Meanwhile, scrub clean the parsnips before slicing off their tops and tails and peeling them. Cut into small dice and stir into the spiced onions, ensuring that they are well coated in the oil. Cover and cook over a moderately low heat for 5 minutes, stirring regularly to prevent them from catching.

Peel, core and dice the apples. Mix them into the parsnips. Cover and continue to cook for a further 5 minutes, stirring occasionally. Add the water and bring to the boil. Lower the heat, season to taste and simmer for 30 minutes or until the parsnip is meltingly soft. Liquidize and strain the soup, then chill, covered, until you need it.

When you are ready to serve, reheat the soup before adding the cream. Add a little water if you prefer a thinner soup, but once the cream is added do not let the mixture boil or it may split. Sprinkle with the chives and serve piping hot.

Denhay ham and rocket salad with apple cheese

Modern British chefs are increasingly rediscovering all manner of pickles and preserves, but instead of restricting themselves to the traditional uses (see over), they are experimenting with wonderful new combinations. Fruit cheeses, for example, are often served as part of an appetizer with finely sliced dry cured ham, smoked venison or lightly grilled goat's cheese. Alternatively, they can be served with robust-flavoured roast or grilled meat. (Serves 4)

100g/3½oz rocket, trimmed
½ tablespoon champagne or
   white wine vinegar
1½ tablespoons hazelnut oil
salt and freshly ground black
   pepper

225g/8oz apple cheese (see
   over)
12 thin slices Denhay ham

Gently wash the rocket in cold water and spin dry. Whisk the vinegar and hazelnut oil together and season to taste.

Dip a sharp knife into a jug of very hot water and cut the apple cheese into 1cm/½ inch thick rounds. Keeping the knife hot and clean, cut each round into diamonds.

When you are ready to serve, divide the ham between 4 plates. Dress the rocket with the vinaigrette and divide in an attractive manner between the plates, before scattering with the apple cheese diamonds.

Apple cheese

In the sixteenth century Britain became enamoured with the latest Italian craze for a new course which became known as dessert. This consisted of serving exquisite sugared fruit sweetmeats along with beautiful arrangements of fresh fruit. Different coloured fruit pastes or cheeses, as they were called, were arranged in complicated patterns and savoured at the end of a meal. Quince, damson and apple were the most popular, to such a degree that different varieties of apples were grown for their ultimate colour when made into cheese. The custom of serving such sweetmeats at the end of a meal has remained in Britain, damson cheese being served with port while apple cheese is sometimes accompanied by thick cream and fresh hazelnuts.

Fruit cheeses are traditionally potted in straight-sided jars. Their flavour improves with age. They will keep indefinitely in a cool dark place; if you are of a nervous disposition, store them in the fridge. (Makes 850g/1lb 14oz)

850ml/1½ pints cider	1 small stick cinnamon
4 strips finely pared lemon rind	1.4kg/3lb cooking apples
	vegetable oil
4 cloves	granulated sugar

Place the cider, lemon peel, cloves and cinnamon in a non-corrosive saucepan and boil vigorously until the cider has reduced by one third. Roughly chop the apples, pips, skin and all, mix well and simmer for about 1½ hours or until the apples are reduced to a pap.

Wash your jars or moulds and leave to dry in a very low oven. Lightly oil them with vegetable oil and set aside. Push the mushy apples with their juice through a fine sieve. Measure out the purée and allow 340g/12oz sugar to each 565ml/1 pint of apple purée.

Place the sugar and apple pulp in a heavy-bottomed saucepan over a low heat. Stir until the sugar has dissolved, then bring to the boil and continue to cook, stirring all the time, until the mixture is so thick that the spoon leaves a clean line when drawn across the bottom of the pan. This process will take about 25 minutes and as the purée thickens it will turn a beautiful dark amber. It will also spit ferociously, so keep your arms well covered.

Carefully spoon the hot apple cheese into your pots. Press a small waxed disc, waxed side down, on to the cheese and once cold, seal, label and date.

Note: Apple cheese is sometimes confused with apple butter. The only difference between the two is that fruit cheeses are cooked to a firmer consistency than butters, otherwise they are identical.

Sautéed pork with apples and pears

British cooks have collected and reinterpreted French recipes for centuries. The following combination of pork, apples and cider can still be traced back to Normandy, although its current method is firmly rooted in late twentieth-century Britain. (Serves 4)

2 tablespoons runny honey
1 clove garlic, finely chopped
285ml/½ pint dry cider
3 sprigs parsley
2 sprigs rosemary
1 lemon, finely grated
680g/1½lb trimmed pork fillet
3 tablespoons olive oil

Caramelized fruit
2 small apples, for example,
   Cox
½ lemon, juiced
2 small pears, ripe

40g/1½oz butter
3 tablespoons Calvados
15g/½oz unrefined golden
   caster sugar
salt and freshly ground black
   pepper

Gravy
285ml/½ pint chicken stock
   (see page 339 or buy ready
   made)
140ml/¼ pint dry cider
30g/1oz butter

Mix together the honey, garlic, cider, herbs and lemon zest in a bowl. Cut the pork fillet into 1cm/½ inch thick rounds and add to the marinade. Cover and chill for up to an hour.

Peel, quarter and core the apples and pears. Cut into neat, fat slices and toss in the lemon juice.

Melt the butter in a small non-stick frying pan. As soon as it begins to sizzle add the apple and pear slices and fry briskly until they begin to soften and colour. Add the Calvados and set alight – standing well back as the flames shoot up. Vigorously shake the pan and as soon as the flames have gone out sprinkle with the sugar and continue to fry until the fruit is well coloured. Season to taste, remove from the heat and keep warm.

In a separate pan reduce the chicken stock and cider until they taste good. Keep warm while you finish cooking the pork. Remove the pork fillets from their marinade, pat dry and season. Brush with oil and either grill on a ribbed cast-iron oven-top grill or pan-fry over a high heat in a non-stick frying pan. Just before you are ready to serve the pork with the caramelized fruit, quickly whisk the butter into the hot stock and serve separately.

Crab apple jelly

Many small gardens will contain a pretty crab apple tree when they have no room for an ordinary apple tree. This simple, intensely flavoured recipe is one of my favourite preserves and is just as good eaten with game as it is added to fruit pies and cakes. Making jellies has become much easier with the arrival of a special fold-away jelly-bag kit. This consists of a muslin bag and a four-legged plastic stand which you are supposed to clip on to your bowl. The jelly-bag is then suspended from the stand so that it can neatly drip into the bowl. (Makes 455g/1lb)

2kg/4½lb crab apples, for example, Siberian	1.7 litres/3 pints water preserving or granulated sugar

Wash the crab apples and cut into quarters, no matter how small. Place in a non-corrosive saucepan with just enough water to cover the fruit. Bring slowly to the boil, then simmer gently for an hour or until the fruit is pulpy. Remove from the heat and drain through a jelly-bag for 12 hours. Measure the liquid and allow 455g/1lb sugar to every 565ml/1 pint of liquid.

Preheat the oven to low and warm the sugar along with some washed jam-jars.

Pour the juice into a jam pan and clip a thermometer on to the side of the pan. Warm the juice, then add the warm sugar and stir over a low heat until it has dissolved. Increase the heat and boil rapidly until the thermometer registers 105°C/221°F – jam setting point. If you do not have a thermometer, chill a saucer in the fridge before you begin. Allow the jelly to boil for no longer than 10 minutes, then remove from the heat and place a small drop of jelly on to the cold saucer. As soon as it is cool gently push the jelly with your finger; if it wrinkles, setting point has been reached. If not, return the pan to the heat and continue to boil for a further minute or two more.

Once you are satisfied that your jelly has reached setting point, remove from the heat, skim off any scum and pour into your warm jam-jars. Press a small waxed disc, waxed side down, on to the jelly and, once cold, seal, label and date.

Apple charlotte

This is a modern interpretation of a pudding that dates back to the latter part of the eighteenth century. Originally, apple charlotte was made by encasing a thick apple purée in butter-soaked bread in a charlotte mould. It spawned countless other intensely flavoured apple purée and bread based puddings, usually called Charlotte or Brown Betty. As charlotte moulds are not found in the majority of kitchens today, including mine, I usually make this dish in an 850ml/1½ pint pudding basin. The apple filling can be prepared in advance if wished. (Serves 4)

Filling
2 tablespoons dried
   cranberries
2 tablespoons dried sour
   cherries
2 tablespoons dried
   blueberries
200ml/7fl oz cider
4 apples, for example, Charles
   Ross

115g/4oz caster sugar or to
   taste

Charlotte
170g/6oz butter, melted
extra caster sugar
1 good cottage loaf*

Place the dried fruit in a non-corrosive saucepan with the cider and simmer gently for 5 minutes. Peel, core and neatly dice the apples, mixing them in with the cider as you prepare them. Sweeten to taste and simmer for a further 5 minutes. Set aside.

Preheat the oven to 200°C/400°F/gas 6. Brush the pudding basin with some of the melted butter before liberally dusting with caster sugar. Cut out a round slice of bread to fit the bottom of the basin. Dip this in the melted butter and snugly fit in the bowl.

Cut the bread slices into neat, crustless strips or wedges, long enough to fold over the filling. Lightly dip these in butter and line the basin sides, ensuring that there are no gaps. Tightly pack with the apple mixture and fold the bread flaps over the top so that the filling is completely encased.

Bake for 30 minutes or until the bread is crisp and golden. Allow to cool a little before tipping out and serving warm with thick double cream and extra sugar.

*Note: If possible, ask your baker to slice your bread lengthways as this makes it far easier to line the pudding basin.

Apple pie

The late Lord Dudley could not dine comfortably without an apple pie, as he insisted on calling it, contending that the term tart only applied to open pastry. Dining, when Foreign Secretary, at a grand dinner at Prince Esterhazy's, he was terribly put out on finding that his favourite delicacy was wanting, and kept on murmuring pretty audibly, in his absent way: 'God bless my soul! No apple pie.'

Abraham Hayward, Q.C., *The Art of Dining*, 1852

This is a latterday interpretation of Florence White's recipe in *Good Things in England* (1932). She covered her apples with a fragrant layer of old-fashioned cottage rose petals before moistening them with a syrup made from simmered apple trimmings. (Serves 4)

225g/8oz chilled puff pastry (see page 338)	2 tablespoons rose water or to taste
905g/2lb cooking apples	3 tablespoons water
115g/4oz granulated sugar or to taste ·	½ egg white, beaten
	1 tablespoon granulated sugar

Preheat the oven to 220°C/425°F/gas 7. Roll out the pastry on a lightly floured surface to roughly the same shape as your pie dish only larger. Cut a ribbon from the edge of the dough and press it firmly on to the rim of the pie dish.

Wash the apples and remove any blemishes before peeling. Cut the apples away from their cores and quickly slice into chunks. Mix in the sugar and rose water, tip into the pie dish and sprinkle with the water.

Brush the pastry rim with some of the beaten egg white. Then loosely roll the pastry on to a rolling pin and lift on to the pie dish. Using a fork or spoon, firmly press around the rim so that the two pastries are glued together in an attractive manner. Cut off the excess pastry. Prick the lid with a knife and paint with some more egg white, then sprinkle with the remaining granulated sugar.

Place the pie dish in the centre of the preheated oven and bake for 20 minutes, then reduce the temperature to 180°C/350°F/gas 4 and bake for a further 15 minutes or until the pastry has turned golden.

Serve hot, warm or cold with plenty of thick double cream or home-made custard.

See also
Almond cake with apple and blackberry salad (page 71)
Roast pheasant with bread sauce (page 228)

BACON

'Is there nothing neat or decent to be had in this horrid place?' 'What think you of some eggs and bacon, madam,' said the landlady. 'Are your eggs new laid? are you certain they were laid to-day? and let me have the bacon cut very nice and thin; for I can't endure anything that's gross. Prithee try if you can do a little tolerably for once, and don't think that you have a farmer's wife, or some of those creatures in the house.' The landlady begun then to handle her knife; but the other stopt her, saying, 'Good woman, I must insist upon your first washing your hands; for I am extremely nice, and have been always used from my cradle to have everything in the most elegant manner.'

Mrs Honour, lady's maid to the beautiful Sophia, taking on airs at one of the many inns that Henry Fielding satirizes in *Tom Jones*, 1749

Bacon and eggs is as essential to British life as Wellington boots and umbrellas. A stalwart race, there are few things that we cannot do without, if forced. Bacon, however, is one of them. I was appalled to discover on landing in America that they did not sell back or even middle back bacon. The prospect of a couple of years without the pleasures of crisp smoked back bacon for breakfast filled me with horror. Not even my secret hoard of Marmite could console me against my loss. After all, who can take a blueberry muffin seriously when you could be eating a bacon butty? The smell of bacon and eggs on the morning air is enough to tempt any Briton into the dingiest of greasy spoons. Its allure is indefinable but is rooted in an ancient taste for peasant food that has been acknowledged since at least the sixteenth century:

Bacon is good for carters and plowmen, the whiche be ever labouring in the earth or dunge . . . I do say that coloppes (slices of bacon) and egges is as holsome for them as a talowe candell is good for a blereyed mare.

A Compendyous Regyment, or a Dyetary of Health by Andrew Boorde, 1542.

Of course, bacon is and always has been used in a wide variety of dishes in Britain. Its robust salty flavour has added a delicious depth to everything from soups and stews to stuffings and dumplings. Until the law changed in the 1870s, pigs were kept in every British town and village, often in people's homes. Although some were reared as porkers (destined to be eaten as fresh pork) the majority were kept as bacon pigs. As such they were valued for their ability to produce long sides (flitches) of bacon rippled with creamy fat, which could then be sliced as needed through the winter. Their legs were usually removed and cured separately for ham. The Tamworth is a classic bacon pig, yielding particularly long sides of bacon and fine heavy hams. Different breeds were favoured in different parts of the country, for example, Gloucester Old Spots were prized in Gloucestershire for their rare ability to fatten on orchard windfalls. Naturally, many farmers developed their own local cures to preserve and complement their home-grown bacon.

By comparison the modern pig somehow seems to be a rather unromantic creature. His menu is carefully controlled to produce meat with just the right proportion of fat to lean rather than his own particular flavour. And modern cures are more influenced by marketing appeal than by taste. As ever, it is a question of trying to combine quality with an acceptable price. Happily, some of the smaller producers are returning to more traditional farming methods, such as feeding their pigs on the whey left over from their cheese-making or developing excellent new dry cures. Such bacon commands higher prices but is beginning to establish its own market.

Curiously, bacon still links us in strange ways to our culinary past. It remains as much a food for the poor as for the rich. I for one used to add bacon to my limited diet of soups, salads, risottos, pastas, tarts and sandwiches when I could afford no other meat. Its deliciously savoury nature transformed a simple tomato chive salad into an addictively exciting dish. Yet echoes of the past can also be found in our current use of bacon in ragouts, stuffings and even vegetable dishes. The ancient combination of bacon and beans has been transformed over the centuries into a stylish piquant dish, while the pleasures of eating a roast fowl are infinitely enhanced by the addition of a succulent, bacon-infused stuffing.

Practical guide

Bacon is made from the entire side of a pig, except its legs. The different cuts, namely, streaky, middle back and back bacon, come from different parts of the side and have varying degrees of fat. Back bacon is the leanest while streaky, which comes from the rib end, contains the most fat. Middle back falls between the two.

There are two basic methods of curing bacon sides: dry cure or salting and wet cure or brining – the end result is 'green' (unsmoked) bacon. Traditionally, meat was dry cured by being set on a specially designed draining-board before being covered with dry salt which was replenished as the meat wept salty juices. The loss of liquid causes the meat to lose weight and this, along with the fact that it takes longer to cure than brining bacon, makes dry cured bacon more expensive to produce and therefore less popular among producers. However, compared to industrially produced wet cured bacon it results in a superior, firmer-textured bacon and therefore should be bought in preference. It has a pure bacon flavour that becomes even more apparent if you eat some crisply grilled streaky or middle back slices.

Wet cures can be done in two ways. The pork side can either be submerged in a salt solution, which is often flavoured with sugar (or treacle) and spices, or it can be injected with brine by hundreds of tiny needles. The latter method often includes various preservatives which not only help cure the meat but can, in some cases, act as an attracter of water, thus increasing the weight of the meat. In either case, the bacon usually releases a certain amount of liquid or white curds as it cooks. Legally, all bacon is allowed to contain up to 10 per cent unspecified water, so according to Joanna Blythman in her book *The Food We Eat*, if labels state that they contain not more than 15 per cent water it actually means that they could contain up to 25 per cent extra water. Wet cures can range in taste from the bland to the well-rounded, a hint of sweetness complementing a rich bacon taste.

After bacon has been salted it can then be smoked. In some instances this is still done in a traditional manner, but unfortunately some manufacturers now take short cuts by spraying the meat with a synthetic flavouring product known as 'liquid smoke' which infuses it with a smoky taste. This will not be mentioned on the label, so you will need to look out for key descriptions such as 'smoked over oak chips' or 'oak smoked' to indicate that traditional methods have been used.

Bacon is cut to different thicknesses across the country. As a rule of thumb the further south you travel the thinner you will find your bacon cut. Occasionally bacon is still sold with its tough rind attached. Snip this off before using. Melted bacon fat can be used for cooking as it contains lots of flavour; however, health-wise it is probably better to stick to sunflower oil.

Taste notes

◊ Streaky or middle back bacon is often cooked with drier meats, for example, rabbit, pheasant, partridge, grouse, chicken and pigeon. All benefit from its slow release of fat and salty flavour.

◊ A wide variety of fresh green vegetables are cooked with bacon, in particular, all forms of greens from cabbage to lettuce, broad beans and peas. Modern taste dictates that it is lightly fried in olive oil with garlic and spring onion, before the greens, broad beans or peas are added. The latter two benefit from a little stock or water and a touch of mint or parsley.

◊ Dried pulses taste gorgeous with bacon, either slowly simmered in soup or added at the last minute to salads.

◊ The salty nature of bacon emphasizes the sweetness of fish, in particular white fish or shellfish, for example, monkfish, prawns and scallops. It also tastes good eaten in the Welsh way with laverbread.

◊ Bacon and eggs normally refers to fried eggs or occasionally poached eggs served with fried or grilled bacon. However, crisp bacon is lovely folded into creamy scrambled eggs or poached with asparagus and cream in baked eggs (*oeufs en cocotte*). Alternatively, add bacon to omelettes with mushrooms or serve simply with egg-soaked fried bread.

Tomato salad with bacon vinaigrette

In recent years crispy bacon has become an increasingly popular addition to salads, in particular with spinach and avocado. Here is my favourite variation. (Serves 4)

680g/1½lb good tomatoes
8 slices back bacon
2 tablespoons vegetable oil
½ teaspoon smooth Dijon
   mustard
1 clove garlic, crushed
3 tablespoons finely sliced
   chives

2 tablespoons white wine
   vinegar
6 tablespoons extra virgin
   olive oil
salt and freshly ground black
   pepper

Halve and slice the tomatoes, discarding each end. Arrange in a shallow bowl.

Trim the bacon of any fat (unless you like crisp bacon fat) and cut into small dice. Heat the vegetable oil in a frying pan and when hot add the bacon. Fry over a moderate heat until crisp, then drain on some kitchen paper.

Meanwhile, whisk together the mustard, garlic, chives, vinegar and olive oil. Season to taste and mix into the tomatoes. The salad will improve if allowed to sit for 5 minutes. Finally mix in the bacon and serve with crusty bread to mop up the juices.

Scallop, spinach and bacon pasta

This recipe is very much of the modern mode, the salty taste of the bacon enhancing the delicate sweetness of the other ingredients. (Serves 4)

455g/1lb queen scallops

8 slices unsmoked back bacon

200g/7oz prepared baby
   spinach

salt

½ tablespoon vegetable oil

400g/14oz spaghetti

6 tablespoons olive oil

1 fat shallot, finely sliced

2 cloves garlic, crushed

1 teaspoon thyme leaves

freshly ground black pepper

6 tablespoons dry Martini

Gently wash the scallops and, if necessary, remove the tough muscle and black digestive thread attached to their waist. Pat dry and set aside. Trim the bacon of any fat and cut into small dice.

Bring a large pan of water to the boil and add the spinach and a pinch of salt. Wait a few seconds until the spinach changes colour, then immediately drain and cool under cold running water. Squeeze out as much water as you can and roughly reshape into leaves. Set aside.

Add the vegetable oil and some salt to a large pan of boiling water then drop in the spaghetti. Dried pasta will take around 10−15 minutes, while fresh pasta takes only a few minutes to cook.

About 5 minutes before your pasta is ready, pour half the olive oil into a frying pan and fry the bacon until it is just beginning to turn crisp. Add the shallot, garlic and thyme and continue to fry for a further 2 minutes before removing from the pan. Add the remaining olive oil to the frying pan and increase the heat to high. As soon as it is hot, season the scallops with salt and pepper and quickly stir-fry for 2−3 minutes. Return the bacon and spinach to the pan with the dry Martini and adjust the seasoning to taste. As soon as the mixture is hot, toss the drained pasta into the mixture until it is evenly coated and serve immediately.

Mushroom bacon tart

Deliciously savoury bacon tarts have become an essential part of the British diet. (Serves 4)

225g/8oz shortcrust pastry
  (see page 335)
225g/8oz smoked back bacon
2 tablespoons olive oil
1 onion, finely diced
170g/6oz button mushrooms,
  trimmed

1 large egg
1 large egg yolk
200ml/7fl oz double cream
salt and freshly ground black
  pepper
55g/2oz roughly grated
  Gruyère

Preheat the oven to 220°C/425°F/gas 7.

Roll out the pastry on a lightly floured surface into a 30cm/12 inch circle and loosely wrap around the rolling pin. Hold the pin over a 23cm/9 inch tart dish and carefully unroll, gently pressing the pastry into place. Prick the bottom with a fork, press some aluminium foil or greaseproof paper into the middle, and fill with rice or old dried beans before chilling for 30 minutes.

Place the tart in the centre of the preheated oven and bake blind for 15 minutes. Remove the covering and continue to bake for another 5 minutes, until the pastry has become dry but not coloured and has lost that raw sweaty look. As soon as you have removed the pastry case reduce the oven temperature to 200°C/400°F/gas 6.

While the pastry is cooking, trim the fat from the bacon and cut into small dice. Heat the oil in a frying pan and sauté the bacon for 3 minutes. Add the onion and continue to cook until soft and lightly coloured. Meanwhile, wash and quarter the mushrooms. Stir these into the fried onion and continue to fry for a further 3 minutes. As soon as they are lightly cooked tip the entire mixture into the half-baked pastry case.

Beat together the egg, egg yolk, cream and seasoning. Pour over the mushrooms and sprinkle with the cheese before returning to the oven. Bake for a further 20–25 minutes or until golden and slightly risen. Serve hot, warm or cold.

Capon with white wine and chestnuts

I came across a reference to a recipe of Mr Cooper, gentleman chef to Charles I, for roasted capon with white wine, bacon, chestnuts and pistachios. It sounded so good I felt I had to create a modern version.

Strictly speaking capons are emasculated cockerels, that grow plump and tender as a result of their misfortune. Slightly larger than your average chicken, they have delicate well-flavoured flesh that roasts beautifully. They can easily be ordered from the butcher and are not expensive.

Before cooking this recipe, check that your bird will fit into a large ovenproof saucepan with a tight-fitting lid. At worst you can always cheat by tightly covering the pan with a double thickness of foil. Heavy cast-iron enamelled pans such as Le Creuset are perfect for pot roasts. As capons can vary in size, weigh your bird after it has been stuffed and allow about 30 minutes for each 455g/1lb. (Serves 4–6 depending on whether you like having left-overs for the next day.)

Stuffing	30g/1oz shelled pistachio nuts
30g/1oz butter	115g/4oz cooked and peeled
1 small onion, finely diced	chestnuts, roughly chopped
1 clove garlic, crushed	
4 slices smoked back bacon	*Roast capon*
225g/8oz minced pork	1 plump oven-ready capon
1 medium egg	55g/2oz butter
2 lemons, finely grated	1 tablespoon olive oil
3 tablespoons finely chopped	24 button onions
parsley	6 slices smoked back bacon,
salt and freshly ground black	diced
pepper	285ml/½ pint dry white wine

Preheat the oven to 170°F/325°F/gas 3. Begin by making the stuffing. Melt the butter in a frying pan and gently fry the onion and garlic until soft. Roughly dice the bacon, fat and all, and place in the food processor. Quickly mince in the machine before adding the minced pork, egg, lemon zest, parsley and seasoning. Process briefly for a few seconds to mix together, then tip into a bowl. Stir in the pistachio nuts, chestnuts and buttery onions.

Check the seasoning by frying a small patty of the mixture and adjusting according to your taste.

Remove any excess fat from the capon and, if necessary, wipe inside and out with a damp cloth before seasoning with salt and pepper. Pack the stuffing into the neck and wrap any excess in foil.

Meanwhile, melt the remaining 55g/2oz butter with the olive oil in your chosen ovenproof saucepan. Add the capon breast side down, and colour. Turn the bird until each side is nicely coloured, then remove and set aside. Stir in the button onions and diced bacon and gently fry for 3 minutes until lightly coloured. Then stir in the wine, return to the boil and return the bird, breast side down in the juices. Quickly baste, making sure that the onions stay in the liquid, before covering and placing in the centre of the oven. Roast gently for 2½ hours, remembering to turn the bird the right way up half-way through cooking. Place the foil-wrapped stuffing in the oven at this stage.

Test to see if the capon is cooked by inserting a skewer between its breast and thigh. If the juices run clear it is ready. Serve piping hot with the delicious pan juices. It also makes an excellent cold dish.

Mustard bacon beans

This is an autumnal recipe that is part salad, part vegetable, depending on the weather and your mood. If you feel like a hearty meal, try serving with pan-fried duck breasts. (Serves 4)

225g/8oz black-eyed beans
1 bay leaf
3 teaspoons whole grain
   mustard
2 cloves garlic, crushed
6 tablespoons finely chopped
   parsley
1 teaspoon finely chopped
   tarragon
4 tablespoons sherry vinegar

9 tablespoons extra virgin
   olive oil
salt and freshly ground black
   pepper
225g/8oz honey-cured back
   bacon, trimmed and diced
2 shallots, finely diced
2 inner sticks celery, finely
   diced

Soak the beans for 12 hours in plenty of cold water. Drain and rinse before placing in a pan with plenty of cold water and the bay leaf. Bring up to the boil and bubble vigorously for 10 minutes, skimming off any scum. Reduce the heat and simmer gently for 30 minutes or until tender. Drain and set aside.

Whisk together the mustard, garlic, herbs, vinegar and 6 tablespoons of olive oil. Season to taste and set aside.

Heat the remaining oil in a saucepan and fry the bacon until it is crispy. Add the shallots and celery and fry for a minute before adding the beans and the mustard dressing. Warm through, then remove from the heat and serve.

Bacon butties

Everyone has their own recipe for a bacon butty and much is dependent on the mood of the eater. It is a dish much favoured by those wishing to recover from the night before, although it can be enjoyed at any time – hunger and a craving for salty bacon being the only two prerequisites.

As far as I am concerned the bacon is best either in soft warm baps or between thick slices of freshly baked cottage loaf. However, warm French bread or breakfast rolls are also good. (Serves hungry 2)

4 soft baps
3 tablespoons vegetable oil
12 slices back bacon
2 tomatoes or 4 free-range
  eggs

salt and freshly ground black
  pepper
butter for spreading

Warm the baps in the oven while you are preparing the ingredients. If you are making a fried egg and bacon sandwich, you might as well fry your bacon, otherwise you can choose between grilling and frying. Heat the oil in your favourite frying pan. Once it is sizzling hot, add the bacon. As soon as the bacon begins to colour, turn it over and continue to cook until both sides are well coloured and the fat has become brittle and crispy.

In the meantime, slice the tomatoes and season with salt and pepper. Otherwise, stack the bacon to one side of the pan (or keep warm in the oven) and gently break your eggs into the frying pan. Fry according to your taste.

As soon as your rolls are warm, spread with butter. Break the bacon up and divide between the 4 baps before covering with tomato slices or fried eggs. Squidge each roll together, cut in two and serve with lots of hot coffee and a bottle of Taittinger.

See also
Avocado, bacon and shrimp salad (page 261)
Chicken and leek pie (page 168)
Mushroom barley risotto (page 38)
Rabbit and cucumber fricassée (page 82)
Roast pheasant with bread sauce (page 228)
Sweet spiced ham (page 287)

BARLEY

Sow barley in March, in April, and May,
the later in sand, and the sooner in clay.
What worser for barley, than wetness and cold?
what better to skilfull, than time to be bold?

Who soweth his barley too soon, or in rain,
of oats of thistles shall after complain:
I speak not of May-weed, of Cockle and such,
that noieth the barley, so often and much.

March's Husbandry in *Five Hundred Good Points
of Husbandry* by Thomas Tusser, 1573

The hay-like scent of freshly harvested barley can briefly be recaptured by sniffing a newly opened packet of pearl barley. In an increasingly urban world it is easy to forget the pleasure of wandering past fields of rustling corn and tentatively nibbling the sweet grains of barley or wheat. Barley has been grown in Britain for some 10,000 years and yet we barely notice it. Strange, as so many of us suck lemon barley sweets or drink it malted in beer and whisky. It sits on the supermarket shelves, sidelined by more fashionable pulses, waiting to be sprinkled into the odd soup and old-fashioned stew. Its aromatic grains, which have sustained us for generations in simple pottages and fruit-enriched cereals, are too good to be forgotten, so next time you see a packet, stop and buy it.

Once cooked, its firm almost nutty grains become plump and soft with a complex, slightly woody taste. They will eventually form a soft pink jelly if over-cooked. This was once hawked by street sellers across London for those of a delicate constitution. Originally, barley was grown throughout Britain, although it was particularly favoured in the north and west where the weather was too wet or cold to guarantee a good wheat harvest. In some areas it was mixed with other cereals to create rustic breads and savoury pottages, while in others it dominated much of the cooking. Barley bannocks and brose still survive in certain pockets of Scotland. However, by the eighteenth century barley was transformed into subtle-tasting creams and puddings, flavoured with orange-flower water, sugar, cream, lemon, mace, raisins or currants. It was infused into health-giving cordials, flavoured with wine for the sick and boiled in a savoury pudding with Easter-ledge (bistort – a wild green plant) as an annual spring tonic.

Today barley is often relegated to the ubiquitous Scotch broth, although it makes excellent salads, risottos and puddings. The grains need only a brief cooking for salads, before being tossed warm into a vibrant vinaigrette and left to cool. Tiny cubes of courgette, cucumber and red pepper, along with handfuls of fresh herbs, can then be added, with diced ham or smoked chicken. Luscious wild mushroom risottos and creamy lemon baked puddings need a little longer.

Practical guide

Theoretically, several different forms of barley are available in Britain. However, pot or Scotch barley is quite difficult to find. An oatmeal brown, only the outer husk has been removed from the grains. It has to be soaked in water overnight before a long, gentle cooking. Those who use it either eat it as an alternative to rice or add it to slow-cooking earthy stews.

Pearl barley is far more common. It is the polished version of pot barley and, just to add to the confusion, is usually added to Scotch broth, as well as to other soups, stews, puddings and drinks. It can also be sold ground as barley flour and should not be confused with barley meal. Barley meal is made from ground pot barley. Both can be found in some health food shops and should be bought in small quantities as they have a limited life span. All forms of barley should be stored in an airtight jar in a cool dark place.

Lastly, there is beremeal. As far as I know, only one man in Britain currently mills it and he is able to buy it from only one farmer in the north of England. Beremeal is made from the grains of an ancient hardy variety of barley (*Hordeum vulgare*). Evidence suggests that Neolithic man grew this strain of barley, or bere grain as it became known. As other varieties of barley were developed its use became limited to small pockets in Scotland and the Orkneys, where it was made into bannocks and a form of brose (similar to porridge). It has a strong, almost astringent flavour. If you are keen to try it, contact your local health food shop and see if they will order any from Mr Morrison at Golspie Mill, Golspie, Highlands and Islands, KW10 6RA.

To cook barley for a salad, soup garnish or as a starchy accompaniment, place in a pan of cold water, bring to the boil, drain and rinse. Transfer to a fresh pan. Tie together a peeled carrot, cleaned leek and parsley sprig, add to the barley, and cover with plenty of cold water or a good home-made stock. Bring up to the boil and simmer for 20 minutes or until just soft and nutty. Drain and serve. Allow 140g/5oz uncooked weight for a salad for 4 people.

Taste notes

◊ The robust flavours of barley work well with celery, chives, tarragon, shallots, garlic, mushrooms and carrot.
◊ A small amount of cooked pearl barley can be added as a chewy garnish to a thin, smooth soup such as cream of mushroom or prawn bisque.
◊ Liquorice root, lemon and orange all taste good with barley water, as do clary sage, borage flowers and sweet Muscat wines.

Spring vegetable barley soup

Barley has been cooked in a meaty broth with vegetables for hundreds of years. In Scotland it was mixed with kale and hough (shin of beef), in England it was often cooked with lamb or veal's head – a popular dish with the Puritans in the seventeenth century after the beheading of Charles I. Happily, modern tastes have become a little more sophisticated, preferring quick, fresh-tasting dishes to the heavier earthy flavours of slow-cooked soups. Choose the first of the season's young vegetables, changing them to suit your taste. (Serves 4)

850ml/1½ pints good chicken or vegetable stock (see pages 339–40 or buy ready made)

30g/1oz pearl barley, washed

115g/4oz young turnips, peeled and diced

2 young carrots, peeled and diced

2 small leeks, cleaned and diced

2 inner celery stalks, finely diced

2 tomatoes, peeled, quartered, seeded and diced

85g/3oz baby spinach, finely sliced

140ml/¼ pint double cream

2 tablespoons finely chopped parsley

2 tablespoons finely sliced chives

1 lemon, finely grated

salt and freshly ground black pepper

Pour the stock into a large saucepan and bring up to a full rolling boil. Add the barley and simmer for 15 minutes before adding the diced turnip, carrot, leek and celery. Return to the boil, then simmer for a further 5 minutes.

Add the diced tomato and spinach, return to the boil, then stir in the cream, herbs and lemon zest. Adjust the seasoning to taste and serve immediately.

Note: If wished you can add tiny broad beans, young peas or asparagus tips with or instead of some of the vegetables.

Mushroom barley risotto

Barley risotto is an interesting slightly nutty-flavoured alternative to Arborio rice provided it is lightly cooked – go too far and it becomes too gelatinous. Vegetarians can omit the bacon and substitute a good vegetable stock (see page 340) for the chicken stock. (Serves 2–3)

30g/1oz dried wild mushrooms or 115g/4oz fresh wild mushrooms
6 slices back bacon
3 tablespoons olive oil
2 cloves garlic, crushed
2 inner sticks celery, finely diced
2 carrots, finely diced
115g/4oz pearl barley
4 tablespoons dry vermouth
850ml/1½ pints chicken stock (see page 339 or buy ready made)
2 tablespoons finely chopped parsley

If using dried mushrooms, carefully wash them in a bowl of water before soaking for 30 minutes. Otherwise wipe your fresh mushrooms clean before trimming and cutting or ripping into bite-sized pieces.

Trim the bacon of any fat and finely dice. Heat the oil in a heavy-bottomed saucepan and add the bacon, garlic, celery and carrot. Fry gently over a moderate heat until soft and golden. Add the mushrooms to the softened vegetables and continue to fry for a further 3 minutes.

Meanwhile place the barley in a pan of cold water. Bring to the boil, drain and rinse under the cold tap. Shake off the excess water and stir into the mushrooms. Fry for 2 minutes then increase the heat and pour in the vermouth. Allow it to bubble up and reduce by half before adding the stock. Return to the boil, then reduce the heat to a gentle simmer and cover the pan. Cook gently for 40 minutes or until the barley is tender and the liquid is absorbed. Stir in the parsley and serve piping hot with a crisp green salad.

Lemon barley pudding with summer fruits

Here is an eighteenth-century-inspired pudding. The summer fruit is a luxurious option for all those who used to enjoy strawberry or raspberry jam with their rice pudding. If serving in winter, try cooking the barley with some dried fruit of your choice. (Serves 4)

Lemon barley pudding
15g/½oz butter
115g/4oz pearl barley
425ml/¾ pint single cream
285ml/½ pint milk
1 tablespoon orange-flower
   water
55g/2oz caster sugar
2 large lemons, finely grated
salt
ground mace

Summer fruits
225g/8oz strawberries, hulled
115g/4oz redcurrants, stripped
   from their stems
115g/4oz caster sugar
3 tablespoons water
225g/8oz raspberries

Preheat the oven to 150°C/300°F/gas 2 and liberally butter an ovenproof dish.

Wash the barley and place in a saucepan of cold water. Bring to the boil and drain immediately.

Mix the blanched barley together with the cream, milk, orange-flower water, sugar and lemon zest. Add a pinch of salt and mace and pour into the buttered dish. Bake for just over 2 hours or until the barley is tender.

Shortly before serving, halve the strawberries and place in a non-corrosive pan with the redcurrants, sugar and water. Place over a low heat until the sugar is melted and the strawberries are releasing plenty of juice. Stir in the raspberries, warm through and remove from the heat.

Serve the barley pudding and accompanying fruit hot, warm or cold according to your taste.

Barley wine cordial

I feel it is high time to revive the cooling delights of home-made barley wine and barley water. Both are utterly delicious and should not be lost to the inevitable rise of ready-made drinks. The most fragrant recipe that I have come across was in *The Compleat Housewife* by Eliza Smith (1758). Mrs Smith not only mixes her barley water with lemons, sugar, wine and rose water, but also adds borage water and clary water. Her clary water was made by infusing large quantities of clary flowers (a form of sage that imbues the water with the flavour of Muscat) in borage water and sack (similar to sherry). She remarks of her barley wine that 'it is very pleasant in hot weather, and very good in fevers'. (Makes 1.285 litres/2¼ pints)

115g/4oz pearl barley, washed
2 litres/3½ pints water
55g/2oz caster sugar or to
  taste
285ml/½ pint flowery white
  wine

2 small unwaxed lemons,
  finely pared
borage or mint sprigs

Place the barley and water in a large non-corrosive saucepan. Bring to the boil and skim off any scum, then boil vigorously until the water has reduced by half. This will take about 25 minutes.

Meanwhile, place the sugar, wine and lemon zest in a china bowl. When the barley water is sufficiently reduced, stir it, barley and all into the sweetened wine. Lightly cover and leave until cold. Check the taste and add more wine or sugar if wished, then strain into a jug. Cover and chill until needed.

Serve chilled with sprigs of borage or mint.

BEEF

'Laura Pyke,' said young Bingo with intense bitterness, 'is a food crank, curse her. She says we all eat too much and eat it too quickly and, anyway, ought not to be eating it at all but living on parsnips and similar muck. And Rosie, instead of telling the woman not to be a fathead, gazes at her in a wide-eyed admiration, taking it in through the pores. The result is that the cuisine of this house has been shot to pieces, and I am starving on my feet. Well, when I tell you that it's weeks since a beefsteak pudding raised its head in the home, you'll understand what I mean.'

Jeeves and the old school chum, from *Very Good, Jeeves* by P. G. Wodehouse, 1930

It would be impossible to consider British food without beef. For centuries a fine joint of roast beef was as much a symbol of our national identity as John Bull or his growling bulldog. There are few who do not love its gorgeous flavour, whether it be eaten as a steak or in a pie. Such a passion can be traced back thousands of years, or so the vast quantities of beef bones found on fourth-millennium BC habitation sites would suggest. Hard as it is to believe now, in time, BSE (bovine spongiform encephalopathy) or mad cow disease will become a terrible memory rather than a living problem. Hopefully, this will be sooner rather than later. However, I should add a few words of caution. There is still a large amount of research being conducted on the current safety of eating beef and all its products. Inevitably advice and information will change in the forthcoming months, so readers need to keep themselves abreast as new developments arise. Ideally, cooks should only buy from certified BSE-free herds.

In the past our consumption of beef was linked with our capacity to improve farming practices. The union between Scotland and England saw vast droves of black highland cattle driven down to the southern markets. Every part of the animal was eaten or used and with the onset of winter whole sides were salted and smoked. The introduction of Dutch farming techniques in the eighteenth century finally established beef as our national dish. Land was enclosed to grow special fodder for cattle and new breeds were developed to produce tender, richly flavoured meat. Unlike much of Europe, Britain bred separate dairy and beef herds. Huge cuts of beef, rippled with fat, were transformed into succulent roasts and sumptuous puddings that became the pride of the nation. In the course of a long period of war with France, it is hardly surprising that beef was adopted as a national emblem, particularly when complicated foreign recipes were considered an excuse to disguise bad produce. No wonder the French referred to us as 'rosbifs'.

Such a legacy is hard to lose, as has been seen with the politicization of BSE. Nevertheless, before its arrival our cooking habits were beginning to change. The relatively high cost of prime cuts transformed beef from a staple to a luxury food, while the popularity of fast-food burgers has been seen by many as an Americanization of our taste, despite the fact that we have always enjoyed the delicious contrast of savoury meat with piquant relishes. So in honour of old favourites, I have decided to keep this chapter relatively conservative, although I have no doubt that in a few years it will be as natural for the British to cook a spicy beef and ginger stir-fry as a steak pudding. Incidentally, I apologize for not including any recipes for roast beef and Yorkshire pudding, steak and kidney pie and beef stew with dumplings, but they are already in *Modern British Food*, and, where possible, I did not want to duplicate any recipes.

Practical guide

In simple terms, the best way to buy a good piece of beef is to go to a good butcher, preferably a member of the Q Guild, the ultimate sign of excellence in butchery awarded by the Meat and Livestock Commission. This is the only way that you can hope to buy meat from a known herd, which has been farmed sensibly and hung properly. The taste, texture and colour of beef is influenced by the sex, breed, feed and treatment of the animal and only a good butcher will be aware of these factors and hang his beef accordingly.

Ideally a side of beef should be hung for about 10–14 days to maximize its flavour and tenderness. However, some advocate a mere 7 days while others prefer 21 days. The longer the beef is hung the more pronounced will be its flavour and the less it will weigh as it loses moisture. Well-hung butcher's meat should be a deep plum red with white or cream-coloured fat. Grass-fed cattle tend towards the latter. Supermarket pre-packed beef cannot be judged in quite the same way, as despite being hung it is often deceptively red in colour. This is because it is packed in nitrogen and carbon dioxide flushed packets that contain insufficient oxygen to darken the meat naturally. Ideally all beef should contain fine flecks of fat or *marbling* throughout the lean meat. This melts and bastes the meat as it cooks and keeps it deliciously tender.

All meat must be kept chilled and loosely covered. It should always be stored on the shelf below cooked meat and should never come into contact with any other foods. Unwrap whatever you have bought and place in a clean, lightly covered bowl, so that air can circulate around the meat.

In theory there are countless different cuts available to the cook. To further complicate matters, each cut can be sold by several different names, depending on the locality and custom. For simplicity, I will divide these by cooking method rather than anatomy.

Roasting

Fillet, rib, rolled sirloin and topside all make good roasts. Try to buy a decent sized 905g/2lb joint as, with the honourable exception of fillet, it is difficult to control the degree of cooking with smaller cuts and they also have a tendency to shrink. The smallest rib roast should be 2 ribs. Where possible, choose joints with a nice layer of creamy fat, as this will reduce the need for basting, add flavour and give you excellent dripping. Some cuts are sold encased (barded) with a layer of beef fat, but others will require a regular basting with butter or olive oil. Meat roasted on the bone is always more succulent than boned joints.

Estimated quantities uncooked weight
Whole fillet: 115−140g/4−5oz per person
Rib roast: 340−425g/12−15oz per person
Rolled sirloin: 140−225g/5−8oz per person
Topside: 140−225g/5−8oz per person

Roasting table estimated per 455g/1lb of average thickness

Cut	220°C/425°F/gas 7	170°C/325°F/gas 3	Degree
Whole fillet	8−10 minutes		Rare
	14 minutes		Medium
	21−22 minutes		Well done
Rib roast	15 minutes initially	16 minutes	Rare
(2 ribs = c. 2.3kg/5lb)	15 minutes initially	25 minutes	Medium
	15 minutes initially	31−32 minutes	Well done
Rib roast	15 minutes initially	15 minutes	Rare
(4 ribs = c.5kg/11lb)	15 minutes initially	20 minutes	Medium
	15 minutes initially	25 minutes	Well done
Rolled sirloin	15 minutes initially	15 minutes	Rare
	15 minutes initially	25 minutes	Medium
	15 minutes initially	35−37 minutes	Well done
Topside	15 minutes initially	15 minutes	Rare
	15 minutes initially	27 minutes	Medium
	15 minutes initially	37 minutes	Well done

Traditional accompaniments

Aside from a good gravy made from the roasting juices, horseradish sauce and a fine mustard are considered essential accompaniments to roast beef. Most would feel deprived without an accompanying Yorkshire pudding to sop up the juices and plenty of crisp roast potatoes. Some consider roast parsnips another important accompaniment, while others like their carrots, despite the fact that these are traditionally served with boiled salted beef. Green vegetables have always been served with roasts and vary according to the time of year. In my home, no roast meal was complete without *mop*, thick slices of white bread to soak up the last of the gravy.

Grilling

The loin, rump and rib are all used for steaks. Rump steaks are cut from the unfortunate animal's rump or bottom. Many consider these to be the most flavoursome of all the steaks.

The loin follows and contains the fillet and the sirloin. The fillet can be divided into several different types of steaks. Its thickest end produces the Châteaubriand, a very large steak that is grilled in one piece and served as a filling meal for two or three people. Fillet steaks are cut from the centre of the fillet, followed by the tournedos and then the medallion. Tournedos are thinner than fillet steaks but not as small as the medallion, which is cut from the tail end of the fillet.

Sirloin, entrecôte and Porterhouse steaks are all cut from the sirloin and have a firmer texture than the buttery soft fillet. Occasionally, T-bone steaks were also sold in Britain. These are cut through the T-shaped bone across the sirloin and include a piece of fillet with the sirloin meat.

Beef burgers are best made at home with a mincer. Alternatively, order your beef and ask the butcher to mince it for you so that you can guarantee that it is made with pure muscle. Choose a good cut, such as topside, but make sure that it contains about 10 per cent fat so that it does not dry out as it cooks; 225g/8oz of lean topside needs about 2 tablespoons of finely chopped beef suet mixed into it.

If you are using a normal grill, preheat to its full setting for 20 minutes while at the same time allowing your steaks to come up to room temperature from the fridge. Season the steaks with freshly ground black pepper and brush with olive oil. You can also season them with a hint of crushed garlic or some Worcestershire sauce. Place the steaks about 7.5cm/3 inches away from the heat and grill according to the chart below. The only exception to this rule is the Châteaubriand, which needs to be placed nearer 13cm/5 inches away from the heat. Alternatively, you can use a barbecue or a ribbed cast-iron oven-top grill.

Grilling time per side for individual steaks

Cut	Weight	Thickness	Cooking time	Degree
Rump, sirloin or Porterhouse	225g/8oz	3cm/1¼ inches	2 minutes	Blue
			3 minutes	Rare
			4 minutes	Well done
Fillet	140g/5oz	3cm/1¼ inches	2 minutes	Blue
			3 minutes	Rare
			3½ minutes	Medium
			4–4½ minutes	Well done
Tournedos	115g/4oz	4cm/1½ inches	3 minutes	Blue
			4½ minutes	Rare
			6 minutes	Medium
			7–8 minutes	Well done
Châteaubriand	455g/1lb	3cm/1¼ inches	7 minutes	Blue
			9 minutes	Rare
			10–11 minutes	Medium
			12–13 minutes	Well done
T-bone	425g/15oz (including bone)	2cm/¾ inch	3 minutes	Blue
			4 minutes	Rare
			6 minutes	Medium
			8–9 minutes	Well done
Beef burger	170g/6oz	2.5cm/1 inch	4 minutes	Rare
			6 minutes	Medium
			8 minutes	Well done

Traditional accompaniments
Aside from the accompaniments already mentioned under roasting, savoury butters or sauces are still the favourite accompaniment to a good steak or beef burger. Although some still adore steak with Béarnaise sauce, many are turning to piquant salsas and relishes – fresh tomato and shallot, for example, or roasted pepper, tomato and olive. Cold butters can be made with roasted garlic, black or green olives, fresh herbs, blue cheese or anchovies. All are excellent melted on to the sizzling meat. However, perhaps our favourite

accompaniment is crisp yet fluffy chips, although grilled or fried onions, mushrooms and tomatoes are all perfectly acceptable.

Frying
All the cuts of meat mentioned under grilling can be fried. Ultra-thin minute steaks should also be fried, as they need an intense heat to cook quickly and prevent them from becoming tough. Finely sliced, they are often used in stir-fries and sautés, as they remain tender with a quick cooking.

As has already been stated, stir-fries are becoming an increasingly favoured manner of serving beef. Aside from soy sauce, sake and mirin, oyster sauce, black beans, Thai curry pastes and fish sauce are all popular flavourings. In the same way garlic, ginger, chilli, lemon grass and lime leaves, along with mushrooms, green beans, red or green peppers and spring onions all taste delicious cooked with beef.

Stewing
The tougher cuts of beef are used for stewing, as these will become meltingly tender if slowly cooked. Traditionally the best cuts are considered to be the rump, topside, brisket (flank) and the upper part of the shin. I have to say I find brisket far too gelatinous when stewed, but it is, of course, purely a matter of taste. Supermarkets usually label stewing meat as just that, so you have to second guess which part of the cow you are dealing with. I suspect that it is usually either rump or topside. In any case, trim off any excess fat and remove as much sinew as you possibly can. There is nothing worse than eating gristly stew.

At this stage it is probably sensible to avoid anything other than pure muscle – in other words avoid ox tail, neck, marrow and any offal.

If you are braising a whole piece of beef such as rump or topside, ask the butcher to lard it for you to keep it succulent while cooking. Otherwise cut the meat into the required size by following along each muscle seam. This yields tender stewing meat.

Traditional flavourings
The typical image of a British beef stew comes complete with plump parsley-speckled dumplings and jolly carrots. In reality, they range from delicate almond and saffron scented curries to robustly flavoured red wine and olive casseroles. All manner of alcohol can be added, from brandy to Guinness, and every conceivable vegetable has probably been added at one time or another. Oven-dried orange peel, fresh herbs and lemon peel are all popular

flavourings, as is the late addition of fried mushrooms and caramelized button onions. Bacon works well with beef, while oysters can be added at the end of a plain beef stew. However, they must be added at the last minute as they quickly turn into rubber balls if over-cooked.

Beef ragout

Originally, British ragouts were a form of stew where a highly flavoured sauce was added towards the end of cooking. Modern recipes are simply piquant stews. Try serving with a pilaff or buttery jacket potatoes. (Serves 4)

905g/2lb lean stewing beef, trimmed
salt and freshly ground black pepper
5 tablespoons olive oil
3 tablespoons cognac
1 medium onion, finely sliced
2 cloves garlic, crushed
565ml/1 pint full-bodied red wine
400g/14oz can chopped tomatoes
3 strips finely pared lemon rind
1 sprig parsley
1 small sprig rosemary
16 green olives, stoned
3 tablespoons finely chopped parsley

Remove any fat or sinews from the meat, cut it into 2.5cm/1 inch dice, and season with salt and pepper. Heat the olive oil in a non-corrosive saucepan and brown the meat in batches over a moderately high heat. Too much meat added at any one time will reduce the temperature of the pan and cause the meat to stew in its own juice rather than fry. Return the meat to the saucepan and pour over the cognac. Immediately ignite it and quickly stir the beef around the pan until the flames go out.

Set the meat aside and add the onion and garlic to the pan. Gently fry until soft then add the wine, scraping the bottom of the saucepan as you do so. Allow it to boil vigorously until it has reduced by half. Then stir in the chopped tomatoes, lemon rind, parsley and rosemary sprigs, olives, meat and any juices. Season to taste and simmer very gently for just under 1½ hours or until tender. Remove the lemon rind and herb sprigs and add the chopped parsley just before serving.

Beefsteak pudding

A classic British dish. Use an 850ml/1½ pint pudding basin (Serves 4)

455g/1lb lean chuck steak, trimmed
3 tablespoons vegetable oil
seasoned flour
1 medium onion, finely diced
2 carrots, cut into rounds
4 field mushrooms, peeled, trimmed and roughly diced
285ml/½ pint water
115ml/¼ pint red wine
1 strip lemon rind tied together with 1 sprig parsley and 1 sprig thyme
salt and freshly ground black pepper
225g/8oz suet pastry (see page 336)

Remove any fat or tough fibres from the meat before cutting into 2.5cm/1 inch chunks.

Heat the oil in a heavy-bottomed saucepan or casserole dish over a moderate heat. Toss the beef in some seasoned flour. Then add in two batches to the hot oil and stir until nicely brown on all sides. Set aside.

Reduce the heat and, if necessary, add a little more oil before adding the onion and carrots to the pan. Fry gently for 5 minutes, then stir in the mushrooms and continue to cook for a further 2 minutes. Return the meat to the pan and stir in the water, wine, lemon rind and herbs. Adjust the seasoning to taste and simmer gently for ¾ hour. The stew can now be set aside and chilled until needed. Remove the herbs and lemon zest before tipping into the lined pudding basin.

Two hours or so before you wish to serve your beef pudding, follow the instructions for suet pastry on page 336. Then boil your pudding for 2 hours, remembering to keep the water level replenished with extra boiling water. When you are ready to turn the pudding out, remove it from the water and allow it to sit for a couple of minutes before removing the foil and greaseproof paper. Place a warm serving plate over the top and invert both together, giving a few gentle shakes until you feel the pudding slip out.

Beef Wellington

I felt I had to include this much-loved British dish. I do not know when it was invented or how it came by its name. To call it boeuf Wellington, as was the case in the late seventies, somehow seems rather cheeky. It became a favourite director's dining-room dish that every young deb was expected to be able to cook. It can also be made as individual steaks.

Do not be discouraged by the length of the recipe – each stage is very straightforward and the final result is well worth the effort. The chicken liver pâté and mushroom filling can be made the day before if wished or you can buy some ready-made pâté. (Serves 6)

Chicken liver pâté
55g/2oz butter
1 small onion, finely diced
1 clove garlic, crushed
225g/8oz chicken livers
salt and freshly ground black
   pepper
3 tablespoons sherry

Mushroom filling
30g/1oz butter
2 shallots, finely diced
1 clove garlic, crushed
225g/8oz button mushrooms,
   finely diced

1 lemon, finely grated
2 tablespoons finely chopped
   parsley

Beef Wellington
1.1kg/2½lb beef fillet,
   trimmed
Worcestershire sauce
2 tablespoons olive oil
225g/8oz puff pastry (see
   page 338)
½ small egg beaten with 1
   tablespoon milk

Preheat the oven to 220°C/425°F/gas 7.

Melt 55g/2oz butter in a frying pan over a low heat. Add the onion and garlic and fry until soft and golden. Place the chicken livers in a colander to drain off any blood. Cut away any discoloured yellowish areas along with any sinews.

As soon as the onions are soft, increase the heat and add the chicken livers. Stir-fry briskly until well coloured. Season generously and pour in the sherry. Allow it to bubble up and reduce by half, then remove and purée in the food processor. Adjust the seasoning to taste, cover and chill until needed.

When you are ready to make the mushroom filling, melt the butter in a non-stick frying pan. Add the shallot and garlic and fry over a moderate heat until soft. Add the mushrooms and continue to fry until they begin to release their liquid. Add the lemon zest and seasoning and increase the heat, stirring regularly until the liquid has evaporated. Stir in the parsley and transfer to a bowl. Chill, covered, until needed.

Season the fillet with Worcestershire sauce and black pepper. Tuck (and tie if wished) its thinner tail underneath if it is of an uneven thickness. Heat the oil in a small roasting tray over a high heat. Carefully add the fillet – keeping its shape – and colour evenly. Transfer to the oven and bake for 10 minutes. Remove and place on a cooling rack to drip dry. Save the juices to make a gravy in the normal manner if serving hot.

Once the beef is cold, roll the pastry into a thin oblong, large enough to envelop the meat. Save any trimmings. Arrange the mushrooms down the centre, so that they match the length of the fillet. Remove any string and spread the chicken liver pâté along the length of the fillet, then lay the meat, pâté side down, on to the mushrooms. Brush the pastry edges with the egg and milk and neatly wrap around the meat. Flip it over and arrange on a greased baking sheet.

If wished, roll out your trimmings into pastry leaves or roses. Brush the meat with the egg and milk, then embellish with leaves and cut 4 or 5 slits in the top as air vents. Chill for 20 minutes.

Bake for 40 minutes at 220°C/425°F/gas 7. Remove and serve hot or cold with horseradish sauce, fresh watercress and a good red wine gravy if wished.

Note: Steak or beef en croûte is made in exactly the same way, but you omit the chicken liver pâté.

Blue cheese burgers

Beef burgers were assimilated into the British diet after the Second World War with the rise of cheap, modern eating houses. The arrival of Wimpy, McDonald's and Burger King created a new image of fast food that has had a deep impact on the British tastebuds. Regardless of what you might think of a fast food burger, it contains those essentially satisfying components of sweet, sour and salty which appeal to our national taste. There is no comparison between the flavour of home-made and mass-produced beef burgers. You have the added advantage of knowing exactly what your burger contains if you have chosen the meat and supervised the mincing. (Serves 4)

Blue cheese butter	Beef burgers
55g/2oz Stilton cheese	680g/1½lb lean topside,
55g/2oz softened butter	coarsely minced
2 tablespoons finely chopped	6 tablespoons shredded beef
chives	suet
1 tablespoon lemon juice	3 tablespoons finely chopped
salt and freshly ground black	parsley
pepper	1½ teaspoons garlic salt
	1–2 tablespoons olive oil

Preheat the grill to its highest setting.

Beat together the Stilton, butter, chives and lemon juice. Season to taste and spoon on to a piece of greaseproof paper in a roughly cylindrical shape. Roll the paper up and lightly roll under your fingertips until it forms a smooth even sausage. Chill.

Mix together the minced beef, suet, parsley, garlic salt and freshly ground black pepper. Fry a tiny patty of the mixture and adjust the seasoning to taste. Shape into 4 patties and chill, loosely covered.

When ready, place the beef burgers on a grill rack. Brush with olive oil and place 7.5cm/3 inches beneath the grill. Cook according to your taste, following the timings on page 47.

Slice the blue cheese butter into rounds and place on the beef burgers just before you remove them from the grill. Serve with chips and a green salad, or tuck into lightly toasted and buttered rolls with thin slices of sweet pickled cucumber, thinly sliced red onion and lots of crisp lettuce.

BEETROOT

A friend of mine had a large hamper of vegetables sent her from the country. Amongst them were a great number of beetroots. What to do with them she did not know. 'There is only one way to use them,' she remarked, 'and that is as a pickle. But I cannot live on pickled beetroots, I *must* get rid of them.'

'Try and invent some dishes,' I replied, which was done; and here are a few of them.

'The Red Root', an anonymous article published in *Home Cookery*, March 1914

The British are, to say the very least, ambivalent about beetroot. For some, being force fed pickled beetroot, spam and boiled grey potatoes at school has led them to renounce for ever the pleasures of this sweet-tasting vegetable. Yet for others beetroot is as essential to their well-being as pickled onions and pork pies. Like it or not, the beetroot has become an essential part of our culinary identity. Country cooks still boil tiny, freshly pulled beetroot and serve them tossed in butter or roasting juices with spring lamb; and city cooks still transform small vinegared beets into jewel-like winter salads with oranges and walnuts.

References to beet in Britain can be found as early as the thirteenth century, listed with sorrel, orach (mountain spinach) and mallow as a useful herb for the ubiquitous pottage. But it was not until the sixteenth century that our familiar red or Roman beet became established, introduced along with cucumbers, pumpkins, cauliflowers, spinach and chard by the green-fingered Protestant refugees. Its glorious colour made it perfect for ornate Elizabethan salads, while its distinctive sweet flavour made it ideal for pickling. Its fate was sealed, for despite some experimental cooking in the eighteenth century, which included such delicacies as pink pancakes and strange fish-shaped beetroot fritters, the majority of cooks have preferred, until recently, to serve it as a simple vegetable, salad or pickle.

Beetroot is currently enjoying a quiet renaissance, as will be shown by a quick glance down some of the more recherché seed catalogues. Today you can grow not only red, white or golden-coloured beetroot, but round or easy-to-slice long beetroot, as well as the extraordinary Chioggia, which when cut open displays pretty pink and white rings. Specialist growers now supply restaurants with some of these delicacies, but few shops will sell them as they are too temperamental for large-scale commercial growers. Thus gardeners and restaurants have the advantage over the urban cook, who has enough trouble trying to find ordinary raw red beetroot, as greengrocers still prefer to sell them boiled and saturated in spirit or malt vinegar.

In the matter of cooking, there is no doubt that chefs are leading the way. Tiny roasted beetroot are served as an accompaniment to hare and venison or tossed with ceps and capers as a tart sauce for pan-fried breadcrumbed sweetbreads. They are grated into clear game soups, deep fried as crisps or used to colour home-made pasta. For the domestic cook, often short of time, a simpler approach is adopted. Piquant relishes can be quickly made and used to great effect from the ready cooked (and vinegared) beetroot, flavoured with lime, honey and dill. Raw beetroot can be effortlessly boiled before being tossed in crème fraîche with succulent young salad onions or added to a fragrant summer salad. The possibilities are endless.

Practical guide

Beetroot, or *Beta vulgaris*, can be divided into four distinct categories: our familiar culinary beetroot, sugar beet, mangel-wurzels and various types of chard. Modern sugar beet has been developed from the White Silesian beet and is grown purely to make sugar, while the orange-coloured mangel-wurzel is fed to cattle. Since chard is grown for its leaves rather than its roots, I will not deal with it in this chapter.

If buying raw beetroot, where possible choose roots with fresh, green tops and avoid any with misshapen roots, as this can indicate bolting and consequently a disappointing taste and texture. They can be kept for a couple of weeks in the bottom of the fridge. Twist their tops off about 2.5cm/1 inch from the root before storing, as these can turn slimy within a few days. Some cookery books advocate eating very young beetroot leaves, but as many varieties can be bitter it is wise to test-nibble a leaf. If you like it, prepare your leaves like spinach by pulling the tougher stalks away from the leaves when necessary and lightly cooking. Alternatively, use the tiny thinnings from your garden in salads or stir-fries.

Home-grown beetroot can be picked from mid May to the end of October. Different coloured beetroot has the same flavour as red beet. Burpee's Gold produces a fine yellow beet, while Albina Vereduna is a good culinary variety of white beet and Bull's Blood the darkest of red beetroot. When shopping during the summer months, choose the smallest beets you can find, as they will taste like tiny sugar lumps. In the winter, use medium-sized, firm-textured beetroot, as these will have retained their moisture during storage.

How to cook beetroot
Gently wash the roots under cold running water before cooking. Never trim or peel them, as this will cause bleeding with a loss of colour and flavour. Traditionally beetroot is either baked or boiled. To my mind boiling produces a sweeter-tasting vegetable than baking, probably because the roots

have been cooked more quickly. Beetroot the size of a large egg will take about 45 minutes to bake at 170°C/325°F/gas 3 and 30 minutes to boil if added to boiling water. Always try to cook the same sized roots so that they are ready at the same time. You can test if they are tender by rubbing their skin with your thumb; if it peels easily they are cooked.

Beetroot is baked by wrapping it in a baggy oiled foil or greaseproof paper parcel. If using paper, try stapling it together for ease. Make sure that the beets are spread out within their parcel and roast at 170°C/325°F/gas 3. Alternatively, add them to plenty of boiling salted water, remembering to top it up if you are cooking particularly large or old roots. Trim and peel once cool enough to handle, wearing rubber gloves if you don't appreciate shocking pink hands. Your beetroot can then be finished as you wish.

Taste notes

◊ The sweet flavour of beetroot is enhanced by the addition of some form of acid, even with hot dishes. Good quality wine, sherry and balsamic vinegar all make excellent seasonings, as does lime, lemon or orange juice.

◊ Cold beetroot, lightly seasoned with a good vinegar, is excellent eaten with smoked fish, cold meats and cold meat pies. It is also surprisingly good sliced in herb-flavoured cream cheese rye bread sandwiches, especially if accompanied by sweet pickled cucumbers. Hot beetroot is lovely with lamb, venison and the stronger-flavoured game. Try tossing in the roasting juices or butter with a light sprinkling of herbs.

◊ Horseradish, pickled cucumber, chives, shallots, spring onions and parsley are all traditional accompaniments, while orange juice, nut oils, honey, dill, apples, walnuts, celery, lamb's lettuce, watercress and sour cream are more recent pairings.

Smoked salmon with beetroot lime relish

Salmon and beetroot are not commonly associated with each other, but curiously they work beautifully together, the sweet and sour taste of the beetroot enhancing the smoky richness of the salmon. You can use shop-bought cooked and vinegared beetroot for this recipe. (Serves 6)

½ tablespoon runny honey
1 tablespoon finely chopped
   dill
1 lime, finely grated and juiced
255g/9oz cooked beetroot
½ cucumber, peeled
salt and freshly ground black
   pepper
115g/4oz good cream cheese

9 thin slices good brown
   bread
370g/13oz finely sliced
   smoked salmon

Garnish
2 limes, cut into wedges
6 sprigs dill

Mix together the honey, dill, lime zest and juice. Trim and peel the beetroot before cutting into fine matchsticks. Add to the honey dressing. Slice the cucumber into rounds before cutting into like-sized matchsticks. Mix into the beetroot and season to taste.

Spread the cream cheese evenly over the bread slices. Cover with the smoked salmon and trim the crusts before cutting each slice into 4 triangles. Divide the smoked salmon 'points' between 6 appetizer plates and arrange in an attractive manner. Quickly grind some black pepper over them, and add the relish in a little pile on each plate. Garnish with lime wedges and fresh dill and serve immediately.

Beetroot parsley salad

The fresh taste of the herbs makes this a fragrant summer salad. (Serves 4)

455g/1lb cooked baby beetroot
1 lemon, finely grated
3 tablespoons flat-leaf parsley
  leaves
3 tablespoons sliced chives
1 tablespoon finely shredded
  mint leaves

2 tablespoons tiny capers,
  rinsed and drained
1 tablespoon balsamic vinegar
3 tablespoons extra virgin
  olive oil or walnut oil
salt and freshly ground black
  pepper

If necessary, peel and trim the beetroot before cutting it into quarters. Place in a bowl with the lemon zest and herbs. Squeeze any excess liquid out of the capers and add to the beetroot. Whisk together the vinegar and oil, season to taste and thoroughly mix into the beetroot.

Baby beets in crème fraîche

Although the cream turns a wild pink, beetroot tastes very good dressed like this and served with grilled meat. In the past hot beetroot tended to be served either tossed in butter or meat juices with roasted button onions, or lightly seasoned with vinegar and dressed with reduced cream. Herbs were added according to the taste of the cook. (Serves 4)

455g/1lb raw baby beetroot
salt
1 bunch fat salad onions,
  trimmed
2 tablespoons olive oil

4 tablespoons crème fraîche
1 lemon, finely grated
¼ teaspoon finely chopped
  sage
freshly ground black pepper

Wash the beetroot and trim the leaves, leaving 2.5cm/1 inch of stem attached. Add them to a pan of boiling salted water and cook for 20–30 minutes or until tender. Drain and spread out to cool on a plate. Peel and trim them as soon as it is comfortable to hold them.

Quarter or halve the salad onions, depending on their size. Heat the olive oil in a saucepan and gently fry the onions for 2–3 minutes or until they begin to soften. Add the beetroot, crème fraîche, lemon zest, sage and seasoning to taste. As soon as it is hot, remove and serve.

Note: Salad onions look like spring onions with fat white bulbs – if none are available, just substitute the fattest spring onions you can find.

Beetroot crisps

There are only a certain number of dishes that large beetroot are fit for, and crisps is one of them. Different vegetable crisps have become very popular in Britain, to such a degree that they can now be bought as a savoury snack food. But they taste even better home-made, particularly as a delicious accompaniment to game and duck. They can even be added to salads. As is so often the case with cooking, all the normal rules governing the preparation of beetroot are ignored for this particular recipe. (Serves 4)

4 large beetroot	1 teaspoon finely chopped
vegetable oil for deep frying	thyme
salt	

Preheat the oven to 130°C/250°F/gas ½. Scrub the beetroot clean under cold running water. Cut away their roots and stems and peel before finely slicing. Use either a food processor or a mandoline. Wrap your knuckles in an old tea towel if you are using the latter, as beetroot are tough and it is easy to slip. Unfortunately the tea towel will probably be stained permanently.

Heat the oil to 180°C/350°F. Slip the beetroot slices in small batches into the oil and cook for about 2 minutes or until they become speckled with tiny blisters. Do not cook until brown or they will taste bitter. Remove and drain on kitchen paper before spreading out on a baking sheet. They will not become crisp until they begin to cool. Repeat until you have finished all the crisps. Then place in the oven for 30 minutes so that they gently dry out further, before tipping into a large mixing bowl. Sprinkle with salt and thyme and serve warm or cold.

The crisps can be made in advance and reheated in a low oven.

BLACKBERRIES

They have what no grown up has – that directness – chatter, chatter
chatter, on Ann goes, in a kind of world of her own, with its seals &
dogs; happy because she's going to have cocoa tonight, & go black-
berrying tomorrow: the walls of her mind all hung round with such
bright vivid things, & she doesn't see what we see.

The Diary of Virginia Woolf, 1924

The taste of wild blackberries eaten straight from the briar evokes for many a very British flavour redolent with childhood memories: secret expeditions to a favourite blackberry patch punctuated with indignation if some unknown hand had already pillaged the sweetest, plumpest berries. Until recently blackberries were affectionately regarded in Britain as a plentiful free food, perfect for the home and nursery, but not for the more refined interpretations of British cooking. The few recipe books that mentioned them did so in a manner more reminiscent of a social conscience than gastronomic pleasure. Mrs Rundell, for example, in *Modern Domestic Cookery*, 1853, epitomizes this attitude with her entry under blackberry jam:

In families where there are many children there is no preparation of fruit so wholesome, so cheap, and so much admired, as this homely conserve. The fruit should be clean picked in dry weather, and to every lb. of berries put ½lb. of coarse brown sugar; boil the whole together for ¾ of an hour or 1 hour, stirring it well the whole time. Put it in pots like any other preserve, and it will be found most useful in families, as it may be given to children instead of medicine; makes excellent puddings; and even if the fruit be purchased in London, the cost will not exceed 8d. per lb.

Even *Farmhouse Fare*, published in 1946, is filled with useful country recipes to cure colds and sore throats with blackberry cordials and syrups. Consequently the majority of our traditional recipes are designed to preserve large quantities of freshly picked wild blackberries. They were partnered with apples, elderberries and occasionally sloes, all of which were gathered at the same time. It was only the excess that was used fresh in puddings, such as that definitive if dull dish of apple and blackberry pie.

Although blackberries are indigenous to Britain, they were rarely cultivated for anything other than game cover until early in the twentieth century, despite the fact that the Americans had begun to domesticate them by the mid 1830s. Their invasive briars were considered too thorny and unpleasant for British gardens. However, in recent years they have begun to become more popular, both commercially and in domestic gardens. Supermarkets now sell them throughout much of the year, although to my mind these berries lack the sweet subtlety of wild brambles. Somehow, the majority of imports seem very tart and watery. Nevertheless, it assures us of a plentiful supply of native berries in the autumn and there are many urban cooks who are grateful for an excuse to cook a gooey hazelnut crumble. This sudden abundance has also benefited chefs, who as a result have introduced grouse with blackberry jelly, Calvados-soaked apple and blackberry pies, velvety blackberry lemon cream pots, bramble ice creams and soft meringues topped with cream and warm blackberries on to their menus.

Practical guide

Although there are at least 400 micro-species of blackberry growing wild in Britain, most experienced pickers only differentiate between blackberries and dewberries – the latter being covered by a dull white bloom and having fewer nodules to their fruit. Some maintain that dewberries have the finer flavour. In reality different species fruit at different times, some early, others late, and each tastes subtly different. They can be found growing everywhere, from the back garden to scrubland, hedge, heath and woodland.

Wild blackberries (or brambles as they are also called in some parts of the country) flower from May until October and will fruit from August to November. The first crop yields the best fruit, while the smaller secondary crop is good for jam and fruit purées. Remember that black fruit must be soft before it will taste sweet. If you wish to go picking, make sure that you wear thick, protective clothing and wellington boots, no matter how hot the weather, as the thorns will inevitably scratch you and bare legs and arms make easy targets. It is worth taking a walking stick to hook back aggressive canes, and plenty of plastic carrier bags that can be conveniently stuffed in the pockets until needed. Always choose a patch away from fields that may have been sprayed or heavily polluted roads.

Once home, gently tip small batches of the berries on to a clean white tray. This will allow you to pick off any little wiggly creatures before serving or freezing the berries. Washing should be avoided unless it is an emergency, in which case place the berries in a colander and dip in a sink filled with cold water. This also applies to home-grown and bought berries. Although blackberries taste best eaten at room temperature, they should be stored in the fridge as they quickly turn mouldy after picking.

Domesticated blackberries have become an increasingly popular garden fruit, perhaps because of their enormous size. I find them a little too sharp to enjoy raw but they are excellent cooked. If you crave that wild taste in your garden, you should choose a near relation such as Ashton Cross. If you desire large fruit free from thorns, then Loch Ness is your bramble. Alternatively, Fantasia has taken the lead in the domesticated flavour stakes, while the more acidic Bedford Giant continues to be a popular early fruiter.

Commercially grown blackberries can now be bought for much of the year. However, they should be used as a culinary fruit as their dark colour belies their tart taste. They are at their best in August and September.

Taste notes

◊ Add a few unripe red berries to blackberry jam or jelly – their acidity will add flavour and help the mixture to set.

◊ Traditionally blackberries have been partnered with apples, in particular with the early windfalls. These are made into jam, jelly and chutney as well as pies, crumbles and autumn puddings. The proportions are a matter of taste – Jane Grigson, for example, recommends half the weight of blackberries to the weight of apples in fruit puddings. It is worth remembering that they also taste wonderful cooked with peaches, nectarines, pears or raspberries.

◊ Add a light spicing of cinnamon, allspice, cloves, Chinese five-spice, peppercorns or fresh chillies to enhance their deliciously musky scent, and use unrefined sugars for extra depth of flavour. For more delicate flavourings use fresh scented geranium leaves, mint leaves, lemon or orange zest, vanilla pods or almond essence.

◊ A splash of fruit liqueur such as blackberry, raspberry, blackcurrant or kirsch can add a surprising richness to a simple pudding, while savoury fruit sauces can be enhanced with port.

◊ Over the last twenty years or so, blackberries have been transformed into jellies, sauces and relishes to serve as an accompaniment to grouse, partridge, pigeon, duck and venison.

Duck with blackberry relish

A modern variation of blackberry sauce. (Serves 4)

1 small fresh red chilli, finely
chopped
3 tablespoons finely chopped
coriander
2 tablespoons lime juice
2 ripe nectarines
salt and freshly ground black
pepper

225g/8oz fresh blackberries
caster sugar to taste
4 duck breasts, with their skin
attached
¼ teaspoon five-spice powder

Place the finely chopped chilli and coriander with the lime juice in a small mixing bowl. Stone the nectarines, then neatly dice and mix into the lime juice. Season to taste before adding the blackberries. Finally sweeten to taste if necessary.

Shortly before you are ready to serve, trim the duck breasts by removing any tough sinews. Add some salt and black pepper to the five-spice powder. Lightly score the duck fat into diamonds and rub the breasts all over with the spiced mixture.

Set a non-stick frying pan over a moderately high heat and arrange the duck breasts skin side down in it. Fry for 5 minutes, then flip the breasts over and cook for a further 5 minutes if you like your duck medium rare. You may need to tip off some of the excess fat as they cook.

Serve the sizzling hot duck accompanied by the blackberry relish, which is at room temperature.

Lemon blackberry cream pots

This is a fruity variation of burnt cream (crème brûlée), with the obvious difference that the top is not caramelized. It is equally good with a caramel topping – just sprinkle with demerara sugar and set under an exceptionally hot grill or use a blow torch. Choose the fattest, sweetest blackberries that you can find. (Serves 4)

3 lemons, finely pared	6 tablespoons caster sugar
565ml/1 pint double cream	225g/8oz blackberries
4 large egg yolks	

Place the finely pared lemon peel in the cream and gently heat to scalding point. Cover and leave to infuse for 20 minutes.

Whisk the egg yolks with the sugar in a large bowl until pale and creamy. Slowly add the cream, beating all the time. Return the mixture to a clean saucepan and place over a low heat, stirring continuously until the custard begins to thicken. It will take about 20 minutes to reach the right consistency. If you think the custard is getting too hot, just lift the pan off the heat and continue to stir. Gradually you will feel the custard thickening. Once it begins to become thick and velvety, remove from the heat and continue to stir until it cools a little. Place over a bowl of iced water if wished.

Divide the blackberries between 4 small ramekins. If they are sharp, toss them in some extra sugar. Strain the lemon cream through a fine sieve and pour over the blackberries. Cover and chill for 2 hours or until the cream is completely cold and set.

Blackberry geranium jelly

Pots of blackberry jelly are the stuff of winter teas, melting into hot butter-soaked crumpets or scones. However, they also make an excellent addition to fruit pies and some game sauces. The custom of adding a herbal flavouring to jams and jellies is also peculiarly British. I first came across this combination of flavours in Elizabeth David's *Summer Cooking*. Scented geraniums (pelargoniums – *P. radula*) are widely available from garden centres. Simply crush a leaf between your fingers to ascertain its scent – rose, lemon, cinnamon . . . Choose your favourite variety for this recipe, ensuring that it is home-grown and free from pesticides.

Blackberries only contain a moderate amount of pectin, so they have to be either mixed with a pectin-high fruit such as cooking apples, or given some pectin artificially, to allow them to set properly. The addition of a few unripe red blackberries or the juice of 1 small lemon will also help to set the jelly. (Makes around 455g/1lb)

8 scented geranium leaves,	granulated sugar
freshly picked	15g/½oz butter
1.1kg/2½lb fresh blackberries	½ bottle Certo, an apple-
285ml/½ pint water	based pectin extract

Gently rinse the geranium leaves in cool water before placing in a large pan with the blackberries and water. Bring up to a boil, then simmer for 30 minutes or until very soft. The blackberries should have released all their juice.

Remove from the heat and drain through a jelly bag for 12 hours. Measure the liquid and allow 455g/1lb sugar to every 565ml/1 pint of liquid.

Preheat the oven to low and warm the sugar along with the washed jam jars.

Pour the juice into a jam pan and clip a thermometer on to the side of the saucepan. Warm the juice before adding the warm sugar, and stir over a low heat until it has dissolved. Add the butter and Certo, increase the heat and boil rapidly until the thermometer registers 105°C/221°F – jam setting point. Once it reaches this point, boil for a further 2 minutes before removing from the heat.

If you do not have a thermometer, chill a saucer in the fridge before you begin – then allow the jelly to boil for no longer than 10 minutes before removing from the heat and placing a small drop of jelly on to the cold saucer. As soon as it is cool, gently push the jelly with your finger – if it wrinkles, setting point has been reached. If not, return the pan to the heat and continue to boil for a further minute or two.

Once you are satisfied that your jelly has reached setting point, remove from the heat, skim off any scum and pour into the warm jam jars. Press a small waxed disc, waxed side down, on to the jelly and once cold, seal, label and date

Almond cake with apple and blackberry salad

This can be served for tea or as a pudding, but in either case you may well find yourself pressed by your guests for the recipe. (Serves 6)

170g/6oz softened butter	1 lemon, finely pared and
170g/6oz caster sugar	juiced
3 large eggs, separated	55g/2oz granulated sugar
85g/3oz self-raising flour,	3 dessert apples, such as Cox's
sifted	Orange Pippin, cored and
285ml/½ pint dessert wine e.g.	sliced
Sauterne	225g/8oz fresh blackberries
85g/3oz ground almonds	

Preheat the oven to 170°C/325°F/gas 3 and butter a 20cm/8 inch spring-form cake tin. Beat the butter and caster sugar until pale and fluffy, then gradually beat in the egg yolks followed by 2 tablespoons flour and 85ml/3 fl oz dessert wine. Lightly fold in half the almonds, followed by half the remaining flour, then fold in the remaining almonds and the last of the flour.

Immediately whisk the egg whites in a clean, dry bowl until they form firm peaks. Quickly fold them into the cake mix, then spoon the mixture into the cake tin and place in the centre of the oven. Bake for 40–50 minutes or until a skewer comes out clean. Turn out and place on a cooling rack over a deep-rimmed plate.

While the cake is baking, place the lemon peel, granulated sugar and 140ml/¼ pint of water in a small, non-corrosive saucepan. Dissolve over low heat, then simmer gently for 10 minutes. Remove from the heat and stir in the remaining wine and lemon juice.

Prick the warm cake with a fork, then slowly pour over half the syrup. Leave to cool. Reheat the remaining syrup and add the sliced apples. Once the mixture is cool, add the blackberries and serve in a pretty glass bowl as an accompaniment to the syrupy cake. Those of an extravagant disposition can accompany it with lots of thick double cream.

Bramble hazelnut crumble

This is one of my favourite recipes. The crumble has become an essential part of our post-war repertoire of puddings that are now considered quintessentially British. Its criteria are that it must have a juicy filling and a crisp topping that melts into an exquisite goo as it sinks into the fruit filling. The rich, port-like flavour of elderberries enhances the taste of the blackberries in a surprisingly gorgeous way. If you do not have any jelly, pick 8 sprays of ripe elderberries. You will also need to add extra sugar – around 115g/4oz extra.

The following method for making the crumble topping is unorthodox but delicious. If you do not have a food processor you will have to buy ground hazelnuts. Work the butter into the flour by hand, then stir in the sugar and nuts. (Serves 4)

720g/1lb 9½oz blackberries	*Crumble topping*
4 tablespoons elderberry jelly or cordial	170g/6oz plain flour
115g/4oz unrefined caster sugar or to taste	55g/2oz whole unblanched hazelnuts
½ teaspoon ground cinnamon	115g/4oz nearly frozen cold butter, diced
	55g/2oz unrefined caster sugar

Preheat the oven to 200°C/400°F/gas 6.

Place the blackberries, elderberry jelly, sugar and ground cinnamon in the pie dish and gently mix together. If using fresh elderberries, wash them in plenty of cold water, watching out for all the wildlife, especially those long-legged spiders, then strip the berries from their stems and mix into the remaining fruit.

Place the flour and hazelnuts in a food processor. Whizz until the nuts form fine crumbs, then add the diced butter. Briefly process for a minute or two, until the butter forms fine breadcrumbs. Remove to a bowl and mix in the sugar.

Cover the fruit with the crumble mixture and press down lightly but evenly. Place in the centre of the preheated oven and bake for 25 minutes before reducing the temperature to 190°C/375°F/gas 5. Continue to bake for a further 15 minutes. Best served hot or warm with lots of thick cream or home-made custard (see page 88).

CUCUMBER

The pride of the Gardeners about London chiefly consists in the production of Melons and Cucumbers at times either before or after the natural season.

Richard Bradley, 1719

Elegant hothouse cucumbers have graced British tables for centuries, long before the invention of the sandwich in 1762 or indeed of cooling glasses of Pimm's in the late nineteenth century. We appear to have acquired a taste for this refined vegetable fruit from the late sixteenth century on; despite the gloomy writings of Robert Burton in 1621, who cited cucumbers along with coleworts, gourds, melons and cabbages as a cause for melancholy, provoking troublesome dreams and sending black vapours to the brain. Obviously natural good taste prevailed and the hothouse cucumber was developed for the benefit of cooks who then stewed, stuffed, baked and pickled it. Such dishes were not without risk if bought from the grocer, as Mrs Rundell points out in 1853 in *Modern Domestic Cookery*:

As an additional reason for preparing them [pickled gherkins] at home, it is indeed well known that the very fine green pickles are made so by the dealers using brass or bell-metal vessels, which, when vinegar is put into them, become highly poisonous.

Fortunately, such dangers have long since been eradicated and most modern cooks prefer to buy ready-made pickled cucumbers and gherkins.

Our taste in preparing cucumbers may have changed, but the critical comments regarding unseasonal tasteless crops persist. Cucumber can be found in a wide variety of dishes from salads to salsas. Its subtle flavour is blended with influences from as far afield as Thailand and India as well as the more familiar traditional accompaniments. Chilli-spiced sweet vinegar sauces, for example, reflect Thai influences as much as Victorian tastes, while yoghurt-based sauces and soups hint at Indian or Middle Eastern influences. The current popularity of the salad has allowed the cucumber to rise above that grim invention – the mixed green salad. Who can remember without dread that awful concoction of limp lettuce, woolly tomatoes, tasteless cucumbers and salad cream? Modern salads are heavenly by comparison – delicate cubes of cucumber, for example, mixed with juicy cubes of pear and radish and lightly seasoned with lemon juice, salt and pepper. The only area where the cucumber appears to have dwindled in popularity is as a cooked vegetable. Simply peeled, seeded and sliced before being fried in butter, it makes a lovely dish, especially when finished with dill and crème fraîche.

Perhaps restaurants will re-establish its reputation as an accompaniment when they serve elegant strips of cucumber mixed with leeks, carrots and mouli.

Practical guide

Cucumis sativus, commonly known as cucumber, can be divided into two main types: smooth green indoor varieties, sometimes referred to as English or greenhouse cucumbers, and outdoor or ridge varieties. The latter gained their name from the practice of growing them along ridges to improve the soil drainage. Ridge cucumbers can be subdivided into traditional cultivars which tend to yield small, roughly textured cucumbers; Japanese cultivars which have slightly longer (around 30cm/12 inches) smooth-skinned fruit; round fruited cultivars, which yield very juicy apple-shaped fruit; bush cultivars which do not climb in a vine-like manner, and gherkins, which yield tiny cucumbers perfect for pickling. Gardeners can pickle or sauté any excess small cucumbers from their plants, whatever their variety.

In Britain tender indoor varieties are available throughout the year, while ridge cucumbers tend to be sold more widely during their season, which runs from July until October. There is no agreement as to whether one variety tastes better than another, so the most sensible approach is to be guided by the appearance of the cucumber. Always choose fruit that looks plump and juicy. Avoid any that feel spongy when pressed or have begun to wrinkle. Unfortunately, since most cucumbers are waxed you cannot judge whether they have a good natural gloss.

They can be stored for up to a week in the salad drawer of a fridge, but never let them get too cold as their high water content freezes easily and on defrosting turns the cucumber into an unpleasantly slimy green sausage. Undoubtedly they taste best if eaten as soon as possible.

There is much advice given in cookery books on whether to peel and/or salt cucumbers. Cucumber peel is reputed by some to induce wind and by others to prevent it. Certainly, some tough-skinned varieties such as the round apple cucumber should be peeled before eating as their skin makes them unpleasantly chewy. Otherwise, it is purely a matter of taste. The custom of salting cucumber is easier to understand. Indoor cucumbers do not need to be salted or soaked in vinegar. The practice probably originated with the French, who have predominantly grown ridge cucumbers. These can turn tough and bitter late in the season and these problems can be remedied by salting. To find a bitter cucumber these days is unusual, so the only reason for salting is if you wish to remove any excess juice from your cucumber before adding it to a sauce or mousse, or if you wish to make your slices particularly soft and pliable. If you wish to seed your cucumber, slice in half lengthways and use a teaspoon to neatly dig out and discard the seeds.

Taste notes

◊ Thin slices of cucumber or strips of cucumber rind make a cooling addition to Pimm's, summer punches, iced wine or champagne cups. They work particularly well if accompanied by borage flowers, as these have a delicate cucumber aroma.

◊ A wide variety of herbs complement cucumbers, including dill, tarragon, mint, borage, chives, chervil and parsley.

◊ Cucumbers are commonly used as an accompaniment to fish and shellfish – oysters, prawns, lobster and crab as well as salmon, sole, monkfish, sea bass, halibut and hake.

◊ Traditionally, cucumbers were also served hot with lamb, pigeon, duck and chicken.

◊ Cucumbers cool quickly, so they should be cooked at the last possible moment and served immediately. They can be cooked in butter and if wished finished with stock and/or cream.

◊ Cold cucumber sauces can be flavoured with tarragon vinegar, cream, crème fraîche, Greek yoghurt, black pepper, cayenne pepper, ground roasted cumin seeds, garlic and any number of herbs.

Cucumber sandwiches

Cucumber sandwiches are very easy to make, their excellence depending more on the quality of the ingredients than the skill of the cook.

½ cucumber, peeled

sea salt

unsalted butter, softened

8 slices good white bread

freshly ground black pepper

Slice the cucumbers thinly, so that you can see the knife blade through the cucumber slice as you cut. Lightly salt and leave to drain in a colander for 10 minutes.

Quickly butter all the bread on one side. Then neatly cover 4 of the buttered slices with cucumber. Season with some freshly ground black pepper before covering with the remaining bread. Press gently together, then trim the crusts and cut into the required shape. Serve immediately.

Cucumber salad

This is one of my favourite summer cucumber salads. Its zingy flavours are very refreshing and work well with grilled food. The contrast between the sweetness of the pear and the pepperiness of the radishes perfectly complements the cucumber. (Serves 4)

½ cucumber, peeled
2 bunches (or packets)
   radishes
2 ripe pears

½ lemon, juiced, or to taste
salt and freshly ground black
   pepper

Cut the cucumber into medium-sized dice and place in a salad bowl. Wash and trim the radishes, cut into similar sized dice, and add to the cucumber.

Peel and quarter the pears. Remove their cores and cut into the same sized dice. Add to the salad and immediately mix in some of the lemon juice. Season with salt and pepper to taste and adjust the lemon juice. Serve within 30 minutes of making.

Grilled prawns with spiced cucumber dressing

A wide variety of cucumber sauces have been created to accompany fish dishes. Cold sauces have included mayonnaise or tarragon-flavoured creams. However, the Victorian taste for cucumber flavoured with a chilli vinegar has been unwittingly reinterpreted in Thai style to make this delicious modern sauce.

Buy the large headless prawns or whole langoustines for this recipe. If the langoustines are plump and large, reduce the number you buy accordingly. In either case they should be allowed to defrost slowly in the fridge. Mirin is a form of sweetened sake. (Serves 4 as a starter)

24 raw prawns or langoustines	½ teaspoon dried chilli
1 clove garlic, crushed	flakes
1 tablespoon soy sauce	5 tablespoons boiling water
1 tablespoon mirin	2½ tablespoons white wine
2 tablespoons sesame oil	vinegar
	1 cucumber, peeled, seeded
Cucumber dressing	and finely diced
2 tablespoons granulated	
sugar	

Peel the prawns, then cut a tiny slit down the length of their backs. Pull away the black digestive cord (if it is there) and gently rinse. Pat dry and place in a bowl with the garlic, soy sauce, mirin and sesame oil. Cover and chill for up to 1 hour.

Place the sugar and chilli flakes in a small mixing bowl. Pour on the boiling water and stir until the sugar has dissolved, then add the vinegar. Mix in the diced cucumber and season to taste with salt. Cover and chill until needed.

Preheat a ribbed cast-iron oven-top grill. When it is hot, add the prawns, in batches if necessary. Within a couple of minutes they will begin to turn a rosy pink, at which stage turn them over and continue to cook for a further 2 minutes. As soon as they are cooked, keep them warm until the rest are done, then serve piping hot with the spicy cucumber sauce.

Note: If you are using a barbecue, you will need to thread the prawns on to skewers to help prevent them from falling through the bars. Allowing 6 prawns per person, spear each portion on to 2 parallel skewers, so that the prawns are held rigid and cannot twist around. Place on a very hot barbecue and cook for about 2 minutes per side.

Dover sole with cucumber and tomato

Traditional hot cucumber sauces are quite rich by modern tastes, as they include complex veloutés to which poached and puréed cucumber is added with cream, or unctuous butter sauces to which diced cucumbers are added. Happily the current vogue for quickly prepared, fresh-flavoured foods is creating a demand for new recipes. (Serves 2)

½ cucumber
1 ripe tomato
1 tablespoon finely chopped chives
1 tablespoon finely chopped chervil
2 whole Dover sole, 170g-225g/6–8oz each, skinned

1 tablespoon olive oil
salt and freshly ground black pepper
30g/1oz butter
1 teaspoon lemon juice

Preheat the grill to its highest setting and brush the grid with oil to help prevent the fish from sticking.

Peel and halve the cucumber lengthways. Remove its seeds with a teaspoon and cut into neat dice. Cover the tomato with boiling water for a few seconds, then remove and peel as soon as it is cool enough to handle. Quarter and cut away the seeds. Cut its flesh into the same sized dice as the cucumbers. Mix the herbs in with the tomato.

Brush the fish with olive oil and lightly season. Place under the grill and cook each side for 4–5 minutes.

As soon as the fish is nearly cooked, melt half the butter in a non-stick frying pan. Add the cucumber and fry over a moderately high heat for 2 minutes. Season generously, then add the tomato and herbs along with the lemon juice. Heat through, then stir in the remaining butter and remove from the heat. Plate the fish and spoon over the sauce so that it partially covers the Dover sole.

Note: If you are unable to get skinned sole, do not worry as it is easy to remove. Cut a nick at the tail end, gently insert the handle of a teaspoon under the skin and lift it up. Then, using a cloth to protect your hands from its abrasive skin and give you a firmer grip, pull the skin hard towards the head of the fish. It should peel off. Repeat with the other side. Finally, take a pair of kitchen scissors and trim around the edges and tidy its tail. If you do not like looking at its cooked head, remove this too.

Rabbit and cucumber fricassée

Bunny lovers should despair not, as this recipe can be adapted to skinned corn-fed chicken breast if wished. As this is a quick-cooking recipe, use farmed rabbit rather than wild. (Serves 4)

1 rabbit, boned and jointed (or 4 skinned chicken breasts)	6 slices back bacon, trimmed of fat and diced
salt and freshly ground black pepper	285ml/½ pint well-flavoured chicken stock (see page 339 or buy ready-made)
3 tablespoons olive oil	140ml/¼ pint double cream
3 tablespoons Armagnac	1 cucumber
1 clove garlic, crushed	a pinch of ground mace
2 shallots, finely sliced	

Cut the rabbit (or chicken) into large bite-sized pieces and season. Heat the oil in a large non-stick or heavy-bottomed frying pan. As soon as it is sizzling hot, quickly colour the rabbit (or chicken) in batches until golden. Once finished, return the meat to the hot pan, pour over the brandy, stand well back and ignite. Stir the rabbit (or chicken) as the flames shoot into the air, then remove with a slotted spoon and set aside.

Reduce the temperature and add the garlic, shallots and bacon. Cook until the shallots are soft, then add the chicken stock and bring to the boil, scraping vigorously to remove any crispy bits from the bottom of the pan. Keep at a full rolling boil for 3 minutes then stir in the cream. Return to the boil and let it bubble for a further 3 minutes.

At this stage return the rabbit (or chicken) pieces to the pan along with any juices and simmer gently for 4–5 minutes. Meanwhile peel the cucumber and cut in half lengthways. Remove the seeds with a teaspoon and slice the flesh into thick sickle moons. Stir these into the fricassée and continue to simmer for a further 3 minutes. Finally, season to taste with a pinch of mace, salt and pepper and serve piping hot.

See also
Cold tomato yoghurt soup (page 197)
Smoked salmon with beetroot lime relish (page 60)

ELDERFLOWERS

Successive Crys the Seasons Change declare,
And mark the Monthly Progress of the year.
Hark, how the Streets with treble Voices ring,
To sell the bounteous Product of the Spring!
Sweet-smelling Flow'rs, and Elder's early Bud,
With Nettle's tender Shoots, to cleanse the Blood:
And when *June's* Thunder cools the sultry Skies,
Ev'n *Sundays* are prophan'd by Mackrell Cries.

Trivia, or the Art of Walking the Streets of London by
John Gay, 1716

There are certain aspects of British cookery that never cease to fascinate me, and one of these is the extraordinary ability we have to gather up the delicate flavours of our countryside and transform them into exquisite dishes. Sweet-scented violets, primroses, cowslips, lime blossom, elderflowers and roses have been picked by British cooks since time immemorial and converted into fragrant messes. But while primroses, cowslips and lime blossom have slipped from common usage, the elderflower has remained popular.

It is one of those subtle flavourings that makes a dish taste quintessentially British. What Frenchman would dream of adding elderflower to his rhubarb compote? What American would add a dash of elderflower cordial to his spritzer? And surely no Italian would churn a gooseberry and elderflower sorbet? Yet as far as the British are concerned, elderflowers, with their sweet scent of Muscat grapes, add an indefinable charm to countless dishes from cooling drinks to creamy custards.

Traditionally elderflowers, like many other flowers, were infused into vinegars, cordials and wines. This custom certainly dates back to the sixteenth century, but may well have originated far earlier. The flavouring of vinegar with elderflowers continued until well into the nineteenth century. Mrs Rundell, in *Modern Domestic Cookery*, 1853, even goes so far as to suggest adding tarragon to her elderflower vinegar as 'a mixture of both is very agreeable'. Elderflower cordial, Frontiniac, wine and champagne are still made in Britain today, both at home and in some instances commercially. They are made from the delicious combination of elderflowers, lemon and sugar, although Frontiniac also contains raisins and matures beautifully.

Currently, the most popular use of elderflowers is as a flavouring for gooseberries and rhubarb. A single stem cooked with a pan of fruit is sufficient to transform it into an irresistible dish, whether it be rhubarb fool or gooseberry jam. Happily, the revival of British cooking is beginning to lure cooks into exploring other possibilities with this delicate flower. Modern interpretations include elderflower custard, on to which islands of poached meringue can be floated, and elderflower syrup for summery fruit salads. Even the ancient dish of elderflower fritters has been revived on restaurant menus, although it is easily made at home. It must surely only be a matter of time before the custom of adding the tiny flowers to fluffy cake and pancake batters is also revived.

Practical guide

Elder bushes (*Sambucus nigra*) grow literally everywhere in the British Isles except in northern Scotland. They thrive in country lanes, woods, car parks, garden hedges and wastelands. Unnoticed for much of the year, they flower in June and July, blossoming later the further north you travel.

Never pick elderflowers unless you can safely identify them. Choose your sources carefully, avoiding heavily polluted areas and any farmland where they might get sprayed by pesticides. Ideally the flowers should be picked in the cool of the morning, although elderflowers have such a pronounced scent that few recipes will suffer if you happen to pick them later in the day.

Gather the flowers by snipping individual sprays off the tree. Carefully shake off as much insect life as you can before laying them in a basket. Unfortunately, thin long-legged brown spiders do tend to hide in the sprays, so arachnophobics beware. Avoid any blossoms that are infested with insect life or past their best.

Once home, contrary to popular advice, I recommend completely submerging the flowers in a sink of cool water. Any hidden six- or eight-legged friends are then forced to swim rather than drown. I feel that the removal of wildlife justifies any slight loss of flavour. Gently shake the water from the flowers and leave to dry on paper towelling if making fritters or freezing, otherwise add to your recipe as required.

Elderflowers freeze very well and can be added frozen to a dish as a flavouring. Prepare as above, allow to dry, then package in small, single-portion polythene bags. They can be kept in the freezer for six months. Never defrost before use, as they turn a nasty brown and smell rotten. Alternatively, you can buy dried elderflowers from good herbalists such as Culpeper's in London. Tie them in a small square of muslin and add in moderation, just as you would dried herbs, as they have an intense flavour. Store in an airtight container in a cool, dark place.

Taste notes

◊ Elderflower vinegar is easily made (see lavender vinegar, page 154) and makes a superb seasoning for fish. Otherwise, add a dash of sugar, a twist of lemon and lots of iced soda and enjoy as a refreshing summer drink.

◊ Elderflower syrup (see lavender syrup, page 154) is a good way of pre-serving the flowers, although it can also be bought from some supermarkets. Add it to fruit puddings just as you would the flowers.

◊ Traditionally, elderflowers were used as a substitute for Frontignan, a sweet Muscat wine, as they taste remarkably similar. Elderflower wine makes an excellent addition to icing – simply moisten the icing sugar with the wine and a little lemon juice. Butter icing can also be flavoured in this way.

Floating islands

This romantically named pudding certainly dates back in name, if not in content, to the eighteenth century, as Hannah Glasse gives a recipe for 'The Flooting Island, a pretty Dish for the Middle of a Table at a second Course or for Supper' in her *The Art of Cookery Made Plain and Easy*. However, her dish consists of islands of thinly sliced rounds of bread, layered with currant jelly and hartshorn jelly before being topped by the thick creamy froth of syllabub. The thinner, separated liquid from the syllabub is then poured into a pretty glass bowl and the islands are arranged in this. From the nineteenth century floating islands were made from poached meringue and then floated in a sea of custard. These were sometimes covered in a golden cage of spun sugar. A little too sweet for my taste.

The elderflowers will imbue the custard with an exquisite taste that will keep your guests wondering at your genius. If you want to become ultra-sophisticated, try scattering a few poached gooseberries or fresh raspberries into the elderflower custard. Fresh, frozen or dried elderflowers can be used for this recipe. (Serves 4 – makes 12 islands)

Elderflower custard	6 medium egg yolks
4 elderflower heads	
425ml/¾ pint milk	*Islands*
2 strips lemon peel, finely	285ml/½ pint milk
pared	425ml/¾ pint water
115g/4oz caster sugar	3 medium egg whites
140ml/¼ pint double cream	95g/3½oz caster sugar

Gently wash the flower heads in cool water before placing in a saucepan with the milk, lemon peel and half the sugar. Heat to scalding point, stirring occasionally to ensure that all the sugar dissolves. Remove from the heat, cover and leave to infuse for 10 minutes.

Before you begin the custard, fill a large bowl with ice and a little water and set a medium-sized bowl over it with the double cream.

In another bowl whisk the egg yolks with the remaining sugar until they leave a trail. Gradually whisk in the hot strained elderflower milk and immediately return the mixture to the saucepan. Still stirring, with a wooden spoon, set over a low heat and continue to stir until the custard is as thick as runny double cream. Do not let the custard boil or it will split. Quickly pour through a fine sieve into the iced bowl of cream and continue to stir until it is cool. Cover and chill in your serving dish.

Meanwhile, prepare the islands by pouring the milk and water into a wide, shallow saucepan. Bring to a very gentle simmer, so that only the occasional bubble floats up.

Place the egg whites in a large, clean, dry bowl and whisk until they form soft peaks. Slowly add the sugar, whisking all the time, until they form a stiff, glossy meringue. Using 2 dessertspoons, shape the meringue into a lozenge (i.e. a heaped dessertspoon shape) and drop with the help of the other spoon into the barely simmering liquid. Repeat until you have 4 islands poaching in the milky water. Cook for 1 minute, then carefully flip them over and cook for another minute. Do not overcook them or they will disintegrate.

Gently lift the cooked meringues out with a slotted spoon and lay them on a cooling rack to drain. Continue to cook the remaining mixture. Once finished, leave the islands to drip for 30 minutes, so that they will not dilute the custard. Then carefully float them on the elderflower custard and cover and chill until ready to serve.

Note: Fresh raspberries or a brilliantly coloured summer fruit purée can also be added to this pudding. In either case they should be added once the pudding is ladled into soup bowls.

Elderflower fritters

Elderflower fritters date back to medieval times, although these days many cooks prepare them by coating the flowers in a crispy tempura batter. However, on reading Florence White's book *Flowers as Food*, essential reading for any floweraholic, I came across this wonderful early eighteenth-century recipe which is credited to John Nott. I have adapted it slightly for the modern cook but it still makes a superb fritter. Choose the more delicate-stemmed flowers and serve with the gooseberry sauce. (Serves 4)

Gooseberry sauce
225g/8oz gooseberries, topped
   and tailed
115g/4oz caster sugar
140ml/¼ pint double cream

Fritters
12 elderflower heads
2 tablespoons good brandy
4 tablespoons sweet white
   (dessert) wine

1 lemon, finely grated
a pinch of cinnamon

Batter
55g/2oz plain flour
pinch of salt
2 large eggs, separated
115ml/4fl oz sweet white
   (dessert) wine
vegetable oil for deep frying
caster sugar

The gooseberry sauce can be made ahead. Place the gooseberries in a non-corrosive saucepan with 3 tablespoons of water. Simmer gently until they begin to release their juices, then increase the heat and cook until they form a mush. Purée and strain before sweetening to taste with the sugar. Stir in the cream and allow to cool.

Gently wash the elderflower heads in cool water, lightly shake off the excess water and spread out to dry on some paper towelling. Leave in a shady spot while you mix together the brandy, white wine, lemon zest and cinnamon. Break each flower head into 2–4 pieces and soak head down in the brandy. Lightly cover with some damp paper towelling and leave for 1 hour.

Shortly before you are ready to serve, sift the flour and a pinch of salt into a large mixing bowl and make a well in the centre. Separate the eggs, placing the whites in a clean, dry mixing bowl. Beat the wine into the yolks and slowly stir into the flour well, beating all the time to ensure that no lumps form.

Heat the oil to 180°C/350°F. Whisk the egg whites until they form soft peaks, then carefully fold into the batter. Holding an elderflower head by its stalk, dip into the batter until well coated, then drop into the hot oil. Repeat with the remaining blooms, frying them in batches until crisp and golden. Remove from the fat and quickly dry on paper towelling before snipping away the excess bitter stalks and arranging on a plate. Serve immediately, liberally dusted with caster sugar, with the gooseberry sauce.

Strawberry, cherry and elderflower salad

The delicate flavour of elderflowers works beautifully with a wide variety of summer fruit from early English strawberries to sweet cherries. Fresh, frozen or dried elderflowers can be used for this recipe. (Serves 4)

3 large elderflower heads	140ml/¼ pint dessert wine
½ lemon, finely pared and	140ml/¼ pint water
juiced	285g/10oz fat red cherries
115g/4oz granulated sugar	340g/12oz small strawberries

Gently dip the elderflower heads in cool water before placing in a non-corrosive pan with the lemon peel, sugar, wine and water. Dissolve the sugar over a moderate heat and simmer gently for 10 minutes. Remove from the heat, stir in the lemon juice and leave to cool slightly.

Wash and stem the cherries before cutting them in half and removing their stones over a mixing bowl, so that you capture their juice. Wash and hull the strawberries. Cut them in half if they are on the large side and mix into the cherries. Strain the warm (not hot) syrup over the fruit, pressing the juice from the flower heads. Leave to macerate until you are ready to eat.

See also
Gooseberry elderflower sorbet (page 101)
Rhubarb elderflower fool (page 249)

GOOSEBERRIES

As to the time and temperature for gooseberry eating opinions differ.
A friend tells me that the moment of moments and the day of days is
on the return from church at 12.30 on a warm July day when the fruit
is distinctly warm.

The Anatomy of Dessert by Edward Bunyard, 1929

Ribes grossularia, the parent of our modern gooseberry, is not native to Britain. In fact the first record of a British gooseberry bush appears in 1275, when Edward I imported some direct from France at 3d a bush for his garden at the Tower of London. Despite this relatively late start, the gooseberry made up for lost time until by the turn of the nineteenth century Britain was considered to be at the cutting edge of gooseberry cultivation.

The supreme adaptability of this unassuming plant to the British diet has fuelled our obsession. Initially its tender leaves were valued in spring salads, while its fruit, the first of the season, could be made into excellent wine and verjuice (a vinegar-like substance as essential to early British cooking as olive oil is to the modern cook). As the climate cooled, gooseberries began to replace grapes in the commercial production of wine, before later, with the arrival of cheap sugar, becoming a popular jam along with strawberries and plums. However, there is no disputing the fact that once people began to taste gooseberries freshly cooked with sugar they were smitten. Their lively flavour appealed to the national palate and transformed our much-loved fruit tarts, pies and fools into exquisite delicacies. In the same way their natural piquancy when cooked in a sauce enhanced the rich taste of roast pork, goose or duck, as well as the first spring mackerel.

By the early eighteenth century we were addicted, and gooseberry mania ruled the country. Northern gooseberry clubs were formed and competed fiercely to grow the largest and best tasting gooseberry. Each club carefully recorded every new variety grown by its members, until by 1826 the Horticultural Society listed 185 strains in its first catalogue. Market gardeners eagerly tried to extend its natural season, which runs from May to August, so that by 1722 gooseberries were being sold in Covent Garden as early as 3 April, while a century later Henry Phillips described in his *Pomarium Britannicum* (1827) how to keep gooseberries fresh on their bushes until Christmas. Cooks became so knowledgeable in gooseberry matters that writers cited appropriate varieties for certain recipes.

Inevitably, gooseberries suffered from the wide variety of fruit that became increasingly available throughout the year. Until recently, fresh gooseberries could only be found in country kitchens while city cooks rarely saw a green let alone a dessert gooseberry. Happily, the fortunes of the goosegog are on the ascendant once more as the supermarkets revise their sales policies and promote gooseberries as a speciality. Sweet-tasting translucent yellow and red dessert gooseberries can be bought in punnets like strawberries, while the sour green culinary gooseberries are sold from mid-June until August.

Practical guide

Traditionally gooseberries have been categorized by their colour, size and hairiness. Thus a gardener can choose between a green, yellow, white or red gooseberry, all of which are then subdivided into smooth or hairy categories which in turn can be divided into large- or small-fruited varieties. These include the large sweet dessert strains as well as the sharper flavoured culinary breeds. According to Edward Bunyard in his *Anatomy of Dessert*, green gooseberries have the best flavour, although the remainder still have an excellent taste. Leveller, a large yellow dessert gooseberry, is often thought to be one of the best sweet dessert gooseberries with its almost Muscat-like flavour, while Invictor and Careless are popular green cooking varieties. Red gooseberries appear to divide cookery writers over their merits, but the consensus for the moment appears to be that although they have a distinctive sweet taste, it is not quite as exquisite as the best yellow gooseberries. The red Whinham's Industry is often sold in the supermarkets.

The gooseberry season currently lasts from May through to the end of August, with the sweeter strains ripening towards the end of the season. The best way to buy gooseberries is from pick-your-own farms, as they can be selected according to the degree of ripeness you desire and, if necessary, in large quantities.

Gooseberries can be picked at several stages of their development. According to Ken Muir in his eminently useful *Grow Your Own Fruit* booklet, a gooseberry crop should be thinned in late May so that the later crop grows fatter. This first thinning can be pickled or used in tart sauces. The second picking should be made when the gooseberries are nearly at their full size but not yet ripe, which is when they have a good flavour. These are often referred to as green gooseberries, whatever colour they may actually be, and are always used for cooking. They are excellent in pies, tarts, ices, curds, sauces and pickles. Their high pectin content makes them ideal for both jam and jellies. Finally, gooseberries can be left until they are sweet and tender. If you are feeling smart, serve them washed, trimmed and prettily arranged in small silver bowls with a few of their leaves, as a summer dessert.

The fruit should always be washed before trimming, as the tiny hairs can harbour dust or worse. Opinion differs as to the easiest way to top and tail a gooseberry. Some use knives, others find a small pair of nail scissors better and a few just use their fingers to nip off the stalk and tiny brown calyx. Jane Grigson gives the very sensible advice that if you are going to make a gooseberry purée you do not need to top and tail your fruit as it is going to be strained, although I have to admit that I still do.

Taste notes

◊ The distinctive taste of gooseberries makes them a difficult fruit to match with other flavours. Elderflowers are their most common partner, although they can be mixed with fennel, mint and parsley. Curiously, lemon and lemony flavours such as mace or nutmeg also work well with them. They are frequently partnered with other astringent ingredients ranging from sorrel to rhubarb.

◊ As has been stated above, gooseberries can be served as a tart accompaniment to a wide variety of richly flavoured meat and fish. This can be in the guise of a sauce, pickle or onion and breadcrumb based stuffing. They can also be used to accompany oily fish such as mackerel or salmon.

◊ Pickled gooseberries can be served in all manner of dishes from piquant salads to elegant plates of cold meat, cured fish or even cheese.

◊ Dessert gooseberries should be served very simply. If you wish to make a more formal pudding, try dressing the sliced berries in an elderflower syrup (see page 92) or steeping them in a fragrant dessert wine.

Fennel, pickled gooseberry and salmon salad

Given the British predilection for pickles it is hardly surprising that gooseberries have also been preserved in this form. This is a very quick pickle to make but it improves with age. Use small tart green berries and remember that they will shrink as they mature.

If you wish, you can use the ready-sliced gravad lax available from most supermarkets. To make at home, ask the fishmonger to fillet a small salmon. This should yield 905g/2lb of salmon fillet. Rub its flesh with 1 tablespoon brandy, then liberally coat with 35g/1¼oz of coarse sea salt mixed with the same amount of granulated sugar and 3 tablespoons of finely chopped dill. Wrap the 2 fillets, flesh side together, in clingfilm in a shallow dish and cover with weights. Leave in the fridge for 24 hours, turning once. Thinly slice in the same way as for smoked salmon. (Serves 6)

Gooseberry pickle
(fills a 455g/1lb Kilner jar)
310g/11oz small green or red
   gooseberries
225ml/8 fl oz white wine or
   cider vinegar
225g/8oz granulated sugar
1 tablespoon yellow mustard
   seeds
1 tablespoon coriander seeds,
   lightly crushed

1 red or green chilli
4 cloves garlic, thinly sliced

Fennel salad
1 tablespoon lemon juice
3 tablespoons extra virgin
   olive oil
salt and freshly ground black
   pepper
2 bulbs Florence fennel
18–24 slices gravad lax

Begin by sterilizing a suitable jar, see (page 180). Make sure that the top is plastic-coated and therefore vinegar-proof. Wash, top and tail the gooseberries, drain thoroughly and pack tightly into the jar.

Put the vinegar, sugar, spices, chilli and garlic in a non-corrosive saucepan and stir gently over a low heat until the sugar is dissolved. Bring to the boil, then simmer gently for 5 minutes. Pour over the gooseberries and cool before sealing. Store in a cool dark place. The longer you leave it, the better it will taste. It will keep for at least a year.

To serve the salad, whisk together the lemon juice, olive oil and seasoning. Trim the fennel, cut in half and wash. Cut into thin fan-like slices and place in a bowl with a handful of drained gooseberries. Dress with the lemon vinaigrette and divide between 6 appetizer plates. Weave the slices of gravad lax between the fennel and serve with thinly sliced buttered brown bread.

Grilled mackerel with gooseberry relish

From at least the seventeenth century the arrival of the first mackerel at the end of May was often accompanied by the first of the season's gooseberries. Over the centuries a wide variety of sauces have been used, ranging from a simple dish of stewed gooseberries, as was enjoyed by Parson Woodforde in 1796, to cooked gooseberries thickened with a little béchamel or cream as suggested by Jane Grigson in *English Food* in 1974. As modern tastes are returning to spicier food, here is a new interpretation of that classic combination. (Serves 4)

Gooseberry relish
85g/3oz granulated sugar or
    to taste
1 small red or green chilli,
    seeded and finely diced
2.5cm/1 inch cinnamon
    stick
3 black peppercorns
a pinch of mace
2 strips lemon peel
1 tablespoon white wine
    vinegar

115ml/4fl oz water
340g/12oz gooseberries,
    topped and tailed

Mackerel
4 medium-sized mackerel,
    filleted
½ tablespoon olive oil
salt and freshly ground black
    pepper
1 lemon, cut into wedges for
    garnish

Place the sugar, chilli, spices, lemon peel, vinegar and water in a non-corrosive pan and dissolve the sugar over a low heat. Simmer gently for 3 minutes before adding the gooseberries. Coat them in the spicy mixture, then cover and simmer gently for 6–8 minutes or until they are soft but still holding their shape. Using a slotted spoon, remove the gooseberries to a clean bowl, leaving the spices in the syrup. Boil this liquid until it is thick and syrupy, then mix into the gooseberries. Serve warm or cold according to your mood but remember to remove the whole spices just before serving.

Preheat the grill to its highest setting and line the grill pan with foil. If you are using a ribbed cast-iron oven-top grill pan, preheat over a moderate heat.

Place the mackerel fillets flesh side down on a board and lightly make 3 evenly spaced diagonal slashes across the skin of each fillet. This should stop them curling up as they cook. Brush each fillet with a little olive oil and season. Once the grill is searingly hot, grill the mackerel fillets skin side up if they are under a grill and skin side down if they are on a ribbed cast-iron oven-top grill pan. As soon as their skin begins to blister and turn golden, turn them over and continue to cook for a further 5 minutes. Allow about 8–10 minutes total cooking time depending on the size and thickness of your fillets.

Serve with the lemon wedges and the spicy gooseberry relish.

Note: You can keep this relish for several days, if kept covered in a clean container in the fridge.

Roast goose with gooseberry sorrel sauce

The custom of serving gooseberries as a savoury sauce with meat has slipped from fashion. Originally it was used to accompany (among other foods) a tender young unstuffed roast green goose. According to the *Concise Oxford Dictionary*, this is a bird that is killed under four months old and eaten without stuffing. Unless you know someone who breeds geese it is impossible to buy. Butchers sell only older corn-fed geese and these are available only in the last two weeks of September so you will have to freeze your gooseberry sauce. (Serves 6)

Gooseberry sorrel sauce
680g/1½lb gooseberries, topped and tailed
55g/2oz granulated sugar or to taste
30g/1oz fresh sorrel

Roast goose
4.5kg/10lb goose
salt and freshly ground black pepper

2 large cooking apples, roughly chopped

Gravy
2 tablespoons plain flour
285ml/½ pint dry white wine
425ml/¾ pint chicken stock (see page 339, or buy ready-made)

Put the gooseberries in a non-corrosive pan with a tablespoon of water and cook over a moderate heat until very soft. Add the sugar and sorrel, purée and strain. Season to taste and set aside (or freeze) until you are ready to serve.

Preheat the oven to 200°C/400°F/gas 6. Wipe the goose inside and out with a damp cloth before pricking it all over with a fork and rubbing with plenty of salt. Lightly season with pepper then stuff its cavity with the chopped apple and place it breast side up on a rack in a large roasting tray.

Roast in the centre of the preheated oven for 20 minutes, then reduce the temperature to 180°C/350°F/gas 4 and continue to cook for 1 hour 40 minutes, basting every 20 minutes or so. Drain off most of the excess fat as it cooks.

Check that the goose is ready by piercing its thigh with a fine skewer. If the juices run clear your goose is cooked. Remove from the oven and allow to rest in a warm place while you make the gravy. Pour off all but 2 tablespoons of the fat. Stir in the flour and cook for 3 minutes before gradually stirring in the wine and stock. Allow to bubble up and reduce down. Once the gravy has thickened a little, season to taste and simmer gently for a few more minutes. Strain into a sauceboat and serve with the roast goose and warm or cold gooseberry sorrel sauce.

Gooseberry elderflower sorbet

There are few gooseberry recipes that have not been partnered with elderflowers at some time or other. The effect is magical and is guaranteed to convert most gooseberry haters into ardent lovers. (Serves 4)

2 elderflower heads	140ml/¼ pint water
455g/1lb green gooseberries, topped and tailed	170g/6oz caster sugar

Wash the elderflower heads by gently dipping them in a bowl of cool water. Any wildlife should drop off when you do this. Put the gooseberries, water and flowers in to a non-corrosive saucepan, cover and place over a moderate heat. Simmer gently, stirring occasionally for 5–10 minutes or until the gooseberries have dissolved into a fragrant mush.

Remove from the heat and stir in the sugar, adjusting the sweetness to your taste. Allow to cool, then remove the elderflowers. Purée in a food processor then pass through a fine sieve. If you are feeling energetic you can simply sieve them immediately. Cover and chill.

Measure out the mixture and add, if necessary, enough cold water to bring it up to 565ml/1 pint. Churn in the normal manner in your ice cream maker or pour it into a shallow plastic container, cover and place in the fast freeze compartment of your freezer. Every 30–40 minutes, mash up the ice crystals with a fork until the mixture has set into a sorbet. Once it is the correct consistency, leave to firm up in the freezer for up to an hour. If you make this in advance, you will need to allow it to soften a little in the fridge for between 30 and 60 minutes.

Gooseberry tart

Gooseberry tart was once as much a national dish as roast beef. As early as 1629 John Parkinson cites green gooseberries being used in tarts, and certainly both Robert May in *The Accomplisht Cook* in 1685 and Hannah Glasse in *The Art of Cookery Made Plain and Easy* in 1747 give recipes. Mrs Glasse's recipe is for red gooseberry tarts. However, the term 'tart' can cause confusion in Britain, as it still refers to a covered pie in Scotland and Ireland, whereas in England it is usually interpreted as an open top pastry. (Makes 6)

225g/8oz shortcrust pastry	455g/1lb green gooseberries,
(see page 335)	topped and tailed
285ml/½ pint water	1 tablespoon apple jelly
340g/12oz granulated sugar	(optional)

Roll out the pastry on a lightly floured surface and line 6 x 9cm/3½ inch greased tart tins. Prick their bottoms with a fork then line with scrunched-up foil and chill for 30 minutes.

Preheat the oven to 200°C/400°F/gas 6 and bake the tartlets blind for 10−15 minutes, until the pastry begins to colour. Remove the foil and return to the oven to dry out for a further 5 minutes.

In the meantime place the water and sugar in a non-corrosive saucepan and dissolve over a moderate heat. Stir in a single layer of gooseberries and simmer gently for 3−4 minutes or until they begin to soften but have not burst their skins. Remove from the syrup with a slotted spoon and spread in a single layer on a large plate. Repeat with the remaining gooseberries until they are all lightly poached. Vigorously boil the remaining syrup until very thick and syrupy. Do not let it caramelize. If you are using the apple jelly, gently dissolve it in the gooseberry syrup.

Arrange the half-cooked berries in an attractive manner in the pastry cases and spoon over some of the thickened syrup. Return to the oven and bake for a further 8 minutes.

Serve warm or cold for pudding or tea but preferably with lots of thick double cream.

Note: As this recipe makes more gooseberry syrup than you need, store the remainder in a clean covered container in the fridge for 2 days or freeze until needed. It can be added to any gooseberry pudding.

See also
Elderflower fritters (page 90)

GREENGAGES

A good plum should have a sweet sugar'd Juice,
a tender melting Pulp and a rich and Exquisite Taste
something perfum'd.

The Practical Fruit Gardener, Stephen Switzer, 1724

Greengages are in one sense a British invention. They are thought to have originated in Armenia, whence they travelled to Greece and on to Italy where they became known as 'verdocchia'. They then spread across Europe, arriving in the early sixteenth century in France, where they were christened 'Reine-Claude' in honour of the wife of François I. It seems they also arrived in Britain around this time, as a basket of greengage stones was recovered by archaeologists in 1982 from the wreck of the *Mary Rose*, which sank in 1545. Certainly a plum listed as Verdoch appears in various records over the next two centuries. However, early in the eighteenth century John Gage, a Roman Catholic priest living in Paris, sent his brother Sir Thomas Gage a collection of plum trees. These were duly planted at Hengrave Hall, near Bury St Edmunds. Legend has it that the label for the Reine-Claude plum tree was lost, so the enterprising gardener called the sweet, green plums 'green gages'. The name stuck and was to become a purely British classification, much to the mystification of other nations. In time any particularly good plum of a green or yellow disposition became known in Britain as a gage.

Modern greengages still suffer from some of the problems described by Edward Bunyard in 1929 in his book *The Anatomy of Dessert:*

In no fruit, except the Cherry, do the shops treat us so scurvily: Greengages from Southern countries, usually as hard as golf-balls, and orchard-grown specimens, small, unripe, and stony, are the best we can find.

Certainly, one can munch one's way though a bag of greengages and be constantly surprised. Each fruit will taste different, ranging from the dull and woolly to the sweet and juicy. A perfect greengage has a sweet fragrance that is difficult to match in any other plum, and such perfection fuels the British passion for these pretty fruits. Apparently the problem lies in the fact that greengages bruise very easily once ripe, so they tend to be picked commercially before they are ripe. Perhaps in time sensitive chilling and careful packaging will eradicate this fault.

Plums, for some peculiar reason I have not yet fathomed, are mainly cooked at home in Britain. They have the air of rusticity about them, which to some degree greengages have managed to avoid. Traditionally, greengages are either made into jam or served fresh as a dessert, preferably with a refreshing Hock. However, they also make excellent puddings and can be transformed into delicate soufflés, fools or ice creams, perfect for the end of summer. Naturally they can also be used in any recipe for cooking plums – just use less sugar. They make sumptuous pies, cobblers, crumbles, sponges and steamed puddings, all oozing with aromatic juices.

Practical guide

Greengages are categorized as dessert plums, which means that they tend to be larger, juicier and have a higher sugar content than culinary plums such as Victorias. They vary in colour from yellowish to deep grassy green, speckled with burgundy. As greengages grow true from seed, we have not introduced many new varieties and Old Green Gage and Cambridge Gage remain the most popular strains.

When shopping choose specimens with a good bloom and no bruising. If you are friendly with a local greengrocer, persuade him to let you sample one. Alternatively visit a pick-your-own farm, as many now also market a wide variety of plums including greengages. Depending on variety and locality, their season spans August and September.

Sybaritic gardeners can indulge themselves by allowing some of their fruit to reach their peak before picking. According to Mr Bunyard, a greengage is ready for the eating when 'a slight shrivelling around the stalk' and 'a deepening of the claret dots' is discovered. However, wasps also adore ripe greengages so you may have to compromise. Unripe fruit will keep for 2–3 days in the salad drawer of your fridge. Arrange carefully to prevent them from bruising, otherwise, lightly cook and freeze.

Some cookery books advocate peeling culinary plums to remove their bitter skin. This is not necessary for dessert varieties such as greengages. In fact, in my opinion it is not necessary at all as plum skin adds a delicious contrast to the flesh.

Taste notes

◊ In theory greengage or plum stones are supposed to yield a delicate almond-like kernel, just like apricots, which can then be cooked with the fruit. However, they are impossible to crack open so I have never been able to test this.

◊ Almonds and vanilla have a natural affinity when cooked with greengages in pies, crumbles, fools and ice cream, while jam makers like to add walnuts and orange.

◊ Greengages taste very good when eaten with crème fraîche or Greek yoghurt or sour cream. Mix with cream in fools, bavarois or mousses.

Greengage soufflé

Soufflés have long suffered from the popular misconception that they are difficult to make. The reason is simple – many years ago ovens were erratic creatures that could vary their temperature with the slightest puff of wind. No cook could guarantee that her oven would sustain the high temperatures necessary for producing an airy soufflé. Modern ovens are far more reliable, and baking a soufflé is now as easy as making a cake. You will need a 1.1 litre/2 pint soufflé dish for this recipe. (Serves 4)

455g/1lb ripe greengages	30g/1oz butter, melted
55ml/2fl oz water	extra caster sugar
85g/3oz sugar	5 medium egg whites
1 tablespoon arrowroot	
2 tablespoons kirsch or a plum brandy	

Halve and stone the greengages. Place in a non-corrosive saucepan with the water. Cover and simmer briskly over a moderate heat for 7 minutes or until they dissolve into a pulp. Purée and sweeten to taste.

Mix the arrowroot with the kirsch then add a couple of tablespoons of the warm greengage purée before stirring it into the rest of the greengage purée. Place over a moderate heat and boil for 2 minutes, stirring continuously until it thickens. Remove and cool.

Preheat the oven and a baking sheet to 220°C/425°F/gas 7. Brush the soufflé dish with the melted butter. Coat with sugar and set aside.

Whisk the egg whites until they become fluffy, add a tablespoon of caster sugar and continue to whisk until stiff and shiny. Loosen the greengage purée with one third of the whipped egg whites, then lightly fold in the remainder.

Carefully fill the soufflé dish. Using a palette knife, smooth off its top before running a knife around its rim. This should help the soufflé to rise evenly. Place on the hot baking sheet and cook in the preheated oven for about 13 minutes. It should still have a soft wobbly centre. Serve immediately.

Greengage yoghurt fool

The end of summer can bring sleepy hot days when a quick and simple fool made with pure fresh flavours is all that the soul could desire. (Serves 6)

680g/1½lb greengages	170ml/6fl oz Greek yoghurt,
140g/5oz caster sugar	chilled
140ml/¼ pint double cream,	
chilled	

Halve and stone the greengages. Place in a non-corrosive saucepan with 3 tablespoons of water and 115g/4oz of sugar. Cover and simmer, stirring occasionally, over a moderate heat for 10 minutes or until the fruit is soft. Purée until smooth, then strain and set aside until cool. Cover and chill.

Whisk the cream until it forms soft peaks. Sweeten the yoghurt with the remaining sugar and fold into the cream. Partially stir this into the cold greengage purée so that the mixture forms pretty green and white swirls. Spoon into 6 elegant glasses or an attractive glass bowl. Cover and chill until ready to serve.

Greengage almond sponge pudding

Fruit puddings can be given countless different toppings, ranging from cobblers to crumbles. Here is an almond variation of a sponge topping for those who are continually looking for new ideas for homely suppers. Serve hot, warm or cold, with lots of thick double cream. (Serves 4)

905g/2lb greengages
55g/2oz caster sugar or to
   taste

Topping
55g/2oz butter, softened
55g/2oz caster sugar

1 large egg
2 tablespoons milk
½ teaspoon almond essence
55g/2oz self-raising flour,
   sifted
55g/2oz ground almonds

Preheat the oven to 190°C/375°F/gas 5.

Halve and stone the greengages and place in a pie dish with the sugar.

Beat the butter and sugar until pale and thick, then beat in the egg, followed by the milk and almond essence. Quickly fold in half the flour, followed by half the almonds, then the remaining flour and remaining almonds. Try to keep the mixture as light as possible.

Spoon the topping evenly, if thinly, over the fruit and bake in the preheated oven for 35 minutes or until well risen, golden and crusty.

GREENS

Bustopher Jones is not skin and bones –
In fact, he's remarkably fat.
He doesn't haunt pubs – he has eight or nine clubs,
For he's the St James's Street Cat!
. . .
When he's seen in a hurry there's probably curry
At the *Siamese* – or at the *Glutton*;
If he looks full of gloom then he's lunched at the *Tomb*
On cabbage, rice pudding and mutton.

'Bustopher Jones: The cat about town' by T.S. Eliot,
Old Possum's Book of Practical Cats, 1939

Over the centuries the British have become notorious for their cooking of greens. It seems that the vast majority of native cooks have felt compelled to subject any green-leafed vegetable to violent over-cooking. Some scientists have conjectured that this habit was acquired far back in Neolithic times when our ancestors tried to rid their wild greens of their intrinsic bitterness by rigorous cooking. Nibble a leaf of wild cabbage, which still grows on the south coast near Dover, and you will quickly taste the problem. Fortunately, for an almost equal number of centuries British farmers (and now botanists) have striven to cultivate sweeter-tasting brassicas. The end result is that not only do we have an amazing diversity of exquisite greens, but we also cook them lightly and sensitively.

Supermarkets now market tender young leaves of curly kale alongside hybrid varieties of spring greens and pointed green cabbages, all of which have lost their bitter stalks. Many a British cook will pick up an exotic pillow packet of mixed tat tsai, choy sum and black cabbage as readily as baby spinach leaves for the evening meal. Such delicate greens need the briefest of cooking, quickly stir-fried with oriental seasonings or lightly blanched before being enriched with crème fraîche or butter.

Curiously the benefit of eating greens has remained deeply imbedded in the British psyche, despite the years of being fed stale cabbage. Somehow they add a natural balance to a meal with their flavour, colour, texture and natural goodness. Such enthusiasm has led to the commercial rediscovery of older greens, such as the beautiful ruby-stemmed leaves of red chard, as well as the introduction of oriental plants, for example pak choi. It has also meant that we have not only maintained our traditional (albeit updated) recipes but have embraced new concepts. Delicate curries of spiced chicken and pak choi are as popular as a spoonful of buttery colcannon. Even wild greens such as nettles have been reinstated. Innovative growers have begun to supply fashionable restaurants, which incorporate such delicacies into creamy soups and rich ricotta stuffings for ravioli. It seems that at the end of the twentieth century we have come full circle in our diet by re-establishing a wide diversity of edible greens.

Practical guide

For the purpose of this book the term 'greens' refers to a wide variety of green-leafed vegetables. It therefore seems sensible to describe some of them briefly, along with their appropriate treatment. Luckily, there are a few principles that can be applied to all of the following. First, in the matter of shopping, you should always choose the freshest, juiciest looking specimens you can find, discarding any that are wilting, yellowing or blemished. When choosing cabbages, spring greens and oriental greens, select those that feel heavy for their size. Second, all greens should be used as quickly as possible after purchase. They should be kept chilled until you are ready to use them. If you have bought tender young greens in pillow packets, leave them unopened until the last minute, as this protects them from bruising and helps to keep them fresh. In the same way, leave the outer leaves attached to spring greens or cabbages until you are ready, as this also helps to preserve them. Lastly, all greens should be thoroughly washed in plenty of cold water as they can harbour both dirt and animal life. It is worth remembering, however, that if you find a slug, snail or caterpillar on your cabbage, it is a good sign as it indicates a lighter use of pesticides.

Cabbages come in a wide variety of forms and colours ranging from white through to red. Although cabbage is available throughout the year, each variety has its own season. Savoy, for example, like most winter hardy cabbages, can be picked from mid-autumn until the following spring. Unlike other brassicas, Dutch white winter cabbages and red cabbages can both be stored throughout the winter. Plain boiled cabbage should literally be cooked for a minute or two if sliced. Over-cooking causes them to release sulphur compounds from their leaves.

Spring greens are also known as winter greens in Britain. Technically they are unhearted or loose-leafed cabbages. When preparing them be completely ruthless and discard all but their innermost hearts. These can then be finely or roughly sliced and washed in several changes of cold water before briskly frying for 2–3 minutes or lightly blanching.

Kale and curly kale, a frilly version of the former, can be prepared in the same way as spring greens. Some shops now sell tiny young curly kale leaves which are not as intensely bitter as their larger counterparts. Excellent in salads and hearty soups.

Spinach can be bought in two forms: normal-sized leaves, which can be smooth or crinkled, and small or young leafed, which is mainly sold by the supermarkets. Both are good, but if you wish to woo a non-spinach lover, you would be advised to start with young spinach as it has a more delicate flavour. To prepare the former, wash thoroughly in three consecutive sinks of cold water. If the leaves are large you may well need to remove their stalks by folding each leaf inwards and pulling the stalk away from the leaf. The leaves can then be sliced if wished. Allow 225g/8oz unprepared large-leaf spinach per person. A 200g/7oz pillow packet of baby spinach will just stretch to two frugal people.

New Zealand spinach, chard, red chard and beet greens are becoming more widely available once more. They all taste similar to spinach, although some chards have fleshy, creamy-tasting stems. They can all be treated in a similar manner. New Zealand spinach is a useful drought-resistant green that was originally introduced into England by Sir Joseph Banks, the botanist on Captain Cook's *Endeavour*. It can be bought from some farm shops and is available from June through to September. Chard and beet greens are related to the beetroot family.

Pak choi, bok choy and choy sum come in many shapes, sizes and spellings. Pak choi can be green- or white-stemmed, stout or elegant. Many varieties are remarkably resilient to cold weather and so can be sold for much of the year. Avoid any with splitting stems or yellowing leaves and use in everything from soups to pickles. Joy Larkcom's book *Oriental Vegetables* is the perfect guide to both growing and eating these delicacies.

Wild greens such as nettles, good King Henry, fat hen and chickweed are becoming increasingly fashionable in some circles. They are usually gathered in the early spring, when at their most tender. As with all wild foods, positive identification is very important and you should only ever pick from a pollution- and pesticide-free source.

Taste notes

◊ All greens act as a delicious foil to roast or grilled meats, in particular lamb, beef, venison, duck, partridge, pigeon, pheasant and hare. Pork is often accompanied by cabbage, usually red, although bacon is often added to green cabbage. Classic veal recipes often use spinach.

◊ Surprisingly, lightly cooked cabbage leaves make a delicate contrast to many fish dishes, particularly when the fish is wrapped in their leaves. Salmon, sole, brill and turbot all taste good cooked in this way.

◊ The creamy taste of many greens can be enhanced by the addition of butter, cream or crème fraîche at the end of cooking. Cheese, particularly ricotta or Parmesan, is another popular seasoning in more complex green dishes. Such cream-based dishes can be seasoned with nutmeg, mace, caraway or paprika.

◊ All greens benefit from an oriental approach, whether it be stir-frying or blanching Japanese style. For the latter see the method for piquant wilted greens (recipe below). Soy sauce, mirin, sake, chilli, garlic, ginger, mustard seeds, sesame oil and sesame seeds are my favourite flavourings with most greens as they enhance their sweetness in a delightful way

Stir-fried chilli curly kale

Use the tiny young-leafed varieties of kale rather than the larger, more bitter leaves. This recipe can be adapted to any green, from pak choi to cos lettuce. Mirin is a form of sweetened sake that is becoming more widely available. It has the effect of slightly softening and balancing the other flavours but the recipe will still taste good without it. (Serves 2)

455g/1lb tender young curly kale leaves
3 thinly sliced rounds fresh ginger
2 tablespoons vegetable oil
2 cloves garlic, cut into fine matchsticks

a large pinch dried chilli flakes
1 tablespoon soy sauce or to taste
1 tablespoon mirin (optional)

Discard any damaged or yellow leaves and wash the kale in several changes of cold water. Drain and set aside.

Trim away the peel from the sliced ginger then cut into fine matchsticks. Heat the oil in a large non-stick frying pan or wok. Once it is smoking add the ginger, garlic and chilli, fry for 30 seconds, then tip in the greens. Stir-fry briskly for a couple of minutes or until they begin to wilt, then mix in the soy sauce and the mirin. Allow it to bubble up and remove from the heat. Serve immediately.

Piquant wilted greens

Serving a dish of grilled or roasted lamb or beef with greens is almost second nature to most British cooks. This is a delicious modern variation and tastes equally good eaten with duck or venison. (Serves 4)

1 shallot, finely diced

1 tablespoon sherry vinegar

5 tablespoons extra virgin olive oil

salt and freshly ground black pepper

680g/1½lb baby spinach leaves

2 cloves garlic, crushed

Whisk together the shallot, sherry vinegar, 3 tablespoons olive oil, salt and pepper. Set aside.

Bring a large pan of salted water to the boil and add a third of the spinach to the water. As soon as it wilts (which will be within 15 seconds), remove from the water with a slotted spoon and cool under cold running water. Return the pan of water to the boil and repeat twice more. Squeeze out as much of the excess water as you can from your spinach.

When you are ready to serve, heat the remaining 2 tablespoons of oil in a saucepan and lightly fry the garlic. Add the spinach and stir-fry until hot. Finally, re-whisk the dressing and mix into the spinach. Adjust the seasoning if necessary and serve immediately.

Note: Fresh mint, finely shredded, makes a gorgeous addition. Just add with the dressing.

Stuffed cabbage leaves

According to Florence White in her intriguing book *Good Things in England*, stuffed or forced cabbage, as it used to be called, is a derivative of the Turkish dolma, for which a certain Mrs Ann Blencowe gave a recipe in her manuscript cookery book dated 1694. Whatever its origins, stuffed cabbage appears regularly in cookery books from the eighteenth century onwards. This particular version was inspired by Mrs Bradley's 1749 Bath recipe in Miss White's book. The cabbage dolmas taste gorgeous.

The original recipe used veal, but you can use lean minced pork instead. If you opt for veal, make sure that you use the darker-fleshed British veal, as this will have been humanely reared. (Serves 4)

1 Savoy cabbage	4 tablespoons finely grated
salt	Parmesan
2 tablespoons olive oil	3 tablespoons finely chopped
1 onion, finely diced	parsley
1 clove garlic, crushed	a pinch of finely grated
2 thick slices white bread,	nutmeg
crusted	freshly ground black pepper
4 tablespoons milk	425ml/¾ pint chicken stock
225g/8oz lean minced veal or	(see page 339 or buy ready-
pork	made)
115g/4oz back bacon, finely	15g/½oz butter
diced	
4 medium hard-boiled egg	
yolks, roughly crumbled	

Preheat the oven to 220°C/425°F/gas 7.

Trim the cabbage by removing any damaged outside leaves. Cut around its core, pointing your knife inwards as you do so, so that you are able to pull out a conical-shaped white core. As you do so the outer leaves will be cut off. Make sure that you have 10 nice leaves, then wash them along with the inner heart in plenty of cold water.

Bring a large pan of salted water to the boil. Drop the outer leaves in and cook for a minute or until tender and malleable. Remove and cool under cold running water. Drop the cabbage heart into the boiling water. As soon as it has returned to the boil, cook for a further 4–5 minutes, then remove and cool under the cold tap. Leave to drain upside down. Pat the individual leaves dry and cut away the tough stalk. Roughly dice the remaining cabbage heart.

Heat the oil in a small frying pan and fry the onion and garlic until soft. In the meantime soak the bread in the milk until soft. Tip the onions into the minced meat, along with the bacon, softened bread, hard-boiled egg yolks, Parmesan, parsley, nutmeg and diced cabbage. Mix thoroughly and season to taste. Fry a small patty of the mixture to check the seasoning.

Divide the stuffing into 10 balls and wrap each ball in a cabbage leaf. Do not worry if it does not completely encase the meat. Secure each parcel with a cocktail stick or tie with fine string and arrange, good side up, in a china baking tray. Heat the stock to boiling point and pour around the stuffed cabbage leaves. Dot with butter and cover with foil. Bake for 30 minutes and serve piping hot, moistened with a touch of stock.

Creamy spiced chicken with pak choi

An elegant modern dish. (Serves 6)

8 skinless chicken breasts	a pinch of ground turmeric
salt and freshly ground black	1 teaspoon ground cumin
pepper	8 tomatoes, peeled, seeded
4 tablespoons vegetable oil	and diced
1 onion, finely diced	425g/15oz baby pak choi
2 cloves garlic, crushed	285ml/½ pint double cream
1 small red chilli, finely diced	

Cut the chicken breasts into large chunks and season. Heat the oil in a saucepan and quickly colour the chicken in batches. As soon as it is flecked golden, remove and set aside. Reduce the heat and stir in the onion, garlic and chilli. Gently fry until soft, then add the spices and cook for a further minute. Add the diced tomato flesh to the onions and continue to fry for 1 minute.

Meanwhile, wash the pak choi and cut into strips, roughly separating the white or pale green stems from the green leaves. Add the stems to the tomatoes, stir-fry for a further 2 minutes, then add the chicken pieces, cream and 285ml/½ pint of water. Return to a simmer, season to taste and cook gently for 5 minutes. Finally, add the green leaves, return to a simmer and cook for 3 minutes. Adjust the seasoning to taste and serve with Basmati rice.

Colcannon

Colcannon, kailkenny, rumbledethumps and champ are all variations of mashed potato and greens, changing according to the location and the whim of the cook. Champ can be made in Ireland with tender young nettle tops and served with a pool of melted butter in the heart of each serving, while in the Scottish borders rumbledethumps contains lashings of butter but no milk or cream. In some parts of Scotland carrots and turnips are mashed into the potato, while in England slices of left-over beef are added to make bubble and squeak. Brave lovers of kale substitute it for the cabbage. (Serves 6)

905g/2lb floury potatoes	115ml/4fl oz creamy milk
salt	70g/2½oz butter
455g/1lb green cabbage,	extra butter for serving
roughly diced	
2 bunches spring onions,	
finely sliced	

Peel the potatoes and cut into large pieces. Place in a pan of cold salted water and bring to the boil. Continue to boil for 20–30 minutes or until tender.

Drain the potatoes and cover with a clean tea towel. Leave to steam dry for 5 minutes before returning them to a clean pan and mashing vigorously until smooth and creamy.

Meanwhile, bring a separate pan of salted water to the boil. Drop in the cabbage and as soon as it begins to return to the boil add the spring onions. Slowly count to 10 and drain thoroughly.

Scald the milk in a clean saucepan, add the butter and as soon as it has melted beat into the potatoes. Finally stir in the cabbage and spring onions and season to taste.

At this stage you can either serve the mixture piping hot with lots of extra melted butter to be poured in a hollow in each serving, or you can fry it as a thick pancake in lots of butter, turning it regularly so that the brown crispy bits become incorporated into the whole dish. Try serving it with crisp grilled rashers of bacon for supper.

See also
Scallop, spinach and bacon pasta (page 28)

HONEY

Oh, is the water sweet and cool,
Gentle and brown, above the pool?
And laughs the immortal river still
Under the mill, under the mill?
Say, is there Beauty yet to find?
And Certainty? and Quiet kind?
Deep meadows yet, for to forget
The lies, and truths, and pain? . . . oh! yet
Stands the Church clock at ten to three?
And is there honey still for tea?

'The Old Vicarage, Grantchester', by
Rupert Brooke, 1912

Honey may be one of the most ancient of foods known to man, but for the British, honey and the keeping of honey bees have come to symbolize Arcadia. The very act of spreading thick, golden honey on buttered bread and then slowly relishing every sticky mouthful is considered by most to be a brief form of escapism. The taste of honey somehow represents the never-never world of the idealized past, rural sunny afternoons filled with the scent of lime blossom, or cosy winter teas, curled up in front of a blazing fire. A stark contrast to the reality of many urban lives, let alone the act of wheeling round a supermarket trolley and selecting your favourite pot of honey; but such is the strange relationship between food, image and reality.

Modern cooks tend to serve honey in what has come to be considered its traditional use as an accompaniment to bread or toast, either for breakfast or for tea. Both are relatively new introductions, beginning with the former, which was first noted in Scotland as Dr Samuel Johnson describes in his *Journey to the Western Islands* in 1773:

Not long after the dram, may be expected the breakfast, a meal in which the Scots, whether of the lowlands or mountains, must be confessed to excel us. The tea and coffee are accompanied not only with butter, but with honey, conserves and marmalades. If an epicure could remove by a wish, in quest of sensual gratification, wherever he had supped he would breakfast in Scotland.

At that time, sweet spreads were virtually unheard of for breakfast in the south.

Honey was the primary form of sweetening in Britain until the sixteenth century. It was used in both sweet and savoury dishes as well as in a wide variety of drinks, in particular, mead and metheglin, a herbal variation of mead. The dissolution of the monasteries marked the beginning of its decline by provoking a national honey shortage in 1536. The dispersed monks suddenly stopped producing it in vast quantities, along with the wax essential for their votive candles. The arrival of increasingly large amounts of sugar in the following century sealed its fate – honey simply could not compete against the culinary advantages of sugar, which rarely fermented and acted as an excellent preservative of fruit. From then on it is scarcely mentioned in cookery books, although it continued to be used in country districts until well into the nineteenth century.

However, national tastes die hard and honey is returning to modern British cooking. Our increasing need for quickly prepared, intensely flavoured dishes makes it the perfect ingredient. Its sticky nature allows marinades and glazes to cling to meats and coat them with a rich caramelized crust. It emphasizes the sweetness of meat, from chicken to lamb, and acts as a subtle balance to oriental flavours, for example, chillies, ginger, soy sauce and sake. Only with puddings should it be treated with care, as its distinct taste can overpower some dishes.

Practical guide

Among connoisseurs each variety of honey is treated like a fine wine, its origins carefully noted from beekeeper to flowers, season and year. Some honeys even improve with age, developing a more full-bodied and mellow taste with time. Just like wines, there are mass-produced honeys and small independent specialist honeys, whose makers religiously transport their hives around the country so that their bees can collect nectar from the apple orchards in Kent or sample the delights of the ling heather on the grouse moors of Scotland. The hives are moved at night, so that not a single sleeping bee is disturbed.

As with all things, selecting which honey to use is a matter of personal taste. Honey can be thick or thin, dark or light, strongly flavoured or fragrant, single-flowered or blended. As a general rule if you buy a light coloured honey, for example acacia, it will have a lighter, more flowery flavour than if you buy a darker honey, such as Greek or French chestnut, which will have a stronger taste. In the same way, the mass-produced brand-name honeys tend to be blends, often of mixed origin, which have been carefully matched together and subjected to flash heating to ensure that they have a uniform texture, flavour and colour. Although they are perfectly acceptable to use in cooking, they lack the exquisite range and depth of flavour that can be found in mono-floral and specialist honeys.

Bees gather nectar from within a 2−3 mile radius of their hive. No keeper can control which blossoms the bees will visit, so naturally the honey varies from season to season and year to year. Technically a single-flower honey must contain a minimum of 50 per cent pollen and nectar from that one flower, although many of the smaller producers try to ensure an 80 per cent content. Certain flowers, such as heather, imbue the honey with a very distinctive flavour, while others, for example lavender or lime blossom, have a lighter, more aromatic taste.

All honey will eventually become thick, but the more fructose a honey contains the longer the honey will remain liquid. Those that contain a high level of glucose, such as honeys gathered from oil-seed rape, set very quickly, while those which contain a low level, for example French lavender honey, can take many years to set. If you wish to thin some of your honey, heat it very gently. If a runny honey begins to crystallize it is a good sign, as it indicates that the honey has been expressed very simply and not submitted to high temperatures.

Honey has the extraordinary ability to keep for ever, provided it is kept in a cool, dark place. However, occasionally it will ferment if it is exposed to dirt or water. The slight sound of fizzing on opening the jar is a warning of fermentation.

Taste notes

◊ The more delicate-flavoured honeys such as lavender or lime are delicious whisked into vinaigrettes or drizzled over fruit puddings.

◊ Stronger-flavoured honeys, for example, heather or French chestnut, are better suited to the robust flavours of meat and can be dissolved into marinades and glazes.

◊ Honey is delicious when mixed with orange, lemon or lime juice. It also tastes good flavoured with ginger, garlic or chilli.

Chargrilled chilli chicken

Soy-based marinades are becoming increasingly popular with British cooks, who contrary to popular belief enjoy piquant food. Try serving these with undressed cos lettuce leaves, spring onions, and thinly sliced cucumber, which has been lightly salted before being mixed in a mixture of sugar and rice vinegar.

The chicken breasts can either be cooked whole or diced and threaded on to skewers. If you wish to grill them whole, place them over a moderately hot barbecue – if they are put on the hottest section the outside will burn before the inside is cooked through – and allow 5 minutes on each side. (Serves 4)

4 tablespoons runny honey	2 cloves garlic, crushed
2 tablespoons soy sauce	1 lemon, juiced
1 small red chilli, seeded and finely chopped	4 corn-fed chicken breasts, skinned
1 teaspoon finely chopped fresh ginger	1 tablespoon vegetable oil
	1 lemon, cut into 8 wedges

Mix the honey, soy sauce, chilli, ginger, garlic and lemon juice in a small bowl and stir until the honey has dissolved.

Cut the chicken breasts into medium-sized pieces and thread on to 4 skewers. Place in a shallow dish, pour over half the marinade, and rub into the chicken. Cover and chill for at least 20 minutes.

When you are ready, gently heat the remaining honey and soy sauce mixture and transfer to a small jug. Brush the chicken brochettes with a little oil and place on the barbecue. Grill for 3–4 minutes on each side and serve with a lemon wedge and the warm sauce.

Honey roast duck

An updated version of the classic sixties dish of glazed roast duck. (Serves 8)

2 oven-ready ducks each
  weighing about 2kg/4½lb
2 teaspoons fine sea salt

Sauce
2 onions, finely diced
4 cloves garlic, roughly
  chopped
4 peeled carrots, finely diced

4 sticks celery, finely diced
1 litre/1¾ pints red wine
5 black peppercorns
3 strips orange peel, finely
  pared

Honey glaze
4 tablespoons runny honey
1 orange, juiced

Preheat the oven to its highest setting. Remove any pin feathers from the ducks and lightly prick all over with a fork.

Rub the salt into the ducks' skin and place the birds upside down in a roasting pan. Roast for 10 minutes, then turn breast side up and roast for another 10 minutes. Remove and cool.

Once the duck is cool, carve each bird into 8 pieces. Begin by removing the whole legs, which are then each cut in half through their joint and neatly trimmed. Continue by cutting the breast meat away from the rib cage and cut each breast into 2 equal sized pieces. Trim once again before covering and chilling until needed.

Roughly chop the duck carcasses and place in a large saucepan over a low heat. They will release their fat and colour at the same time. Stir in the vegetables and soften before adding the wine, peppercorns, orange peel and enough water to cover. Bring to the boil, skim off any scum and simmer gently until the liquid has reduced by two-thirds. Allow a good 3 hours for this. Strain into a clean container and chill once cool.

When you are nearly ready to serve, preheat the grill to medium high and mix together the honey and orange juice. Remove and discard any fat from the top of the stock, transfer to a small pan and boil vigorously until it has reduced down and is well flavoured.

Dip the duck pieces in the honey glaze and place the legs skin side up under the grill for 5 minutes. Add the duck breasts, skin side up and turn over the legs. Cook for a further 5 minutes, then turn all the pieces over, brush once more with the glaze, and cook for another 5 minutes. Serve with the piping hot sauce.

Honey fennel grilled figs

This simple pudding takes literally a few minutes and tastes exquisite. The fennel seeds are an essential ingredient. (Serves 4)

4 tablespoons runny honey	15g/½oz softened butter
1 small lemon, juiced	8 figs
1 teaspoon fennel seeds,	
roughly crushed	

Preheat the grill to medium high. Mix together the honey, lemon juice and fennel seeds in a medium-sized bowl.

Roughly butter a shallow grill-proof dish. Trim the fig stalks and quarter all the figs. Toss them in the honey mixture and tip, juices and all, into the buttered dish. Spread them out so that they can cook evenly and place under a moderately hot grill.

Grill for about 5 minutes or until the figs are hot through, slightly caramelized and oozing with delicious juices. Serve hot or warm with lots of crème fraîche.

See also
Honey walnut ice cream (page 321)
Roast lemon partridge (page 176)
Welsh roast lamb (page 145)

KIPPERS

An American friend, normally most appreciative of English food, says, when he comes to stay, that he bars only two things, Brussels sprouts and kippers. I know just what that indicates: he has been served with large and watery sprouts and town kippers of henna-like complexion and unrefined flavour. I find myself getting quite sad to think that his prejudice will become so set that even when he comes up to the Highlands he will deny himself the luxury of eating a properly smoked, delicately flavoured small Scotch kipper. These are delicacies: not commonplace food.

The Constance Spry Cookery Book, by Constance Spry and Rosemary Hume, 1956

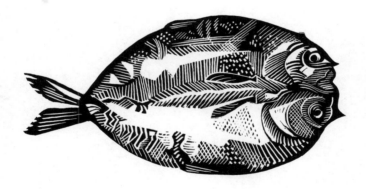

The kipper is a curious dish that is as much an acquired taste as oysters or artichokes. Mr Woodger, a Northumbrian, is credited with its invention in the 1840s, when he adapted the Scottish method of kippering (curing) salmon to herrings. In either case the fish is split open, cleaned, soaked in brine and cold smoked. Applied to herrings, this method gradually overtook the heavier and more pungent whole cured red herrings and Yarmouth bloaters in popularity until it became an essential part of our culinary heritage, cited above many other foods, as being a national delicacy. In the words of George Orwell, writing in *In Defence of English Cooking*:

It is commonly said, even by the English themselves, that English cooking is the worst in the world. It is supposed to be not merely incompetent, but also imitative, and I even read quite recently, in a book by a French writer, the remark: 'The best English cooking is, of course, simply French cooking.'

Now that is simply not true. As anyone who has lived long abroad will know, there is a whole host of delicacies which it is quite impossible to obtain outside the English-speaking countries. No doubt the list could be added to, but here are some of the things that I myself have sought for in foreign countries and failed to find.

First of all, kippers, Yorkshire pudding, Devonshire cream, muffins and crumpets . . .

There then follows a long list of delicious indigenous foods. Yet proffer a kipper to the uninitiated and they will wrinkle up their noses in disgust. Somehow the more I examine popular British foods, the more I am convinced that we enjoy highly flavoured, piquant food. Perhaps this is due to our culinary heritage or our wet and windy weather, but the exquisite smoky sea flavour of the kipper is very much to our taste. Our ancestors were brought up on the famous red herring – a fish that was thoroughly salted before being left to smoke for up to six weeks. The end result was a resilient piece of leathery red fish that had to be soaked in milk or small beer before being lightly grilled in front of the fire, lovingly rubbed with butter and sprinkled with cayenne. The arrival of the Yarmouth bloater, an ungutted herring (hence its name), which was soaked in brine for a mere twelve hours before being briefly smoked for a further twelve hours, weaned them off the intensely flavoured red herrings. The British were ready for the kipper.

It found its place as a simple dish for breakfast or tea, eaten with bread and butter and the occasional lemon. By the turn of the century, small children were affectionately referred to as kippers and Mrs Beeton listed it among her summer breakfast recommendations. So strongly was it associated with the British that in Australia ex-patriates were nicknamed kippers, although this may have referred to the idea that the kippers were gutless! Its popularity remained unabated until the seventies, when the onset of the ban on herring fishing suddenly decimated the industry. During those fallow years, many believed that our partiality to the kipper was lost, but happily people are gradually returning to it despite more recent fishing restrictions. Mail order kippers are booming with the advent of kipper clubs. Once more kippers are being made into delicious marinated salads and fish pastes and tourists are being introduced to the delights of savouring a succulent kipper for breakfast.

Practical guide

Historically, the prime season for smoking kippers was between June and October when the herring had gained enough fat to remain juicy. Certain areas became famous for the excellence of their kippers. The most notable are Craster in Northumberland, Lowestoft in Suffolk, Whitby in Yorkshire, the Isle of Man and, of course, Mallaig, Fraserburgh, Ullapool and Loch Fyne in Scotland.

An average kipper will be soaked in brine for about 30 minutes before being smoked for 16 to 30 hours. Different mixtures of wood and/or peat can be used, and the kipperer will vary his smoking times to take into account the weather and the final flavour of his fish.

Try to choose plump, iridescently golden fish with no artificial colouring. Bright orange kippers should be avoided, as it usually means that they have been artificially coloured. Such fish are normally smoked for a shorter period and consequently taste disappointing. Colouring was first introduced during the First World War to save money, as the kippers lost less weight if their smoking time was reduced. If properly smoked, they can be refrigerated for up to a week, but mass-produced supermarket kippers should be eaten within two days. Vacuum-packed kippers can be stored in the fridge for up to 2 weeks or frozen for up to 3 months.

How to eat a kipper

The most common reason for kipper avoidance is its bones, which many people find distract from the pleasure of eating. However, once the art of tackling a kipper on your plate is mastered such troubles will be forgotten. According to W.C. Hodgson, author of *The Herring and its Fishery*, 'eating a kipper is quite simple if it is laid correctly on the plate to start with, that is, with the skin uppermost . . . With the head towards you, lift up the skin from half of the kipper by running the point of the knife along the edge and fold the skin back. This exposes the flesh on top of the bones, and it is quite easy to remove it in fillets, leaving the bones untouched. When this side has been eaten, turn the kipper round on the plate so that the tail is towards you and repeat the process on the other side.'

Taste notes

◊ Marinated kippers work well with a variety of salads, including beetroot with sweet pickled cucumbers, potato and red onion, or celery and apple.
◊ Simply marinated, they make an excellent addition to a plate of mixed hors d'oeuvres. Alternatively, serve on rye bread as an open sandwich or tiny canapé.

Breakfast kippers

There is no correct way to cook kippers for breakfast, it is purely a matter of taste. If you have never cooked a kipper before it is worth considering the following: grilling will intensify its smoky taste and give it a slight crust, while poaching will slightly lessen its flavour but will make it more succulent. Each school has its ardent supporters.

Personally, I prefer my kippers served plain, but if you are pulling out all the stops try serving them with parsley butter. If you are feeding 4 people, the night before finely chop 2 tablespoons of parsley and beat it into 55g/2oz unsalted butter. Season to taste with lemon juice and black pepper, shape into a small roll and wrap in wet greaseproof paper. Chill until morning, then cut into rounds and serve with the hot kippers.

Grilled kippers

Preheat the grill to medium high and line the grill rack with foil. Liberally dot the kippers with unsalted butter and place under the grill, flesh side up, for 5 minutes.

Poached kippers
Bring a wide pan of water to the boil. Add the kippers, return to the boil and remove from the heat. Leave for 3 minutes then drain well and serve piping hot.

Jugged kippers
The problem with this traditional recipe is that it requires you to have a large heat-resistant jug – those of you who don't can use a large dish or saucepan instead. Place the kippers either in the jug or in the dish and cover with boiling water. Leave for 5–10 minutes, depending on the size and number of your kippers. Remove, drain thoroughly and serve.

Marinated kippers

Variations of this recipe were very popular in the early eighties when marinated fish dishes were all the rage at dinner parties. It tastes too good to be forgotten. (Serves 6)

8 kipper fillets or 4 whole kippers such as Manx kippers	85ml/3fl oz white wine vinegar
1 shallot, finely sliced	1 tablespoon caster sugar
4 sprigs dill, roughly torn	freshly ground black pepper
4 sprigs parsley, roughly torn	
1 lemon, finely grated	*Garnish*
115ml/4fl oz extra virgin olive oil	1½ lemons
	6 sprigs dill

Ease the skin away from the base of the first kipper fillet. Gently pull away the skin – it should come away in one piece. Repeat with the remaining fillets. Kipper fillets sometimes still contain small bones, in which case you are best advised to attack them with an old pair of tweezers. If you are filleting whole kippers, slice off the heads and tails before prising away the bones, some of which will come away surprisingly easily. Finally slice in half lengthways and skin. Remove any dark fat under the skin and lay the kippers in a shallow china dish.

Mix together the shallot, dill, parsley, lemon zest, olive oil, vinegar, sugar and pepper. Pour over the kippers, making sure that each fillet is thoroughly coated. Cover and chill for a minimum of 24 hours.

When you are ready to serve, drain the fillets and pat dry before finely slicing into thin strips. Divide in an attractive manner between 6 individual serving plates. Cut the lemons into 12 wedges and garnish each plate with a sprig of dill and 2 lemon wedges. Serve with plenty of thinly sliced buttered brown bread.

Marinated kipper salad

A luscious variation of the above. (Serves 6)

8 kipper fillets, marinated as above	1 curly endive, trimmed
680g/1½lb new potatoes	a handful of lamb's lettuce leaves
salt	1 tablespoon white wine vinegar
6 tablespoons good mayonnaise	3 tablespoons extra virgin olive oil
6 spring onions, finely chopped	freshly ground black pepper

Prepare and marinate the kippers as above.

Boil the potatoes in plenty of salted water until tender. Cool slightly, cut into chunks, and toss with the mayonnaise and spring onions. Allow to cool.

Meanwhile, using a pair of scissors, trim the head of the curly endive as if it were a mop of hair, removing all the dark green ends and the tough outer leaves. Cut through the root and wash and dry the remaining leaves. Place in a large mixing bowl. Then snip off the lamb's lettuce stalks, gently wash and dry, and add to the curly endive.

When you are ready to serve, whisk together the vinegar and oil, season to taste and dress the salad leaves. Arrange in a pretty manner on 6 appetizer plates with the potato salad. Cut the kipper fillets into thin strips and divide between the plates. Serve immediately.

Kipper paste

Fish pastes, or fish pâtés as they have become known, are still popular, and properly smoked kippers make a truly delicious paste that can be spread on little cocktail canapés or eaten, thickly spread, on hot buttered toast for lunch or tea. (Serves 4)

2 large kippers, e.g. oak-smoked
115g/4oz softened butter, diced
a large pinch of cayenne pepper

1½ lemons, juiced
2 tablespoons double cream
salt and freshly ground black pepper

Bring a large pan of water to the boil and add the kippers. Return to the boil, then remove from the heat and leave for 3 minutes. Drain the kippers and leave to cool. When cold, peel off the skin and carefully remove the fillets from the bones, picking out as many tiny bones as you can.

Place the butter, cayenne and a tablespoon of lemon juice in the food processor. Process until the butter is smooth, then add the flaked kipper. Give a couple of whizzes, then add the double cream, seasoning and more lemon juice to taste. Quickly process once again, being careful not to overwork the fish into too smooth a paste. Adjust the flavourings if necessary and neatly fill 4 small china soufflé dishes. Cover and chill until needed.

LAMB

'What have we for dinner, Betsy?' said the Baronet.

'Mutton broth, I believe, Sir Pitt,' answered Lady Crawley.

'*Mouton aux navets*,' added the Butler gravely (pronounce, if you please, moutongonavvy); 'and the soup is *potage de mouton à l'écossaise*. The side-dishes contain *pommes de terre au naturel*, and *chou-fleur à l'eau*.'

'Mutton's mutton,' said the Baronet, 'and a devilish good thing.'

Vanity Fair by William Makepeace Thackeray, 1848

Historically, lamb, or rather mutton, has taken second place to beef in our culinary repertoire. This is not to say that it was not much loved, simply that it was regarded in a slightly more homely light. Its status, not surprisingly, has changed with the arrival of BSE, and it is now our most popular red meat. It is important, however, to distinguish between mutton and lamb. Few people today have ever tasted mutton, myself included, and it is therefore difficult to appreciate its original role in our cookery.

Sheep were valued primarily for their fleece and were therefore allowed to reach a stout middle age before being surrendered to the pot. As with all forms of livestock in Britain, much energy was directed at improving native flocks, until by the eighteenth century the average sheep had almost doubled in size. This meant that one leg of mutton yielded a respectable meal and became a popular alternative to beef. The resulting meat had a strong, almost gamy taste and needed slow, gentle cooking to render it tender, hence the many recipes for boiled mutton, Scotch broth and stews. Victorian mutton aficionados would recommend their favourite breed for its unique flavour and texture. A far cry from lamb today, which is so young and tender that it is ideally suited for quick cooking and so deliciously sweet as to need only the simplest of accompaniments.

As mutton was gradually replaced by lamb, British cooks slowly began to change their recipes to accommodate the leaner, more tender meat. Roast lamb became a standard Sunday dish rather than the occasional spring luxury. Lamb cutlets and chops became increasingly popular, plainly cooked with the usual trimmings of mint sauce and redcurrant jelly. Mutton broth disappeared with the caper sauce, while mutton stews were readapted to the shorter cooking time of lamb. Today, you are more likely to be given char-grilled lamb brochettes, seasoned with coriander and served with a tomato vinaigrette, than a hearty dish of stewed lamb with turnips accompanied by boiled cauliflower and potatoes.

Practical guide

Indigenous lamb is only available fresh from March until November. 'Spring lamb' reared in the south appears first, followed in June by the first of what the supermarkets refer to as 'hill lamb', which is mainly reared in Wales, the north of England and Scotland. These continue through into September before being replaced by plain 'lamb'. Such meat comes from slightly older sheep, although they rarely get beyond eighteen months. Technically speaking any animal over a year old is called a hogget, but butchers rarely use this term as it is unattractive to shoppers. These older sheep have slightly firmer, more flavoursome flesh than a young lamb but are not nearly as strong as mutton, which technically must come from a sheep older than two. Mutton has to be sought out from specialist suppliers. Try Henrietta Green's wonderful book *The Food Lover's Guide to Britain* for sources. She also lists suppliers of smoked lamb and specialists in rare breeds all of which are supposed to taste different.

From September to May New Zealand lamb is imported into Britain either frozen or chilled. Ironically such lamb is now of a uniformly high quality despite its lower price tag.

Depending on its age, lamb will vary in colour from rosy pink to dark red. It should always be hung by the butcher before sale to ensure tenderness and should smell sweet and clean. A light layering of creamy white fat is useful, particularly on joints as this helps to baste the meat while it roasts. Avoid any whose fat is dry, crumbly or discoloured.

Storage

As with beef, lamb should always be kept chilled and loosely covered. It should be stored on a shelf below cooked meat to avoid contaminating the cooked meat and should never come into contact with other foods. Unwrap whatever you have bought and place in a clean, lightly covered dish, so that the air can circulate around the meat. Never let it sit in a pool of blood.

Roasting

As always in Britain, the same cut of meat can go under several different names depending on the region. However, I will endeavour to give a brief description of the main cuts used. Leg of lamb (gigot) is sold both on the bone and boned and rolled. If you wish to stuff a leg yourself, you usually have to ask for it to be boned, but not rolled. Leg is always taken from the back legs, whereas shoulder is taken from the upper part of the forelegs. This is much fattier than the leg and consequently much cheaper. Due to its lack of meat it is often boned, stuffed and rolled. Some maintain that it tastes sweeter than leg, but they may also have a penchant for fat.

The loin is cut from the back – thus two loins make a 'saddle'. These can be sold singly or jointly, with or without the kidney, and on the bone or boned and rolled with the back fat tied neatly around it. It is considered by many to be the finest cut for roast lamb. Always make sure that your loin is chined, otherwise it is impossible to carve without an undignified struggle.

Best end of neck (rack of lamb) follows on from the loin. It too needs to be chined and can be made into a Guard of Honour by serving two racks with their trimmed rib bones interlocking. Sometimes they are served as a 'crown', tied together in a circle with an appropriate stuffing in the middle. A large rack will feed two and half people, a small one only two. Ideally the exposed bones are supposed to be scraped clean of any meat to prevent them from charring in an unattractive manner. Alternatively the fillet can be removed, trimmed and roasted whole.

Estimated quantities uncooked weight on the bone
Leg: 225–340g/8–12oz per person
Loin: 225–340g/8–12oz per person
Best end of neck (also known as rack of lamb): sufficient for 2 hungry people
Shoulder: 225–340g/8–12oz per person

Roasting table per 455g/1lb for average weight on the bone

Cut	200 °C/400 °F/gas 6	Degree
Leg (1.5–1.8kg/3½–4lb)	22–23 minutes	Rare
	26–27 minutes	Medium (rosé)
	30–31 minutes	Well done
Loin (1.4kg/3lb)	16–17 minutes	Rare
	20 minutes	Medium (rosé)
	25–26 minutes	Well done
Best end of neck (whole)	23–24 minutes	Rare
	30 minutes	Medium (rosé)
	40 minutes	Well done
Shoulder (1.8–2.3kg/4–5lb)	17–18 minutes	Rare
	20 minutes	Medium (rosé)
	22–23 minutes	Well done

Traditional accompaniments

It was widely believed that the accompaniment to roast or indeed grilled lamb should be based on the natural diet of the lamb with a small amount of romantic licence. Thus a moorland lamb should be accompanied by rowanberry jelly, while a lowland lamb should be served with a mint sauce, as mint might grow around local streams. Salt marsh sheep should be eaten with laverbread or samphire, and hill lambs should be flavoured with wild thyme. In reality, most modern sheep taste much of a muchness and your tracklements should be decided according to your mood. A wide variety of delicious sweet jellies can be served – for example, redcurrant, whitecurrant, crab apple and even barberry if you are lucky enough to have access to them. Mint can be added to redcurrant or apple jelly, while port or orange can be added to redcurrant jelly.

Gravy is essential, but ideally should be barely thickened. As to accompanying vegetables, during the summer minted new potatoes and tender young peas are very popular. Naturally, green vegetables are essential for most British diners, but runner beans, green beans or spinach appear to be particularly favoured. Later in the season crisp roast potatoes and a simple watercress salad are also very good.

Lastly, it is important to mention suitable accompaniments to cold roast lamb. Aside from piping hot jacket potatoes and crisp green salads, a variety of pickles, for example spiced damson or piccalilli, make a good accompaniment, as do all the jellies. However, it is worth experimenting with mustard-dressed green bean salads, lettuce tossed with shredded mint leaves and wild garlic, and hot buttered new potatoes.

Grilling

The grilling of a wide variety of foods has become increasingly popular in Britain over the last few years. Lamb has benefited from this new-found enthusiasm, as the smoky taste of the grill brings out its inherent sweetness. Subtle herb or spice marinades can further enhance it, particularly when barbecuing. Whichever cut you choose, it is important to ensure that any excess fat is trimmed off as this can cause the grill to flare and taint the flavour of the meat by direct contact with flames.

Lamb can be grilled in the form of chops, steaks and diced or minced kebabs. Chops can be divided into several different categories: loin, chump and best end (cutlets). The juiciest are loin chops, and they develop a progressively smaller eye of meat as you reach the best end. Steaks can be cut from the leg or from the loin. They can be T-shaped, as with the latter, or rolled into what are commonly called 'noisettes'. Diced kebabs tend to be made from diced leg meat, but they can be made from shoulder or even the best end fillet. The latter requires less cooking time. Minced lamb is usually moulded around a skewer as a kebab, but it can also be made into a lamb burger or patty. The latter should be cooked in exactly the same way as a beef burger.

If you are using a normal grill, preheat to its full setting for 20 minutes, while at the same time allowing your meat to come up to room temperature. The meat should be placed 7.5cm/3 inches away from the heat. Alternatively you can use a ribbed cast-iron oven-top grill or a barbecue.

Grilling time per side

Cut	Weight	Thickness	Cooking time	Degree
Loin chop	115g/4oz	2.5cm/1 inch	4 minutes	Rosé
			6 minutes	Well done
Best end chop	85g/3oz	2.5cm/1 inch	4 minutes	Rosé
			6 minutes	Well done
Chump end	170g/6oz	2cm/¾ inch	4 minutes	Rosé
			6 minutes	Well done
Leg steak	255g/9oz	2cm/¾ inch	4 minutes	Rosé
			6 minutes	Well done
Kebabs (leg or shoulder meat cut into 2.5cm/1 inch cubes)			4 minutes	Rosé
			6 minutes	Well done

Traditional accompaniments

All the accompaniments common to roast lamb can be served with grilled lamb. Alternatively Béarnaise sauce can be offered, as can a wide variety of modern butters and sauces. Simple cold butters can be flavoured with lemon zest and juice and fresh herbs, for example, thyme, marjoram, mint, tarragon, chive, wild garlic, chervil or parsley. Finely diced shallots, black or green olives and even tomato dice can be added, as can anchovies, fresh chilli or roasted garlic.

Salsas and chunky vinaigrettes also make a delicious accompaniment, using tomatoes, olives, roasted peppers and/or herbs as their base. Even yoghurts, raita style, can be wonderful. Many of these accompaniments work particularly well if the meat has been marinated in a subtly flavoured marinade that echoes the taste of the accompanying sauce. The addition of an acid such as wine or lemon juice will tenderize the meat, but it will also imbue the lamb with a slightly gamey flavour. One exception to this rule is if you are making an Eastern-inspired marinade of yoghurt, lemon, garlic and olive oil, where the lamb tastes even more fragrant.

Frying

With the exception of the kebabs, all the information mentioned above under grilling applies to frying.

Stewing

British lamb stews can be divided into several categories, the most obvious being the daube or French style of stew – neatly diced meat flavoured with wine, bacon, herbs and orange or lemon peel – and 'traditional' working-class stews, made with the poorer cuts, sometimes on the bone, such as scrag end, middle neck and the like. These were slowly simmered all day with root vegetables to become Lancashire hotpot, for example, or Irish stew and lobscouse. However, there are also slow-simmered dishes such Scotch broth, poached sheep's head or haggis. For those who are curious about the contents of haggis, it consists of oatmeal, onion and spices mixed with minced-up sheep's liver, lung and heart.

At one time boiled mutton was very popular among the middle classes. Its slow cooking rendered it a tender if drab-looking dish with the added bonus of a fine stock that could be used for soup, another prerequisite of the British culinary past. The decline in mutton sealed its fate and few make it today. However, if ever you are tempted, it should be accompanied by either a fine caper or onion sauce.

Lastly, I ought to mention such dishes as shepherd's pie here, along with lamb pies. Shepherd's pie is distinguished from cottage pie by the fact that it is made with minced lamb rather than beef. I will not weary you with another recipe, as hundreds abound and I have to admit that it is not one of my favourite dishes. Lamb pie used to be made in several forms, either with stewed meat which ranged from leg to lamb's tails covered with a crust, or as a sweet pie, flavoured with spices, apples and dried fruit. Both have dropped from common usage, although I have no doubt that they are still being made in certain homes.

Traditional flavourings

Many traditional lamb soups and stews are flavoured with root vegetables, in particular carrots, turnips, swedes and potatoes. Onions, leeks and barley are also popular with this style of dish. Frenchified versions will include garlic, tomatoes, peas, mushrooms and the like. Luckily, the British have become increasingly enamoured of spices and now make excellent curries with lamb. These are more to my taste, delicately flavoured with cream or coconut, saffron, ginger and cumin. The possibilities are endless.

Welsh roast lamb

Welsh lamb is regarded by some as the sweetest of all the hill lamb. The long slow roasting of this joint helps to ensure a succulent, richly flavoured dish. I cook it until it is meltingly tender and well done, but if you prefer a rosier version, reduce the final slow cooking by 30 minutes. (Serves 6)

2.3 kg/5lb hill lamb	salt and freshly ground black
1 large sprig rosemary	pepper
2 cloves garlic, cut into thin	4 tablespoons thick (Welsh if
slivers	possible) honey
1 lemon, juiced	710ml/1¼ pints dry cider

Preheat the oven to 200°C/400°F/gas 6.

Cut small incisions all over the lamb and insert the rosemary leaves and sliced garlic. Place on a non-corrosive roasting tray and rub all over with the lemon juice. Season with salt and pepper, then rub in the honey. Pour in the cider and place in the centre of the oven.

Roast for 20 minutes then reduce the heat to 150°C/300°F/gas 2 and roast for a further 2 hours 40 minutes. Turn the meat twice while it slowly cooks. It will caramelize to a beautiful golden brown while the cider will reduce down to a dark, flavoursome gravy.

Transfer the joint to a clean dish and leave to rest in a warm place while you finish the sauce. Skim off any excess fat from the juices and place over a low heat. Add more cider if necessary to deglaze the roasting tray before straining into a warm sauceboat. Serve with the lamb.

A good lamb gravy

Known in some circles as 'jus,' there is only one way to produce a truly superb lamb gravy and that is by making a good lamb stock. To quote the Hermit in Lady Llanover's extraordinary book on Welsh cookery, *The First Principles of Good Cookery* (1867): 'No one can have a gravy properly prepared from the same leg of mutton which is just roasted, because there is not time for the fat and gravy which are necessarily mixed together to cool, which process must take place before every particle of the fat can be removed from the gravy.' Although it has become unfashionable to make home-made stock, it is well worth the small amount of effort required. If you are ever in any doubt I suggest you read the ingredients list on a packet of stock cubes, which invariably includes monosodium glutamate, a taste enhancer.

When it comes to stock it is not necessary to worry about exact quantities – rather it is a matter of what you have in the fridge and how large your saucepan is. Naturally the more vegetables you add the more complex the final flavour of your sauce, but treat the following ingredients list as a guide rather than a rule. In the past I have resorted to using the bones and trimmings of 4 lamb racks, omitted the onions and added some dry martini instead of wine and it still tasted good. However, it will taste all the better if you can persuade a friendly butcher to give you some extra bones. If he is particularly kind, ask him to break them into several pieces.

Lamb bones, e.g. leg or shoulder	2 ripe tomatoes, halved
2 small unpeeled onions	½ bottle good red or white wine
2 leeks, roughly chopped	2 large sprigs parsley
3 trimmed carrots, roughly chopped	1 bay leaf
4 cloves garlic	1 sprig thyme
2 outer stems celery, roughly chopped or ½ small peeled celeriac, roughly chopped	3 black peppercorns
	3 cloves

Preheat the oven to its highest setting. Arrange the lamb bones in a large roasting pan and roast until their fat begins to run and the bones are beginning to colour. A wonderful smell of roast lamb will fill the kitchen.

Wash the onions and remove their roots before roughly chopping, skin and all. Add all the vegetables, including the tomatoes, to the lamb bones and mix thoroughly so that they are well coated in fat. Continue to roast, stirring occasionally, until they have turned a beautiful golden brown and the lamb is well coloured. On no account let anything burn, as this will make your stock taste bitter.

Remove from the oven and carefully transfer the lamb bones and vegetables to a large non-corrosive saucepan, leaving as much fat as possible in the bottom of the roasting tray. Pour this off and save for roast potatoes or lamb stews.

Add the wine to the roasting tray and place over moderate heat. Using a wooden spoon, vigorously scrape off any caramelized bits from the bottom of the pan as the wine comes up to the boil. Tip this into the stock-pot along with the herbs, peppercorns and cloves. Finally, add enough cold water to fill the saucepan.

Place over a high heat and bring to the boil, skimming off any scum. Then reduce the heat and simmer gently for about 3 hours. As the stock cooks it will reduce and intensify in flavour. If you have only a relatively small saucepan you may need to replenish the water as it reduces to ensure that you have plenty of well-flavoured stock. The broth is ready once it tastes good.

It is important to simmer stock, as boiling can make it cloudy by suspending tiny particles of fat or debris throughout the broth, rather than letting them float to the surface.

Once cooked to your satisfaction, carefully strain the stock through a fine sieve into a clean container. Allow to cool, then chill. Once cold (and set) a thin layer of white fat will cover the surface of the stock. Remove this, then pour the stock into a non-corrosive saucepan and boil vigorously until it has a wonderfully rich lamb flavour. Do not over-reduce to a syrupy consistency as this will make it taste like Marmite. Chill and freeze what you do not need. Otherwise your gravy is now ready for use. If wished you can whisk a tiny amount of butter into the juices.

Lamb with samphire

Traditionally, lamb that was reared on the salt marshes was served with a slightly salty sea-tasting accompaniment which could either be marsh samphire or laver, a type of seaweed. Samphire comes in two forms, marsh and rock. Marsh samphire, which is also known as glasswort (*Salicornia europaea*), grows wild on the salt marshes and is picked in July and August. It has fleshy, succulent stems and is normally sold by fishmongers and in some health food shops. Rock samphire (*Crithmum maritimum*) is a different plant altogether and grows on cliffs and rocks. Although excellent eaten pickled, fresh or lightly cooked in spring or early summer, it is not normally eaten with lamb. (Serves 6)

1.5kg/3½lb leg of lamb	*Gravy*
1 lemon, juiced	285ml/½ pint reduced home-
85g/3oz softened butter	made lamb stock (see above)
generous pinch of cayenne	55g/2oz cold diced butter
pepper	
sea salt and roughly ground	*Samphire*
black pepper	680g/1½lb samphire
	30g/1oz butter

Preheat the oven to 200°C/400°F/gas 6.

Rub the lamb leg with the lemon juice then coat liberally with the butter. Season with the cayenne pepper, salt and black pepper. Arrange on a roasting tray and place in the centre of the preheated oven. Roast for 1 hour 20 minutes if you like your meat rare, 1 hour 35 minutes for medium rare and 1 hour 48 minutes if you prefer it well done. Baste regularly with the melted butter in the roasting pan.

Thoroughly wash the samphire and snip off any tough woody stems.

Transfer the joint to a clean dish and leave to rest in a warm place for 15–20 minutes. This makes it more succulent, as the juices are re-absorbed into the meat. Meanwhile put a large pan of unsalted water on to boil. Samphire should never be salted as it is quite salty enough.

Heat the reduced lamb stock in a small non-corrosive saucepan. Once it has boiled, check the seasoning then reduce the heat to low and whisk in the butter, a few dice at a time. Immediately transfer to a warm gravy boat.

Drop the samphire into the boiling water, return to the boil and drain immediately. Serve piping hot in a warm dish, dotted with a little butter as an accompaniment to the roast lamb and gravy.

Rack of lamb with black olives

This recipe depends on a well-made lamb sauce as suggested above. Thus prepared it makes a superb dinner party dish, as very little work is required to take it to the table yet it tastes divine. It is particularly good served with a potato gratin. (Serves 6)

2 short cut pairs of best end lamb (also sold as 4 French trimmed racks of lamb), boned and stripped of fat and sinew	3 cloves garlic, crushed freshly ground black pepper
salt	*Sauce*
	140ml/¼ pint dry Martini
Marinade	285ml/½ pint reduced lamb stock
8 tablespoons olive oil	12 black olives, stoned and cut into strips
10 sprigs thyme	115g/4oz cold butter, diced

Rack of lamb is one of the easiest meats to bone, although if you are worried any butcher will do it for you. If you wish to bone it yourself, run your knife down along the bones, following their line, until the tiny ribs come away.

Trim the lamb fillets of any fat and remove the fine blue skin by running a sharp knife just underneath it. Mix together the marinade ingredients and coat the lamb fillets. Cover and chill for 12–24 hours.

Preheat the oven to its highest setting. Shortly before you are ready to serve, reduce the dry Martini to 3 tablespoons by boiling it vigorously in a non-corrosive saucepan. Add the reduced lamb stock, bring to the boil, then add the olives and set aside.

Remove the fillets from their marinade and season with salt. Place a frying pan over a high heat and sear the lamb in this, colouring every side, before transferring to a roasting tray. Spoon over any excess marinade and roast for 10 minutes for medium rare.

Allow to rest while you finish the sauce. Return the black olive gravy to the boil, then reduce the heat and whisk in the butter. Check the seasoning then serve immediately with the lamb, which should be carved into thick slices.

Note: If you are in a rush and need to prepare the lamb quickly, cut the fillets into thick slices and marinate (covered and chilled) for 1–2 hours. Then, when you are ready to serve, heat 2 tablespoons of olive oil in a hot frying pan, season the slices and fry in batches, searing each side until just coloured. Keep warm until all the lamb is cooked.

Coriander lamb brochettes

Although coriander is widely regarded as a recent introduction to British cooking, there is evidence that coriander seeds have been eaten here since prehistoric times. Whether our ancestors used them to flavour their lamb or mutton is another matter. However, such a combination is very much to current taste, influenced as we are by Indian and Middle Eastern recipes. This is delicious eaten with a fragrant saffron pilaff. (Serves 6)

Marinade
3 tablespoons coriander seeds
3 cloves garlic, crushed
6 tablespoons olive oil
freshly ground black pepper

Brochettes
1 kg/2lb 3oz lean lamb leg
    or shoulder meat, cut into
    2.5cm/1 inch dice
3 red onions, cut into 2.5cm/
    1 inch dice
salt

Tomato vinaigrette
6 tomatoes
3 tablespoons white wine
    vinegar
9 tablespoons extra virgin
    olive oil
6 tablespoons roughly
    chopped fresh coriander
2 cloves garlic, crushed

Place the coriander seeds in a small dry frying pan over a moderately high heat and dry roast for about 2 minutes or until they begin to release their scent. Remove from the pan, and crush medium roughly, and transfer to a large mixing bowl. Add the garlic, olive oil and a few twists of black pepper.

Remove any excess fat from the lamb and, if you are dicing it yourself, cut the meat along the muscle seams so that you do not have any tough sinews running through your cubes of meat. Mix the diced lamb into the marinade, cover and chill for at least an hour but preferably for longer.

Cut a small cross in the base of each tomato and cut out the small white core to which the stalk is usually attached. Cover with boiling water and remove as soon as the skin begins to peel. Whisk together the vinegar, olive oil, fresh coriander and garlic, then peel, halve and dice the tomatoes and add to the vinaigrette. Season to taste and set aside until needed.

Preheat your grill, ribbed cast-iron oven-top grill pan or barbecue. Separate the red onion dice and carefully thread alternate pieces of lamb and onion on to 12 x 15cm/6 inch skewers. Season with salt and grill for 7–8 minutes, turning the skewers as you do so. Serve with the tomato vinaigrette.

LAVENDER

Two spoonfuls of the distilled water of the flowers help them that
have lost their voice, the tremblings and passions of the heart, and
fainting and swoonings, applied to the temples or nostrils, to be
smelt unto.

Culpeper's Complete Herbal on the Government and Virtues of Lavender

The scent of lavender on a hot summer's day mixed with the drowsy hum of bees and the occasional coo of a wood pigeon creates that deliciously timeless quality of an English country garden. Lavender, above all other floral scents, somehow smells quintessentially British, yet it has only recently gained popularity as a culinary herb. In 1954 Dorothy Hartley dismissed its place in the kitchen with the following lines:

A few old recipes mention lavender as a cookery herb. Its best eating service is to candy a few small grains to add zest to the Christmas box of candied fruits, and please the few who do not care for the ordinary type of sweet, but like the pungent 'bite' of the lavender.

It is difficult to know what changes national taste, but I suspect that in the matter of lavender, its strangely refreshing taste appeals to our modern palate. We appear increasingly to crave stimulating, lively flavours, and lavender fulfils these criteria while at the same time delivering a delicate flowery taste of summer. Its very name provokes the romantic images of an idyllic rural life that have become so important to urban dwellers.

Curiously, I suspect that the decline of lavender's use as a medicinal herb has also helped it to be reconsidered as a valid flavouring. It is, after all, difficult to imagine cooking with something akin to TCP or Dettol. Happily, gone are the days when nervous aunts dabbed their throbbing brows with lavender water and elderly relations repelled the moths with small sachets of dusty lavender. Instead, chic chefs serve exquisite scoops of lavender sorbet to accompany a peach parfait and smart delicatessens sell elegant bottles of lavender vinegar.

Cooks have begun to use sprigs of lavender in much the same way as they once used rosemary, slipping it into sugar jars in place of a vanilla pod and creating delicate syrups in which summer fruits, such as peaches or rhubarb, are poached. Buttery biscuits and creamy ice creams are enhanced by its presence, as are aromatic salads of smoked fish or goat's cheese.

Practical guide

Lavender loves arid soil, and will grow equally well in beautiful terracotta pots and grandiose herbaceous borders. Choose any varieties from the *Lavandula angustifolia* family, for example, common English lavender, Hidcote or even a miniature such as Munstead.

Gather the flowers when they are just beginning to open, usually at the end of June or beginning of July. They can then either be added fresh to a recipe or dried. Alternatively you can make a lavender vinegar or a lavender syrup. The latter can be stored in the fridge in a sterilized container or frozen in small quantities. A few drops can make a lovely addition to a winter rhubarb compote or lemon jelly.

Lavender needs a light hand – too much can ruin a dish by making it astringent. Added in moderation, it will imbue food with the lightest of flowery flavours. Ideally you should use flowers from your own plant, as you can then ensure that it is not sprayed with pesticides or subjected to heavy pollution. However, you can use dried lavender, provided it is bought from a herbalist who knows that it is to be used in cooking. The majority of florists cannot guarantee that their flowers have not been sprayed.

Lavender syrup
Place 6 sprigs of lavender in a non-corrosive saucepan with 225g/8oz sugar and 285ml/½ pint of water. Set over a low heat and stir occasionally until the sugar has dissolved. Remove from the heat and leave until completely cold. Strain into a sterilized bottle (see page 179 for method) and label or freeze as ice cubes. Use as a flavouring, only ever adding in small quantities.

Lavender vinegar
Buy a very good white wine or champagne vinegar and heat it to scalding point. Slip 6 sprigs of lavender flowers into its bottle before covering with the piping hot vinegar. Seal and leave in a sunny place for 2 weeks, giving the bottle an occasional shake. At the end of this time, decant the vinegar into a sterilized bottle, (see page 179 for method) label and seal. You can, if wished, add a fresh stem of lavender for identification.

Taste notes

◊ As lavender has only been recently reintroduced to British cooking, it is worth experimenting with different flavours. As a vinegar it works well with the richer flavours of smoked fish, in particular eel or salmon; however, it also tastes good added to stir-fried white cabbage, as is suggested by Frances Bissell in her engaging book *A Cook's Calendar*. Lavender makes a good flavouring for fruit jellies, namely apple or rhubarb, which in turn can be used through the year, either as an accompaniment to game and lamb or as a filling for rich almond cakes and hot scones.

◊ Infused into cream as a crème brûlée, lavender is delicious with strawberries, peaches or nectarines.

◊ Try the ancient remedy of burning a few dry lavender stalks to clear the air – the old English version of joss sticks.

Smoked eel salad

This salad makes an elegant starter for a dinner party. You can either use a proper lavender vinegar for this recipe (see above) or cheat with this instant recipe. (Serves 6)

Lavender vinaigrette	Salad
1 sprig lavender flowers	450g/1lb new potatoes
3 tablespoons champagne vinegar	1 lemon, finely grated and juiced
6 tablespoons almond oil or extra virgin olive oil	6 tablespoons crème fraîche
salt and freshly ground black pepper	855g/1lb 14oz fillet of smoked eel
	115g/4oz mixed summer leaves and herbs

Put the lavender and vinegar in a small non-corrosive saucepan and simmer gently for 3 minutes. Remove from the heat and leave to infuse for 30 minutes before straining. Whisk in the oil and season to taste.

Add the new potatoes to a pan of boiling salted water and cook for 15–20 minutes or until tender. Drain and cool a little before peeling off their papery skins. Meanwhile beat the finely grated lemon zest into the crème fraîche and season to taste.

When you are ready to serve, slice the potatoes into rounds, toss in some vinaigrette and arrange in a semi-circle on each of the 6 plates. Drizzle with crème fraîche before partially laying the smoked eel over them. Dress the lettuces in the vinaigrette and arrange in an airy pile on the other side of each plate. Finally pour a little lemon juice over the eel fillets and serve immediately.

Peach compote with almond cream

This simple syrup can be used for a wide variety of poached fruits, pies or fruit salad. Try cooking rhubarb in it, or even slices of eating apples. However, before proceeding I had to include this quote from Eliza Acton's *Modern Cookery for Private Families* (1855):

COMPOTES OF FRUIT
Or Fruit stewed in Syrup

We would especially recommend these delicate and very agreeable preparations for trial to such of our readers as may be unacquainted with them, as well as to those who may have a distaste to the common 'stewed fruit' of English cookery. If well made they are peculiarly delicious and refreshing, preserving the pure flavour of the fruit of which they are composed . . .

So forget your prejudices against the words 'stewed' and 'compote' and try this wonderful modern interpretation. (Serves 4)

115g/4oz granulated sugar	*Almond cream*
285ml/½ pint water	6 ratafia biscuits, roughly
3 sprigs lavender flowers	crushed
1 lemon, finely pared, plus	115g/4oz crème fraîche
juice of ½ lemon	55g/2oz thick double cream
8 ripe peaches	
140ml/¼ pint dessert wine e.g.	
Muscat de Beaumes de	
Venise	

Place the sugar, water, lavender and lemon rind in a wide, non-corrosive saucepan. Dissolve the sugar over a low heat and leave to simmer for 10 minutes.

Quarter, stone and peel the peaches before cutting into thick segments. Add to the hot syrup and simmer for 5 minutes or until tender. Remove the peaches with a slotted spoon and place in a clean bowl. Pour the syrup through a fine strainer into a clean non-corrosive pan and boil vigorously until the juices become syrupy. Stir in the juice from ½ a lemon and the dessert wine. Pour over the peaches and leave to cool.

Meanwhile beat the crushed ratafia biscuits, crème fraîche and double cream together. Cover and chill along with the compote. Serve the peaches in elegant soup bowls, each with a scoop of almond cream.

Lavender pear ice cream

Lavender has become a popular flavouring for British ices, ranging from the purest of sorbets to cleanse the palate to rich ice creams. Here is a classically cool British ice, subtly flavoured for maximum impact. Heaven on a spoon. (Serves 6)

285ml/½ pint double cream
2 sprigs lavender flowers
1 lemon, juiced
3 ripe pears, for example,
　Taylor's Gold

4 large egg yolks
170g/6oz caster sugar
1 tablespoon Poire Williams

Place the cream and lavender in a saucepan over a low heat. Slowly bring up to scalding point then remove from the heat and leave to infuse for 30 minutes.

Pour the lemon juice into a non-corrosive saucepan. Peel, quarter, core and roughly chop one pear at a time. Thoroughly coat in the lemon juice, to prevent the pear discolouring, before continuing with the remaining fruit. Place over a moderate heat and simmer gently for 10 minutes or until the fruit is tender. Purée and set aside.

Whisk the egg yolks with the sugar until thick and creamy. Gradually pour in the lavender cream then return to a low heat, stirring continuously with a wooden spoon until it forms a thick custard. This will take around 20 minutes, but after the first 5 minutes fish out the 2 stems of lavender. You must not stop stirring or leave the custard unattended during this stage, as it can easily split. Remove from the heat and continue to stir as you add the pear purée followed by the Poire Williams. As soon as it is cool, cover and chill.

Churn the cold custard according to your ice cream machine instructions until it reaches a soft set. Otherwise pour it into a shallow plastic container, cover and place in the fast-freeze compartment of your freezer. Every 30–40 minutes, rework with a fork until the mixture has set into a smooth, soft-set ice cream. Serve with lavender biscuits if wished.

Note: Poire Williams is available in miniature bottles from most off-licences, but if you cannot find any pear eau de vie you could use some Calvados, although it does not have as light a flavour.

Lavender biscuits

These make a summery-scented version of shortbread perfect for ice cream or tea. Use open lavender flowers rather than flower buds. Simply pull out the tiny flowers (they come away very easily) and pack into a teaspoon. If you feel it necessary to wash your lavender, rinse the sprigs and allow to dry before stripping the flowers. The biscuits should be eaten freshly baked. (Makes about 16)

115g/4oz softened butter	3 teaspoons lavender flowers
55g/2oz caster sugar	170g/6oz plain flour
1 lemon, finely grated	extra caster sugar for dusting

Preheat the oven to 150°C/300°F/gas 2 and grease 2 baking sheets.

Beat together the butter, sugar and lemon zest until pale and creamy. Mix in the lavender flowers and flour by hand until the mixture forms a stiff dough. Place this on to a sheet of bakewell paper and lay another sheet on top. Then gently press down with a rolling pin and roll out thinly. Lift off the top sheet and stamp out the biscuits with your chosen cutter. Using a palette knife, lift them off the bottom sheet of paper and carefully transfer to the baking sheets.

Bake in the centre of the oven for 30 minutes or until tinged brown. Remove to a cooling rack and liberally dust with extra caster sugar. Serve when cool.

LEEKS

GOWER: Nay, that's right; but why wear you your leek to-day? Saint Davy's day is past.

FLUELLEN: There is occasions and causes why and wherefore in all things. I will tell you, ass my friend, Captain Gower: the rascally, scald, beggarly, lousy, pragging knave, Pistol – which you and yourself and all the world know to be no petter than a fellow, look you now, of no merits he is come to me, and prings me pread and salt yesterday look you, and bid me eat my leek; it was in a place where I could not breed contention with him; but I will be so bold as to wear it in my cap till I see him once again, and then I will tell him a little piece of my desires.

Henry V, by William Shakespeare. And thus the unfortunate Pistol is made to eat Fluellen's raw leek.

Legend has it that on the morning of the great battle between Cadwallon, king of Gwynedd, and Edwin, king of Northumbria, in 632 the Welsh soldiers gathered leeks from a nearby field and placed them in their caps so as to prevent them from mistakenly attacking one another in the heat of the battle. They won the day and so, according to one story, the leek became their national emblem. At that moment it also became the source of many an unkind English joke.

The Romans introduced the British to the pleasures of leeks and they rapidly spread across the land from Scotland to Cornwall. Yet even at the height of their popularity in the Middle Ages, when they were added to everything from pottage to salad, they still suffered from a derogatory image as a result of their natural heat. In a world where each food was believed to affect the four humours, in conjunction with the four elements and the stars, a person's health could be seriously affected by over-indulgence in a particular food. Leeks were regarded as a dangerous food for choleric, lustful people. Chaucer depicts a particularly unpleasant leek-eater in the form of the corrupt, syphilitic Summoner:

> Wel loved he garleek, oynons, and eek lekes,
> And for to drynken strong wyn, reed as blood.

Gradually the leek came to be regarded as too coarse a vegetable for refined palates, although it remained popular in rural areas, especially in Scotland and Wales. This is beautifully illustrated in Susan Ferrier's novel *Marriage* (1818), when the vacuous English bride, Lady Juliana, is introduced to the family of Henry Douglas, her recently acquired Scottish husband:

'Will you take a little soup, love?' asked Douglas. His Lady assented; and Miss Nicky vanished, but quickly re-entered, followed by Tibby, carrying a huge bowl of coarse Scotch broth, swimming with leeks, greens, and grease. Lady Juliana attempted to taste it; but her delicate palate revolted at the homely fare; and she gave up the attempt, in spite of Miss Nicky's earnest entreaties to take a few more of these [*sic*] excellent family broth.

'I should think,' said Henry, as he vainly attempted to stir it round, 'that a little wine would be more to the purpose than this stuff.'

And so the leek has continued to lurk in our food over the centuries, favoured by some in regional dishes, such as cock-a-leekie (made by simmering beef with a capon, leeks and prunes), North Country pudding, Welsh mutton broth or Cornish leek pie, and neglected by others except as an occasional flavouring or as a vegetable. That is until about seventy-five years ago when Louis Diat, the French chef at the New York Ritz-Carlton, invented crème vichyssoise glacée, a chilled leek and potato soup that was based on his mother's recipe and named in honour of the regional cooking of his homeland. Unwittingly, this dish reinstated leeks as a chic dish to eat in Britain, albeit in the velvety form of soup. Gradually they crept back into British cookery, under the pretext of French-sounding salads and tarts. Today leeks are used freely in all sorts of recipes, from elegant leek vinaigrettes to homely chicken pies.

Practical guide

As far as nature is concerned the leek (*Allium porrum*) is a hardy winter vegetable that runs to seed in the spring. As far as the cook is concerned, this means that it develops a woody inner stem that is useless for anything but stock. However, as far as the supermarkets are concerned, leeks are available throughout the year, as they can be imported through the summer months when they are unobtainable here. April leeks should be treated with care by shoppers as they may well hide woody cores.

Despite giant leek competitions, small or medium-sized leeks are best for cooking as they tend to be sweeter and more tender than their over-sized siblings. Always choose leeks as you would a bunch of flowers – their leaves should look fresh and sprightly, while their white stems should be firm and unblemished. They can be stored uncut in the fridge for several days but are best used up quickly.

Leeks are easy to prepare but you must ensure that they are cleaned thoroughly, as their tightly wrapped leaves can harbour mud and grit. Begin by topping and tailing your leeks. Then make a light cut down the length of each leek and peel away the tough outer leaves. These should be discarded, contrary to popular advice which recommends adding them to stocks and soups. In my opinion they are too bitter to be of benefit. Finally cut away the darkest part of the green stem and unwrap this until you reach a tender light green inner core. Use this alongside the white and light green part of your leek.

Alternatively, you can slice or dice your leeks before washing. They can then be soaked and vigorously washed in a sink full of cold water before being scooped out with a sieve. The dirt will fall to the bottom of the sink.

If you are using your leeks whole, you will need to cut a deep cross down from the top before swishing them in plenty of cold water. In theory the mud will loosen and slip out. However, if it looks as though some of the mud has become embedded in the white part of the stem, you will have to make a small cross at the bottom. Sadly there is no easy answer.

Taste notes

◊ Leeks benefit from a light cooking – too long, and they turn unpleasantly slimy. The simplest way to cook them is by lightly frying them, sliced, in olive oil or butter. A touch of thyme or tarragon and, if you are feeling extravagant, a hint of double cream or crème fraîche, and you have a delicious vegetable which can easily be extended into a sauce.

◊ Try cooking leeks in the above manner with shredded spinach, grated carrots or beetroot.

◊ A wide variety of herbs and spices complement leeks, in particular thyme, tarragon, chervil, chives, wild garlic, watercress and parsley. Lemon grass, chillies, coriander seeds and nutmeg are also good.

◊ Although leeks can be served raw, thinly sliced, it is still more to British taste to cook them first. Once lightly blanched, they can then be added to all manner of salads. Their robust flavour will withstand walnut or even sesame oil, while their sweetness tastes delicious when accompanied by shellfish such as grilled squid, prawns, scallops or mussels. A judicious use of herbs will make this a salad fit for the gods.

◊ The smoky flavour of chargrilling seems to enhance the natural sweetness of leeks. They should be lightly cooked and cooled before having any excess water wrung out of them. Pat dry, then very lightly oil them before grilling for a minute or two, just enough to fleck them with grill marks. They can then be marinated and served hot or cold. They are particularly good eaten with Parma ham, roasted peppers, curls of Parmesan or a piquant anchovy vinaigrette as an appetizer.

◊ All dairy products work well with leeks. Cream can be used in everything from rich potato and leek gratins to the simplest of soups. Eggs will transform leeks into subtle savoury baked custards, delicate soufflés and roulades. Cheese will add depth to leek recipes, from pastas to tarts.

◊ Bacon, chicken, beef and lamb are all traditional partners of leeks, while white fish and most shellfish are becoming increasingly popular.

Leek and lemon grass vichyssoise

In the fourteenth century British chefs would make a leek pottage, or white porry as it was called, with the white part of leeks and almonds. Smooth leek soup is, in one sense, an updated version. (Serves 6)

3 cloves garlic, crushed

3 stems lemon grass, finely sliced

4 tablespoons olive oil

2 large potatoes, peeled and diced

1.4kg/3lb leeks

850ml/1½ pints hot water or chicken stock (see page 339 or buy ready made)

salt and freshly ground black pepper

565ml/1 pint single cream

3 tablespoons finely sliced chives or wild garlic

Gently fry the garlic and lemon grass in the olive oil in a non-corrosive saucepan for 4 minutes. Then add the potatoes and continue to fry over a moderate heat for a further 8 minutes until they begin to soften.

Trim the leeks and remove their tough outer leaves. Remove the dark green tops and discard all but the light green inner leaves. Finely slice these along with the white stems. Wash thoroughly in several changes of water and drain well before adding to the potatoes. Continue to fry for a further 5 minutes or until soft.

Add the hot liquid and season to taste. Bring to the boil, then simmer over a moderate heat for 25 minutes or until the vegetables are very soft. Liquidize and pass the mixture through a fine sieve. Adjust the seasoning and stir in the cream. Chill until ready to serve. Garnish with finely chopped chives or wild garlic.

Leek vinaigrette with aubergine caviar

The first recorded English salad to use leeks appears in the late fourteenth century, in a highly flavoured green salad where they were enjoyed finely sliced raw with various herbs, garlic and shallots. Modern leek salads are tamer affairs that are normally served as an appetizer, with whole baby leeks, lightly blanched and marinated in a fragrant vinaigrette. The aubergine caviar accompanying this dish is not true to its Middle Eastern origins as it includes diced, seeded tomatoes. Nevertheless it tastes gorgeous. (Serves 6)

18 thin young leeks, trimmed and cleaned	2 cloves garlic, crushed
salt	4 tablespoons finely chopped parsley
1½ tablespoons sherry vinegar	1 tablespoon lemon juice
9 tablespoons walnut oil	3 tablespoons extra virgin olive oil
freshly ground black pepper	6 sprigs flat-leaved parsley
2 large aubergines	
2 tomatoes, peeled, seeded and diced	

Preheat the oven to 200°C/400°F/Gas Mark 6.

Trim the leeks and remove their outermost leaves. If they have particularly long green tops, trim these down. Make two lengthways cuts in the form of a cross from the top of their leaves to half-way down their stems, and wash in a sink full of cold water. Drop into a pan of boiling salted water and cook for 4–5 minutes or until just tender. Drain and cool under cold water. Pat dry and arrange in a shallow dish. There is nothing worse than watery leeks.

Whisk together the vinegar, walnut oil, salt and freshly ground black pepper. Pour over the leeks, coating them thoroughly. Allow them to marinate for at least a couple of hours, remembering to turn them occasionally.

Place the whole aubergines in the centre of the oven and bake for 30 minutes or until they feel soft and wrinkly. Remove and leave to cool. Meanwhile, peel, quarter and seed the tomatoes. Dice their flesh and place in a bowl with the garlic, parsley, lemon juice and olive oil. Once the aubergines are cold, peel away their skin and cut their flesh into the same sized dice as the tomatoes. Mix them in with the tomatoes and season to taste.

When you are ready to serve, arrange 2 or 3 leeks on each plate with an elegant blob of aubergine caviar. Garnish with a sprig of flat-leaved parsley and serve with lots of crusty bread.

Leek and watercress roulade

This elegant roulade follows the modern mode of reinterpreting classic British ingredients. Serve cold as an appetizer or as a vegetarian main course. (Serves 6)

Roulade
extra Parmesan cheese for
   dusting
455g/1lb trimmed leeks
30g/1oz butter
2 tablespoons flour
140ml/¼ pint milk
3 tablespoons finely grated
   Parmesan
5 large eggs, separated
salt and freshly ground black
   pepper

Filling
225g/8oz cream cheese
4 tablespoons double cream
70g/2½oz watercress, washed
1 tablespoon finely chopped
   tarragon
2 lemons, finely grated
6 ripe tomatoes, peeled,
   seeded and diced

Preheat the oven to 190°C/375°F/gas 5 and lightly oil a shallow baking tray about 33 x 24cm/13½ x 9½ inches in size. Line this with a sheet of greaseproof or bakewell paper, lightly oil and sprinkle with some finely grated Parmesan cheese.

Finely slice and wash the leeks. Melt the butter in a heavy-bottomed saucepan, add the leeks and fry over a low heat until meltingly soft. Stir in the flour and continue to cook for a further 2 minutes, stirring occasionally. Then slowly add the milk, stirring all the time until the mixture thickens into a sauce.

Remove from the heat and beat in the cheese. Transfer the mixture to a food processor and blend until smooth. Beat in the egg yolks, one at a time, and season to taste. Pour into a large bowl and set aside.

Place the egg whites in a large clean white bowl, add a pinch of salt and whisk until they form soft peaks. Slacken the leek sauce with a third of the egg whites before gently folding in the remainder. Pour into the baking tray and bake in the centre of the oven for 15 minutes or until well risen and lightly coloured. Remove and cover with a clean damp tea towel. Leave to cool.

Beat together the cream cheese and double cream until soft. Pick off the watercress leaves and discard the stems. Finely chop and fold into the cream cheese along with the tarragon and lemon zest. Season to taste and chill until ready to use.

When the roulade is cold, carefully invert it on to a large, clean sheet of paper, foil or clingfilm. Peel the greaseproof paper away from its underside. Trim the edges and spread evenly with the watercress cream cheese, leaving the edges free. Scatter the diced tomatoes over the cheese, lightly patting them down as you do so. Then tightly roll it up, starting from the short end, using the paper to help you, until you have a savoury Swiss roll. Wrap this in clingfilm and flip it over so that the roll is held in place. Chill for 2–3 hours to set.

Remove from the fridge 20 minutes before needed. When ready to serve, slice thinly and accompany with a good bread.

Chicken and leek pie

According to Jane Grigson, the custom of serving leek and bacon pies can be found in Wales, Cornwall and northern central France. It seems that similar pies can be found in Flanders but without the bacon. There are many local variants. The addition of chicken makes this perfect for a simple lunch or picnic. (Serves 4)

225g/8oz shortcrust pastry (see page 335)
3 leeks, sliced
30g/1oz butter
115g/4oz lean bacon, finely diced
4 boned and skinned chicken breasts
1 teaspoon roughly chopped tarragon
1 teaspoon Dijon mustard
2 medium egg yolks
140ml/¼ pint double cream
salt and freshly ground black pepper
½ small egg beaten with ½ tablespoon milk

Roll out the pastry into 2 circles, the first measuring about 28cm/11 inches in diameter and the second measuring 23cm/9 inches in diameter. Cover and chill while you prepare the rest of the ingredients.

Preheat the oven to 180°C/350°F/gas 4. Wash the sliced leeks to ensure that no grit is hiding between the rings, and drain thoroughly. Melt the butter in a frying pan and fry the bacon for 3 minutes before adding the leeks. Continue to sauté until they have collapsed, then allow to cool.

Meanwhile slice the chicken into fine strips and place in a bowl with the tarragon, mustard, egg yolks, cream and seasoning. Add the bacon and leeks and mix thoroughly.

Line a 23cm/9 inch pastry ring or flan case with the larger pastry circle, letting the excess pastry fall over the edge. Fill with the chicken mixture and brush the rim with the egg wash. Cover with the remaining pastry circle and seal the pie by pinching the two pastries together with a fork or spoon. Trim and brush with the egg wash before cutting 2 or 3 tiny air holes in the lid.

Bake in the centre of the oven for 45 minutes. Serve warm or cold with a salad.

See also
Luxurious watercress soup (page 329)

LEMONS

In the winter, when flowers are expensive, a silver dish of oranges and lemons is as charming to look upon as flowers.

The Gentle Art of Cookery by Mrs C. F. Leyel and Miss Olga Hartley, 1929

In an age of supermarkets and prepacked prepared foods, it is easy to distance oneself from the physical pleasures of cooking. Yet the sight of rugged Amalfi lemons, nestling in tissue paper, will provoke the sternest of cooks to throw away their shopping list and come home with a bag full of fragrant lemons. They carry with them the promise of warmer climes, clear blue skies and fragrant leaves. Who can resist releasing the exquisite scent of freshly zested lemon peel? Who cannot wish to capture the pure flavour of lemon juice? Everything about lemons is delightful.

Often unnoticed by the casual observer, lemons are one of the most commonly used flavourings in British food. Their presence is not widely advertised, but is nevertheless essential. Their zest is added to the plainest of stews and the simplest of tomato sauces. It finds its way into delicate meatballs, savoury dumplings, stuffings and marinades as well as gorgeous sugar syrups, cakes, biscuits and puddings. Their juice brings alive vinaigrettes, sweet and savoury butters, sauces and marinades, not to mention an enormous range of puddings. In essence lemons can be used either as the focal point of a dish, as with lemon tart, or as a subtle means of enhancing its taste. Lemon juice not only counteracts rich, oily dishes, it also emphasizes natural flavours. Thus a slice of melon, seasoned with a few drops of lemon juice, will taste more intensely of melon than an unseasoned slice. The more aromatic nature of lemon zest, on the other hand, is better used in complex dishes, such as beef ragout or pheasant stuffing, as it slowly imbues them with a lighter, more delicate flavour.

Our native taste for lemons begins at an early age, usually through the sweetened medium of lemon sherbets or dabs, and rapidly progresses to ice lollies and lemon sodas before adulthood is reached with the relative sophistication of a slice of lemon in a cooling glass of gin and tonic. They are subjected to our own unique style of cooking, just as the French or Italians adapt them to their own national taste.

Lemons first began to be imported into Britain in tiny quantities in the thirteenth century. Sometimes they arrived fresh, but more often they were made into what was known as succade, a kind of marmalade. They remained a luxury until well into the seventeenth century, when the arrival of cheaper sugar coincided with greater access to citrus fruit. Their increasing availability soon allowed them to appear in a wide variety of popular dishes, from fragrant rum punches to elegant salad dressings. By the eighteenth century lemons had become *de rigueur* as a garnish, particularly with fish. And during their winter season they were made into syllabubs, creams, marmalades, pickles and cheeses – as in lemon curd. In *The Art of Cookery Made Plain and Easy* (1747) Hannah Glasse gives a recipe for pickled lemons that could have come straight out of a Middle Eastern cookery book with its use of salt and red India pepper. Because of their popularity, jellies, ices, steamed puddings and dumplings were all duly adapted for lemons during the nineteenth century, as were the countless recipes for chutneys and various beverages. Eliza Acton, for example, recommends using her lemon brandy for custard. Naturally, they are still being subjected to the latest style of British cooking.

Our predilection for the lemon has if anything increased, so perfectly does it suit our current taste. In an age when the majority of cooking has to be quick and relatively simple, cooks need to produce food that excites jaded palates. A squeeze of lemon here and a little bit of zest there effortlessly lifts a grill, sauté or salad to new heights. Its pure flavour works wonderfully with many of our currently fashionable ingredients such as natural yoghurt, soy sauce and chillies. It has become as essential an ingredient in the British kitchen as salt.

Practical guide

Lemons come in all shapes and sizes, ranging from large knobbly thick-skinned specimens to small, smooth, thin-skinned varieties, although few British cooks care to distinguish between them, despite subtle differences in flavour and juiciness.

Try to choose lemons that are heavy for their size and free from bruising or soft patches. If they feel light they are unlikely to contain much juice. The smooth thin-skinned varieties are considered better for juicing while the thick-skinned are valued for zesting. Fresh lemons should look shiny, but as the majority are now waxed before sale, it is difficult to gauge their age. Try to buy unwaxed or organic lemons, as their zest tastes superb. They will still need to be washed and should always be refrigerated, as they have a shorter life span.

Once a lemon has been picked it cannot ripen any further. Nor does a green spotted lemon mean that it is unripe. All citrus fruit skin contains chlorophyll, which goes green if left in the warm and fades in the cold. Commercial shippers use ethylene gas to chemically fade these pretty green spots.

The most efficient way to extract lemon juice is to soften the lemon by firmly rolling it under the palm of your hand on a hard surface. The warmer the lemon the more juice it will yield. For the best flavour, always add lemon juice at the very last minute to a hot dish, preferably after it has been removed from the heat, otherwise its taste will change and fade.

Whenever you use lemon peel, try to avoid including the white pith as this will make your dish taste bitter. Always lightly grate lemons, and if you accidentally remove some pith when paring a strip of lemon peel, carefully cut it away before adding the peel to your recipe. A lemon zester is the easiest means of removing pithless peel, but remember that this will disintegrate as it cooks.

If you are adding finely sliced (julienned) lemon zest to a sugar syrup, blanch it for 5 seconds in boiling water to prevent it from hardening in the syrup.

The addition of a small amount of lemon juice is a useful means of preventing certain fruits and vegetables from discolouring, for example, celeriac, avocados and pears. It is also commonly added to jams to increase their acidity, as this helps to release the pectin which in conjunction with sugar sets the jam.

How to prevent lemon wedges squirting juice when squeezed
Depending on whether you like your wedges to look lemon-shaped, cut off the stalk and tail end of the lemon (or not) before cutting in half lengthways. Each half can then be cut into 3 or 4 segments, according to the size of the lemon and your requirements. Finally, slice off the pithy, white core that runs along the top of each segment and slip out any pips. It is this final neatening of the wedges that is supposed to prevent unfortunate accidents with lemon juice.

Taste notes

◊ The acid in lemon juice acts as a useful marinade that will tenderize meat and 'cook' fish. It should therefore be used as a quick marinade and combined with a moisturizing agent such as olive oil or yoghurt. It has the further advantage of forming a delicious caramelized crust on grilled or roasted food.
◊ Never buy ready-squeezed lemon juice when you can buy fresh lemons – they are like chalk and cheese.

◊ Freshly grated lemon zest, combined with freshly chopped parsley and garlic (or other herbs), can be added at the last minute to a dish to lighten its tone.

◊ Squeezed out lemon halves can be crystallized for candied peel if wished. See *Jane Grigson's Fruit Book* for a reliable recipe. Alternatively, if you just happen to be suffering from hands stained by the likes of beetroot, onions or walnuts, liberally coat the lemon halves with salt and scrub on to your hands.

Breadcrumbed fish

As far as the British are concerned, one of the best ways to savour the taste of lemons is to squeeze the juice on the simplest of dishes. There are few more satisfying dishes than crumbed fried fish served with a generous squeeze of lemon and a pile of crisp chips. (Serves 4)

225g/8oz dried breadcrumbs (see method)

2 medium eggs, beaten

7 tablespoons finely chopped parsley

4 teaspoons whole grain mustard

salt and freshly ground black pepper

455g/1lb skinned cod fillet

seasoned flour for dusting

vegetable oil for shallow frying

Garnish

1 lemon, cut into 8 wedges

Begin by making the breadcrumbs. You will need about 310g/11oz of white sliced bread. Spread this out on your oven racks and set the oven to 150°C/300°F/gas 2. Leave until they have dried out and are crisp but not coloured. The time will vary according to the type and freshness of your bread. As soon as the bread is dried to your satisfaction, remove and process into fine breadcrumbs. Any excess can be frozen, provided it has not come into contact with the fish.

Mix the beaten eggs, parsley, mustard and seasoning in a medium-sized bowl. Cut the cod into 4 or 8 pieces. Place the breadcrumbs in a wide bowl. Toss the fish fillets in the flour, shaking off any excess, and dip in the beaten egg. Then completely cover each fillet with the breadcrumbs, pressing them firmly into the egg coating. Arrange in a single layer on a plate, then cover and chill until needed.

Pour about 5mm/¼ inch of oil into a large frying pan and place over a moderate heat. Once sizzling hot, carefully add the fish and fry until each side is crisp and golden. If the cod fillets are unusually thick, you should reduce the temperature a little so as to allow the fish to cook through without burning the breadcrumbs. A normal fillet (around 1cm/½ inch thick) should take 2–3 minutes each side. Drain on kitchen paper, sprinkle with salt and serve piping hot with lemon wedges.

Roast lemon partridge

This is my favourite way of serving partridge informally. Do not expect much gravy, but drizzle the spiced lemon juices over the birds and serve with warm potato crisps and a green salad. The birds taste exquisite.

On mainland Britain the partridge season runs from 1 September until 1 February. However, they are best roasted in October and November while young and tender. (Serves 4)

1 lemon, finely grated and juiced	6 sprigs thyme
1 tablespoon runny honey	4 oven-ready partridges
1 tablespoon olive oil	salt and freshly ground black pepper
¼ teaspoon cayenne pepper	

Place the lemon zest and juice in a medium-sized non-corrosive bowl. Mix in the honey, oil, cayenne pepper and thyme. Clean the birds by carefully wiping each, inside and out, with a damp cloth, picking off any stray pin feathers as you do so. Then place them in the lemon marinade, ensuring that they are thoroughly coated. Cover and chill for a good hour, turning once.

Preheat the oven to 220°C/425°F/gas 7. Place the birds upside down in a small roasting tray. Pour over their marinade, tucking the pieces of thyme under their breasts. Bake in the centre of the preheated oven for 40 minutes, turning them over, breast side up, after the first 25 minutes. Baste regularly.

Test to see if they are cooked by inserting a skewer between the leg and breast of one partridge. If the juices run clear, it is cooked. Remove from the oven and allow to rest in a warm place for 5 minutes before serving with the pan juices.

Lemon meringue pie

For the last 300 years the British have been very partial to pretty tarts filled with an unctuous lemon curd or cheese as it is sometimes known. Such tarts were originally known as lemon cheesecakes, but later evolved into a wide variety of puddings from Manchester to Chester pudding. The latter is in fact what we now know as lemon meringue pie. (Serves 4)

225g/8oz shortcrust pastry
(see page 335)

Lemon filling
3 medium lemons, finely
grated and juiced
115g/4oz caster sugar
40g/1½oz cornflour

285ml/½ pint cold water
30g/1oz butter
2 medium egg yolks, strained

Meringue
2 medium egg whites
115g/4oz caster sugar

Preheat the oven to 200°C/400°F/gas 6.

Roll out the pastry and line a 23cm/9 inch tart dish. Prick the bottom with a fork, line with weighted paper and chill for 30 minutes.

Place the tart in the centre of the preheated oven and bake for 15 minutes. Remove the covering and continue to bake for another 5–10 minutes, until the pastry has become dry but not coloured and has lost that raw sweaty look. Remove and reduce the oven temperature to 150°C/300°F/gas 2.

While the pastry is cooking make the lemon filling. Place the lemon zest, sugar and cornflour in a small non-corrosive saucepan. Using a wooden spoon gradually stir in the cold water so that it forms a smooth paste. Place over a moderate heat and bring to the boil, stirring all the time. Keep stirring for a couple of minutes until the mixture has thickened and become translucent, then remove from the heat and beat in the butter, followed by the lemon juice and finally the egg yolks.

Set aside until the pastry is ready, then spoon it into the cooked pastry case. Immediately whisk the egg whites in a clean bowl until they are stiff. Add half the caster sugar and continue to whisk, gradually adding the remaining sugar. Continue to whisk until it forms soft glossy peaks. Scoop it on to the lemon filling and gently spread it out over the tart so that it touches the pastry rim and seals in the gooey filling.

Return the pie to the oven and bake for 35 minutes or until the meringue has set with a crisp, very lightly browned crust. Allow to sit for 10 minutes before serving warm or serve cold.

Snowdon pudding

According to Eliza Acton, 'this pudding is constantly served to travellers at the hotel at the foot of the mountain from which it derives its name. It is probably well known to many of our readers in consequence.' Never having visited Snowdon, I do not know if it is still customary to serve it there, but I can certainly recommend her recipe, slightly adapted, for anyone wishing to eat a fragrant yet warming pudding. Try serving it either with a light lemon custard or with this rich lemon raisin marmalade sauce. Mrs Acton states that it can also be made with ordinary marmalade. Otherwise, see below for recipe. (Serves 4)

Pudding	85g/3oz lemon marmalade
30g/1oz softened butter	3 medium eggs, beaten
115g/4oz fresh white	
breadcrumbs	
85g/3oz vegetarian suet	*Sauce*
20g/¾oz rice flour	55g/2oz raisins
85g/3oz unrefined caster sugar	6 tablespoons Calvados or
a pinch of salt	brandy
1 lemon, finely grated	225g/8oz lemon marmalade

Place a 710ml/1¼ pint pudding basin in a large saucepan and pour in enough water to come half-way up its sides. Remove the basin, cover the saucepan and bring the water up to the boil.

Liberally butter the pudding basin. Measure the breadcrumbs, suet, rice flour, sugar and salt and mix together in a large bowl. Beat the lemon zest and marmalade into the beaten eggs and stir into the dry ingredients. When thoroughly mixed, carefully spoon into the pudding basin and cover with greased pleated foil.

Gently lower the basin into the boiling water and cover. Allow it to boil steadily for 50 minutes, remembering to replenish the water with more boiling water if necessary as it cooks. Allow to rest for 5 minutes before turning out on to a plate.

Soak the raisins in Calvados while the pudding is cooking. Shortly before serving, tip these into a small non-corrosive saucepan with the extra marmalade. Mix together, simmer gently for 5 minutes, and pour piping hot over the pudding.

Lemon marmalade

Perfect for toast and puddings when your home-made orange marmalade supply runs out before the Seville oranges return to the shops. This will have a soft set. (Makes 1.4kg/3lb)

795g/1¾lb lemons	1.4kg/3lb granulated sugar
1.7 litres/3 pints water	

Wash the lemons and place in a large non-corrosive saucepan with the water. Cover the pan, bring to the boil and simmer gently for 1½ hours. The fruit should be very soft and easily pierced with a knife.

Using a slotted spoon, carefully transfer the lemons to a clean bowl, leaving the cooking liquid in the saucepan. Once they are cool enough to handle, cut each lemon in half and, using a spoon, scrape out all their pulp, pips and most of their pith into a bowl. Mash up the debris before tipping into the saucepan. Boil vigorously until the liquid has reduced by half, then strain it into a jam pan.

In the meantime, cut the fruit skins into fine shreds and set aside. Wash your jam jars in hot soapy water, then rinse thoroughly and dry in a very low oven to sterilize them. Alternatively, use hot but dry out of the dishwasher.

Clip a sugar thermometer on to the jam pan and return the liquid to the boil. Add the sugar and stir over a low heat until it has dissolved. Then increase the heat, watching the thermometer carefully as it bubbles up. Just before it reaches setting point, 106°C/220°F, stir in the shredded peel and continue to boil. Remove from the heat once it has reached setting point and skim if necessary. Leave it to sit for 30 minutes, then stir and pour into your sterilized jam jars. Allowing your marmalade to rest before potting should prevent the peel from floating up to the top of the jar. Cover with a waxed paper disc, allow to cool, then tightly seal. Label and date.

Lemon chutney

Perhaps a national taste for chutney will prove one of the most lasting legacies of our days of Indian imperialism. A pleasant one, I think; I love them all – sweet as jam, sharp as pickles, hot and spicy as the curries themselves.

So wrote Margaret Costa in her magical *Four Seasons Cookery Book*, happily now republished by Grub Street. Certainly no British cookery book would be complete without at least one chutney recipe, and lemon is perhaps the best representative since it spans the boundaries of Indian and British cooking, the Indians being addicted to all manner of lime pickles and the British being more than partial to the taste of lemon. I have halved the quantities of chillies, as I found the original recipe a little too fiery for comfort. Also, if possible buy unwaxed organic lemons, otherwise give them a thorough wash before using. Margaret Costa recommends serving this chutney with curries but I find it equally good with cold meats and cheese.

455g/1lb lemons, finely pared and juiced

4 medium onions, finely chopped

115g/4oz washed raisins, finely chopped

115g/4oz washed sultanas, finely chopped

15g/½oz mild fresh chillies, finely chopped or to taste

455g/1lb granulated sugar

55g/2oz salt

850ml/1½ pints white wine vinegar

Finely dice the lemon peel and mix with the remaining ingredients in a large stainless steel preserving pan. Cover and leave to sit for 2 hours. Bring the mixture up to the boil and then simmer very gently, stirring occasionally, for several hours until it has become dark and thick. The length of cooking time will in part depend on the size of your saucepan, but it should take about 2–3 hours.

Wash your jam jars in hot soapy water, then rinse thoroughly and dry in a very low oven to sterilize them. Alternatively, use hot out of the dishwasher. Once the chutney is ready, pot while piping hot and place a wax disc on top. Allow to cool, then tightly seal. Label and date. The chutney will improve if left to mature for several months.

See also
Lemon barley pudding with summer fruits (page 39)
Lemon blackberry cream pots (page 69)

MACE

How mace came to be the hundred per cent traditional, invariable and indispensable spice of all English potted meats and fish compounds is not clear.

Spices, Salt and Aromatics in the English Kitchen by Elizabeth David, 1970

The delicate, lemony flavour of mace adds a peculiarly British dimension to countless national dishes. It imbues them with a certain lightness in an elegant yet restrained manner. No sausage would be complete without a sympathetic pinch, just as bread sauce sans mace would be dull.

We first developed a taste for it in the thirteenth century, when the Crusaders introduced us to the allure of such exotic spices as nutmegs, cloves, grains of paradise, cubebs, galingale and zedoary. This passion was sustained by the exclusivity of many spices, whose high prices made them deeply desirable. It was only after the collapse of the spice cartels in the eighteenth century that the prices dropped and their popularity waned. At long last the British became more considered in their use, choosing to add one, or at most two flavourings to a dish rather than a baroque mixture of many. Mace began to emerge as a favoured national spice with its warm, subtle flavour, reminiscent of nutmeg yet somehow slightly fresher.

To understand modern British spicing, you have to understand something of the British mentality. Simplicity and style are admired provided it is not apparent how much artifice has gone into the making. Mace is used to enhance the sweet freshness of a dish – you should not be aware that it is there, but you would find the food bland if it were omitted. Thus the simple mixture of trout, butter and salt is transformed into something heavenly by the addition of mace, black pepper and lemon juice.

Today, we use mace with much the same ingredients as we did in the eighteenth century. Now as then, we add it to all kinds of pickles, potted meats, sausages and stuffings; savoury butters, simple fricassées and white sauces. Its delicate fragrance is added to spiced buns, cakes and biscuits, subtle, yet unmistakably British.

Practical guide

Mace comes from the fruit of the nutmeg tree, which is principally grown in Grenada and Indonesia. Once harvested the fruit is split open and its seed (nutmeg), along with its red lacy covering or aril (mace), is removed. The mace is then detached from the nutmeg and dried before being sold either whole as blades of mace or ground. The blades can vary in colour from orange-yellow to orange-red, depending on where they come from. All are extraordinarily tough, so much so that they are not worth grinding at home unless you have a coffee grinder adapted to spices. Most cooks prefer to buy the two articles separately. The blades are perfect for infusions and pickles, while the powder can be used in everything. Some of the supermarkets sell the blades in tiny little jars, but they can also be bought from Indian and specialist grocers.

Like all spices, mace should be stored in an airtight container in a cool dark place. You should always check the sell-by date on your bottle, as once opened it will gradually lose its fragrance. If you have no mace to hand you could substitute it with a tiny pinch of ground nutmeg, remembering that this has a slightly coarser flavour. As mace cooks its flavour will soften and diminish; thus if you require a fresh seasoning, as for potted fish, you should add the mace at the last minute.

Taste notes

◊ The delicate spicing of mace works best with the lighter-flavoured white meats, namely chicken, turkey, pheasant, partridge, veal and pork. In the same way it is used with the lighter-tasting fish ranging from shrimp to salmon.

◊ A touch of lemon zest will emphasize the lemony taste of mace. Try using together in fricassées and stuffings.

◊ It has a natural affinity with most dairy products, but works especially well in white sauces, bread sauce and savoury butters, for example anchovy, lobster or crab. These can be used for sandwiches or partially melted on grilled fish.

◊ The slightly peppery nature of mace makes it an excellent seasoning for watercress and spinach dishes, particularly when cooked in a creamy sauce.

◊ Pickling spice usually contains mace blades along with coriander seeds, allspice, dried birds-eye chillies, black or white peppercorns, mustard seeds and sometimes cloves or dried ginger. It can also include fennel seeds, cinnamon, dill seeds and/or bay leaves.

◊ Most commercial brands of ground mixed spice contain mace along with coriander seeds, allspice, cloves, nutmeg, ginger and cinnamon. It is added to a wide variety of cakes, breads and biscuits, usually with dried fruit.

Potted trout

A classic British dish. (Serves 4)

4 cleaned trout	225g/8oz butter
6 tablespoons lemon juice	a large pinch of ground mace
salt and freshly ground black	
pepper	

Preheat the oven to its highest setting. Lay out a large sheet of foil and place 2 of the trout on top of it. Season them with 1 tablespoon of lemon juice, salt and pepper and dot with 30g/1oz of butter before neatly wrapping them up in a foil parcel. Repeat the process with the remaining 2 trout. Place both parcels in the centre of the oven and bake for 20 minutes, then remove and leave to cool.

Clarify the remaining butter by melting over a low heat in a small saucepan. Let it simmer gently for 3 minutes, then pour through a sieve lined with a clean piece of damp muslin or a clean damp J-cloth. Set aside.

Once the trout are cool, carefully skin, removing their heads and any brown fat. Then gently remove the fillets from the backbone. Most of the bones will remain attached to the backbone, but you will need to flake the fillets methodically to remove any remaining bones.

Place the trout flesh in a bowl and season to taste with the remaining lemon juice, salt, pepper and mace. Divide this between 4 small soufflé dishes. Lightly press down and cover each dish with the warm (not hot) clarified butter. Cover and chill for 12 hours. Serve with hot buttered toast.

Forcemeat balls

Forcemeat balls can be used to accompany roast fowl or game or as a garnish to soups and stews. (Makes 24 balls)

1 clove garlic, crushed	1 lemon, finely grated
1 small onion, finely chopped	300g/12oz finely minced pork
5 tablespoons olive oil	salt and freshly ground black
80g/2¾oz blanched, roughly	pepper
chopped spinach*	a generous pinch of ground
1 medium egg yolk	mace

Gently fry the garlic and onion in 2 tablespoons of olive oil until soft. Squeeze out as much water as possible from the spinach and place in a food processor with the garlic, onion, egg yolk, lemon zest, minced pork and seasoning. Briefly process in a few short bursts until it is well mixed. Then fry a small patty of the mixture to check the seasoning. Adjust if necessary and roll the remaining meat into 24 small balls.

Heat 3 tablespoons of olive oil in a large frying pan and cook the forcemeat balls until crisp and golden. They are now ready to be added to a suitably rich game or beef casserole or served alongside a roast fowl.

*Note: 200g/7oz fresh young spinach will weigh 80g/2¾oz when cooked and squeezed dry.

Pickled onions

These pickles will fill 3 × 455g/1lb Kilner jars. If you decide to use ordinary screw-top jars make sure that their lids are plastic-coated and therefore vinegar-proof. The spices can be altered to taste. Use a pinch of mace if you cannot obtain any blades.

1.8kg/4lb pickling onions	6 black and white peppercorns
455g/1lb salt	6 cloves
1.1litres/2 pints cider vinegar	1 stick cinnamon
2 tablespoons blades of mace	1 tablespoon mustard seeds
1 tablespoon whole allspice	4 dried red chillies
berries	1 bay leaf

Wash and dry the unpeeled onions and place in a large bowl. Dissolve 225g/8oz of salt in 2.3 litres/4 pints of water and pour over the onions. Cover with a plate to prevent the onions coming into contact with the air. Leave for 12 hours.

Drain and skin the onions, using a stainless steel knife, and place in a clean bowl. Dissolve the remaining 225g/8oz salt in 2.3 litres/4 pints water and pour over the onions. Cover with a plate and leave for 24–36 hours.

Meanwhile make up the spiced vinegar. Place the vinegar, spices, chillies and bay leaf in a non-corrosive pan and bring to the boil. Transfer to a clean bowl, cover and leave overnight. The next day strain the vinegar into a jug through a fine nylon sieve.

Wash your Kilner jars in hot soapy water, then rinse thoroughly and dry in a very low oven to sterilize them. Alternatively, use hot but dry out of the dishwasher.

Drain the onions and rinse thoroughly under the cold tap. Pat dry and tightly pack into the clean jars before filling with the cold spiced vinegar, which must be at least 1cm/½ inch above the onions to allow for any evaporation. Then seal the jars. Label and date your jars before storing in a cool, dry, dark place. They will be ready to eat after 2 months, but improve with age.

Cauliflower bacon cheese

Cauliflower cheese has become a famous British dish, although these days it is more likely to be served in the following way as a homely supper dish, rather than as a richly flavoured accompanying vegetable. The mace perfectly enhances the creamy cheese sauce and brings out the sweetness of the cauliflower. A blade of mace can be used instead of a pinch of powder. (Serves 2−3)

Cheese sauce
425ml/¾ pint milk
a pinch of ground mace
4 black peppercorns
1 bay leaf
½ onion
35g/1¼oz butter
35g/1¼oz plain flour
55−85g/2−3oz freshly grated
    Parmesan or Wensleydale
½ teaspoon English mustard
    powder

salt and freshly ground black
    pepper

Cauliflower
1 large cauliflower
1 bay leaf
2 tablespoons olive oil
1 small onion, diced
8 slices back bacon
2−3 tomatoes

Preheat the oven to 220°C/425°F/gas 7.

Begin by making the cheese sauce. Place the milk, spices, bay leaf and onion in a small saucepan. Bring slowly up to the boil but remove from the heat before it begins to bubble. Cover and leave to infuse for 20 minutes, then strain into a measuring jug.

Melt the butter in a heavy-bottomed saucepan over a low heat. Stir in the flour and continue to cook gently for a further minute. Increase the heat to moderate and gradually mix in the warm milk, stirring all the time until it forms a smooth sauce. Keep stirring until it comes to the boil, then simmer gently for 3 minutes. Finally mix in the cheese, mustard and seasoning to taste. Set aside while you prepare the vegetables.

Cut away the leaves of the cauliflower and turn it upside down. Cut in around its stem, so that you can remove a cone shaped core. Gently pull the florets apart, cutting and tidying where necessary. Wash thoroughly in a sink full of cold water. Bring a large pan of salted water to the boil. Add a bay leaf and the cauliflower florets, cover and return to the boil. Then remove the lid and boil for 2−3 minutes until they are just tender. Immediately drain into a colander.

Meanwhile, heat the olive oil in a frying pan over a moderate heat and fry the onion until soft. Quickly trim the bacon of any fat and cut into dice. Immediately add to the onions and continue to fry until just cooked. Cut the tomatoes into eighths, removing their tough white core as you do so.

Arrange the cauliflower florets in a gratin dish so that the flowers are uppermost. Sprinkle over the onion and bacon bits, followed by the tomatoes. Finally pour over the sauce. At this stage it can be chilled, covered, until ready to cook. Place in the oven and bake for 10−15 minutes, depending on whether the cauliflower is hot or cold, or until it is bubbling hot and flecked golden on top.

Note: If you wish to serve as an accompanying vegetable, omit the final onion, bacon and tomatoes.

Wigs

Wigs are thought to take their name from a medieval corruption of the word wedge or wigge. Lighter than air, they are made from a spiced dough that has been enriched with butter and milk. They are then baked into a small round bread that is ripped apart into wedges. Recipes for them are scant, despite many references dating back to the fifteenth century, but they are utterly delicious served hot out of the oven with lots of extra butter.

340g/12oz unbleached organic white flour	2½ teaspoons easy-blend dried yeast
½ teaspoon ground nutmeg	285ml/½ pint lukewarm milk
½ teaspoon ground mace	115g/4oz softened butter
2 teaspoons caraway seeds	30g/1oz caster sugar
a pinch of salt	1 tablespoon milk

Preheat the oven to 220°C/425°F/gas 7 and lightly grease 2 × 18cm/7 inch spring-clip cake tins.

Sift the flour into a large mixing bowl. Mix in the spices, salt and easy-blend dried yeast. If you have a food processor or mixer with a dough hook you can continue by transferring the spiced flour to the bowl of the machine and gradually beating in the lukewarm milk. Otherwise mix together manually until it forms a rough wet dough, then turn out and knead lightly until it becomes supple.

Cream together the butter and sugar. Gradually beat this into the dough until it has been absorbed. If you are mixing the dough by hand you should return the dough to a large bowl before adding the butter, as the mixture becomes very sloppy. Transfer to a large bowl once the butter has been incorporated. Cover and leave to rise for an hour or until doubled in size.

Divide into 2 balls and place one in each cake tin before gently patting into shape. Using a sharp knife score the top of each cake into 8 wedges. Cover with a clean tea towel and leave to rise in a warm place for an hour or until they have doubled in size.

Lightly brush each bread with milk, then place in the hot oven and bake for 15–20 minutes. Turn out and serve warm. Pull apart when ready to eat and serve with lots of butter.

See also
Rabbit and cucumber fricassée (page 82)
Roast pheasant with bread sauce (page 228)

MINT

Mint, Mentha; the Angustifolia spicata, spear-mint; dry and warm, very fragrant, a little press'd, is friendly to the weak stomach, and powerful against all nervous crudities: the gentler tops of the orange mint, enter well into our composition, or are grateful alone (as are also the other sorts) with the juice of orange and a little sugar.

Acetaria, A Discourse of Sallets by John Evelyn, 1699

Sweet-smelling mint can be found in most British gardens growing in rampant clumps in a neglected area, too stony or shady to warrant special care and attention. Look carefully and you will find a well-worn trail from the kitchen door to the mint, as generations of cooks have gathered it through the summer for the new potatoes, peas or mint sauce; just as countless children have tarried by the mint patch, fascinated by its aromatic leaves and buzzing insects, before returning with a handful of sprigs for the iced ginger beer, spiked with lime juice. Mint is to British cooking what basil is to Italian food.

Yet, as is so often the case in Britain, although we believe we only use mint in an archaic if romantic way, the reality is very different. We are continually reinterpreting foreign ideas and incorporating them into our diet. After all, modern cooking, whether it be in the fourteenth century or the twentieth, has always been about synthesizing new ideas into the national diet. Our love of mint, for example, has opened our eyes to the charms of Indian chutneys and the delights of mint-infused yoghurts. In the past we would reinterpret Indian mint chutneys to suit our taste in pickles by including such alien ingredients as apples, sultanas and vinegar. As our tastes change, we are returning to the fresher, more lively flavours of authentic Indian sauces, while choosing to use them in a typically British manner, as a piquant relish for fish dishes such as deep-fried squid. In the same way mint-flavoured yoghurts are now added to a wide variety of recipes, from summer soups to refreshing dips.

Domesticated mint is believed to have been introduced to British cooks by the Romans, who were themselves partial to its fresh flavour. Certainly by the fifteenth century mint was a popular herb for salads, pottages and piquant sauces. Six hundred years later and we still use it, according to the current fashion, in salads, soups and sauces. Even our infamous mint sauce is a direct descendant of the medieval sauce vert, which was made with vinegar, breadcrumbs, parsley, mint, dittany, pellitory and costmary. Modern mint sauces can now also take the form of a creamy home-made mayonnaise or a refreshing vinaigrette combined, for example, with diced tomato and black olives. Both are good eaten with chargrilled chicken or salmon, while mint, lemon balm and lime vinaigrette makes a wonderful marinade for a cold shellfish salad. However, in the height of summer mint is also glorious added to fragrant summer puddings, delicate sweetened creams and ice cold drinks.

Practical guide

Mint belongs to the extended *Mentha* family. The most common variety of garden mint is spearmint (*Mentha spicata*), which has a well-rounded flavour. However, since there is always room for connoisseurs when it comes to food, Bowles' mint (*Mentha × villosa alopecuroides* 'Bowles' Mint') and Moroccan mint (*Mentha spicata* 'Moroccan'), compete with one another as being the ultimate in mintiness. Not having tasted the latter two, I cannot comment. Mint fans should also try to grow ginger mint, lemon mint, apple mint and peppermint. Ginger mint has a slightly hot taste, while the more subtle fruity taste of lemon mint and apple mint make them excellent additions to drinks and fruit dishes. Try crystallizing their leaves by painting them with gum arabic and liberally coating with caster sugar. Spread them out and dry each side for 24 hours. They can be used as a pretty garnish for a wide variety of cakes and puddings. Peppermint leaves are best used for tisanes, as they naturally have a distinctly strong flavour. They come in two forms, black and white, both of which are good.

Mint is an easy herb to grow in a pot, which is lucky since it is an invasive plant and can completely take over your garden. Try to buy it as a plant rather than sowing it from seed, as it does not always grow true. It will grow in most places but must not be planted next to other mints as each species will lose its individual scent and flavour by hybridization. Pots should be kept in the semi-shade. Fortunately for non-gardeners, fresh mint is widely available through the summer months and can be bought in little supermarket pots that can sit on the kitchen windowsill. If you open a packet of fresh mint, wash and dry it before placing in a plastic bag. Blow in some air, so that it inflates like a balloon and seal before storing in the fridge. The mint should stay happily in this state for 2–3 days.

Traditionally, mint was always dried for the winter months. If you enjoy its flavour you should buy it freeze-dried as it is less prone to the musty flavour of dried herbs. Mint sauce will also keep for some months in the fridge if it is stored in a sterilized jar. Alternatively, you can make a mint jelly from apples, gooseberries or redcurrants. The fruit is cooked in the normal manner with a few sprigs of mint. Extra finely chopped mint is added just before the jelly is potted. Some recipes add vinegar at the end of the cooking of the fruit, but before straining.

Taste notes

◊ Mint tastes delicious when cooked with a wide variety of young vegetables. It can also be added in the form of a sprig to a cooked dish of vegetables, or finely chopped with butter. Aside from new potatoes, peas and carrots, it is excellent with young beetroot, globe artichokes, spinach and broad beans. Combined with lightly fried spring onions or garlic, people will marvel at the sweetness of your vegetables.

◊ Used as an accompanying sauce or dressing, mint works beautifully with most shellfish, including prawns, squid and scallops as well as other fish such as salmon or Dover sole. It can be mixed with lime zest, lemon zest or lemon grass, soy sauce, honey, chilli, sesame, olive or nut oils. The possibilities are endless.

◊ Mint makes an excellent addition to wine cups, Pimm's, iced teas and long, cool summer drinks. It should be given a little time to infuse and, if possible, it should be included in each glass so that the drinker can inhale its delicate fragrance.

◊ Mint has a natural affinity with orange. Try seasoning your redcurrant jelly with finely chopped mint, orange zest and juice for an aromatic accompaniment to roast or grilled lamb.

◊ Mint was at one time a popular flavouring for lemon or apple water ices, which were served as part of a main course to cleanse the palate. You could also try this with grapefruit, orange, lime or even grape. Add a touch of salt and pepper to the liquid as this will make it taste even sweeter.

Mint sauce

A bottle of mint sauce is second on Mrs Beeton's list of 'Things not to be forgotten at a picnic', following the most important item of all, a stick of horseradish! Mint sauce, it seems, was not only considered an excellent accompaniment to roast or grilled lamb, but was also advocated as an accompaniment to such delights as 'Roast Porker's Head' and roast veal. There are remarkably few variations, the only major differences being over which type of vinegar or sugar to use. Malt vinegar and brown sugar both have their supporters, although they make too strong a sauce for my taste. (Serves 4)

3 tablespoons finely chopped mint	2 teaspoons caster sugar
1 tablespoon boiling water	3 tablespoons white wine vinegar

Mix together the mint, boiling water and caster sugar. Allow to cool, then stir in the vinegar and leave to sit for 1 hour before serving. If you wish to make large quantities, sterilize your jars according to the instructions on page 179.

Cold tomato yoghurt soup

The simplest of summer soups, perfectly illustrating how modern British cooking absorbs and reinterprets culinary ideas from around the world. If you are short of time use beef tomatoes – buy 6 for this weight. (Serves 4)

1.1kg/2½lb ripe tomatoes	285ml/½ pint thick Greek
2 cloves garlic, crushed	yoghurt
½ cucumber, peeled and finely	½ lime, juiced
diced	salt and freshly ground black
leaves from 3 sprigs mint,	pepper
finely chopped	extra mint to garnish

Cut a small cross at the base of each tomato and neatly cut out the little white core to which the stalk is usually attached. Plunge into boiling water – then as soon as the skin begins to peel, transfer to cold water. Peel and cut into quarters. Place half the tomatoes in a food processor. (Do not purée yet.) Remove the seeds from the remaining tomatoes and add the seeds to the food processor. Purée and push through a fine sieve set over a large mixing bowl.

Neatly dice the remaining tomato flesh and add to the tomato purée along with the crushed garlic, diced cucumber and finely chopped mint. Using a whisk, gradually beat in the yoghurt, so that it forms a smooth creamy soup. Add the lime juice and season to taste. Cover and chill for a couple of hours. Serve icy cold, garnished with extra mint sprigs.

Squid fritters with mint chutney

Mint sauces and mint chutneys litter British cookery books back to medieval times when mint was used in sauce vert. The delicate flavour of fish is beautifully enhanced by this classical Indian mint chutney. (Serves 4)

Squid fritters
115g/4oz plain flour
salt
1 teaspoon easy-blend dried
    yeast
70ml/2.5fl oz lager
70ml/2.5fl oz warm water
1 dessertspoon olive oil
1 small egg white, stiffly
    beaten
455g/1lb cleaned squid

Mint chutney
5 tablespoons finely chopped
    mint leaves
1 tablespoon finely chopped
    coriander leaves

1–2 tablespoons lime juice
1 green chilli, seeded and
    finely chopped
2 spring onions, finely
    chopped
1 teaspoon salt
1 teaspoon caster sugar
½ teaspoon garam masala
½ tablespoon anardana
    powder (ground dried
    pomegranate seeds)
    (optional)*

vegetable oil for deep frying
extra seasoned flour

Place the flour, salt and dried yeast in a mixing bowl and make a hollow in the middle. Using a wooden spoon, slowly stir in the lager, followed by the water, until the batter reaches the consistency of double cream. Stir in the oil, cover and leave in a warm place for 30–40 minutes. The yeast should make the batter bubble alive and rise a little. Just before you are ready to use the batter, fold in the stiffly beaten egg white.

Wash the squid thoroughly under a running tap, squeezing out any jelly-like substances that may still lurk inside its cleaned body. Cut into 1cm/½ inch thick rings and pat dry. If you are using the tentacles, scrape and peel away their tiny suckers under running water and pat dry.

Mix together all the ingredients for the chutney and briefly blend in a food processor. Set aside and cover until ready to serve. Although this chutney will keep for a couple of days in the fridge, it tastes best freshly made.

Shortly before you are ready to serve, preheat the oil in a large heavy-bottomed saucepan or deep fat fryer to 190°C/375°F. Taking a small batch at a time, lightly dust the squid in the seasoned flour before dipping in the batter. Carefully drop into the oil and fry for 2–3 minutes or until golden. Remove with a mesh ladle and drain on kitchen paper. Continue with the remaining squid. Serve piping hot with the mint relish.

Note: Anardana powder can be found in most Indian grocers. It is usually sold among the spices in small cardboard boxes that look as if they belong in the fifties. It imbues food with a sour, fruity taste. While you are there buy some amchoor powder, which is made from dried green mangoes. Traditionally this is added in place of lime juice to the chutney.

Broad bean, mint and feta salad

Current mint vinaigrettes have a cleaner, less complex flavour than their predecessors. In the past they were enriched with sugar and occasionally mustard and hard-boiled egg yolks. Try serving this simple salad as a starter with crusty bread. (Serves 4)

1 clove garlic, crushed	salt and freshly ground black
1 tablespoon finely chopped	pepper
mint, plus 1 sprig	455g/1lb shelled young broad
2 tablespoons white wine	beans
vinegar	4 good sized tomatoes
6 tablespoons extra virgin	200g/7oz feta cheese, diced
olive oil	10 black olives

Whisk together the garlic, mint, vinegar and olive oil and season to taste.

Bring a saucepan of water to the boil. Throw in a pinch of salt, the sprig of mint and the beans. Return to the boil and simmer for 3–4 minutes until tender. Drain and cool slightly under the cold tap. As soon as the beans have dried off a little, discard the mint sprig and tip them into a large mixing bowl. Thoroughly coat in the vinaigrette and set aside.

Cut a small cross at the base of each tomato and neatly cut out the white core to which the stalk is usually attached. Cover with boiling water for a few seconds then remove, peel and cut into quarters. Discard the seeds (the juice can be saved for another vinaigrette if wished) and cut into large dice. Stir these into the bean salad along with the diced feta cheese.

Finally, slice the flesh away from the olive stones and cut into attractive strips or dice. Add to the salad, adjust the seasoning to taste and serve whenever ready.

Chargrilled salmon with mint mayonnaise

The fashion for grilling has swept Britain in the last ten years. Barbecues are *de rigueur* during the summer months, even if you only have the tiniest roof terrace on which to balance an equally tiny disposable barbecue. During the rest of the year, smart kitchens now have ribbed cast-iron oven-top grills which simulate chargrilling. They look a little like a ribbed frying pan. Both fulfil our desires to cook quickly, but they also create the problem of trying to think up new accompaniments. Mint mayonnaise tastes surprisingly good and works beautifully not only with salmon, but also with chicken in rice salads, spiked with chives and lemon. (Serves 6)

Mint mayonnaise
2 large egg yolks
2 tablespoons lemon juice or
    white wine vinegar
1–2 tablespoons roughly
    chopped mint
285ml/½ pint olive oil
3–4 tablespoons double cream

salt and freshly ground white
    (or black) pepper

Chargrilled salmon
6 small salmon fillets
2 tablespoons olive oil
1 lemon, cut into wedges

Place the egg yolks and lemon juice or vinegar in the food processor. Whiz until they turn pale and frothy. Add the mint, then, keeping the engine running, slowly add the olive oil in a thin stream, until it forms a thick mayonnaise. Add the cream, season to taste and transfer to a clean bowl. Alternatively, you can either make it by hand or use an electric whisk. In either case, finely chop the mint before adding.

Rub the salmon fillets with oil and season. Place them, flesh side down, on a hot barbecue or oven-top grill. Cook for about 3 minutes so that they are marked by golden grill lines, then turn to a different angle for a further 2–3 minutes, so that they are covered by an attractive lattice. Flip them over and cook skin side down for a further 3–5 minutes, depending on their thickness.

Serve hot, warm or cold with the mint mayonnaise and lemon wedges. This is particularly good eaten with new potatoes and a green salad or tiny lightly cooked broad beans.

Summer pudding

Mint is not commonly associated with puddings in the minds of British cooks, unless they happen to be from the north of England. Here, they are far more enlightened and create exquisite blackcurrant or bilberry pies, scented with mint, along with sweet pasties, stuffed full of dried currants, raisins, mixed peel and fresh mint. This makes a particularly refreshing variation of summer pudding. (Serves 6)

225g/8oz blackcurrants, washed and stripped from their stalks	225g/8oz blueberries, washed
	225g/8oz caster sugar
	2 tablespoons shredded mint
225g/8oz redcurrants, washed and stripped from their stalks	225g/8oz raspberries
	8–10 medium slices good white bread

Prepare all the fruit, then take a large non-corrosive pan and mix together the currants and blueberries with the sugar, mint and 3 tablespoons water. Cover and place over a low heat for 5 minutes, until the sugar has dissolved and the fruit is releasing plenty of juice. Stir in the raspberries and continue to simmer, covered, for a further 2 minutes. Remove and leave to cool. The fruit should continue to release lots of juice as it cools.

Lightly oil a 850ml/1½ pint pudding basin. Remove the crusts from the bread and neatly line the pudding basin. Cut a circle and place in the bottom of the bowl. Slice the bread into neat triangles or wedges and line the sides, making sure that you have no gaps, otherwise the turned-out pudding will leak and collapse. Set aside one large slice of bread to cover the top.

Tightly pack the fruit into the lined basin. Seal the fruit in by turning over the top of the bread wedges and cover with the last circle of bread. Cover with a saucer. Save the spare fruit and juice. Place the basin in a dish (to catch any juices) and place a heavy weight on the saucer. Leave for a minimum of 8 hours in the fridge.

Before serving, gently loosen the bread around the basin's rim and invert on to a plate, giving it a sharp shake. Pour over the reserved juices so that it looks outrageously glossy, and serve with thick cream. Fresh berries, mint leaves or currant leaves can also be used as a garnish.

Ginger beer drink

This was our favourite drink as children, introduced by my Scottish grandfather who I later discovered enjoyed his with vodka. However, I still love the original non-alcoholic version. Serve in tall glass tumblers.

Rose's lime cordial
ice
mint sprigs

ginger beer, preferably a dry one such as Idris

The quantities are entirely a matter of taste, so use these instructions as a guide. Pour a shot of lime juice into the bottom of each glass. Then add 2 or 3 ice cubes and a lightly crushed sprig of mint. Slowly add the ginger beer until the glass is full. The mint sprig will add a delicious scent to the drink and is best enjoyed tickling the nose. Serve immediately.

See also
Piquant wilted greens (see variation) (page 117)
Summer greens salad (page 218)

OATS

At last the porridge was dabbed on our plates from a thick and steaming spoon. I covered the smoky lumps with treacle and began to eat from the sides to the middle. The girls round the table chewed moonishly, wrapped in their morning stupor. Sick with sleep, their mouths moved slow, hung slack while their spoon came up; then they paused for a moment, spoon to lip, collected their wits, and ate. Their vacant eyes stared straight before them, glazed at the sight of the day. Pink and glowing from their dreamy beds, from who knows what arms of heroes, they seemed like mute spirits hauled back to the earth after paradise feasts of love.

Cider with Rosie by Laurie Lee, 1959

No one knows when oats were first introduced into Britain, but it is thought to have been around the iron age. This extraordinary cereal crop thrives in a cold, wet climate, producing fatter, better-tasting grain the slower it is ripened. It was perfect for the British climate and rapidly became an integral part of our diet. References to it can be found throughout the country, so although it is, and always has been, strongly identified with Scotland, all areas of Britain have grown and eaten oats. Not surprisingly, its resilient nature made it especially popular in the west and north of the country.

When cooking facilities were more primitive, namely a simple pot and bakestone, oats were cooked in a similar way across the land. In the words of Andrew Boorde in 1542, 'Potage is not so much used in all Christendom as it is used in England. Potage is made of the liquor in the which flesh is sodden in, with putting-to chopped herbs, and oatmeal and salt.' If thin such a dish was called 'grewell' and if thick it was known as a 'porray'. Other grains and pulses were also used, but naturally, where oats were the main cereal, they dominated the region's cooking. In the same way, simple oatcakes were made in place of bread as they required no more than a hot bakestone or griddle. Recipes would vary according to the region, but the basic principles were always the same. Thus Welsh oatcakes were rolled out as thin as a penny and as round as a dinner plate, while West Riding oatcakes (haverbread) were made from a yeast-risen batter before being baked into rectangles; but both were made from oatmeal and both were baked and dried.

As is always the case with food, increasing affluence created new social snobberies and oats fell victim to the new refinements sweeping British society. In 1755 Dr Samuel Johnson defined oats as 'A grain, which in England is generally given to horses, but in Scotland supports the people' in his *Dictionary of the English Language*. Boswell was later to retort that 'That is why in England you have such fine horses and in Scotland we have such fine people,' but to no avail. They came to be regarded as a rustic food and consequently fell from favour in many southern circles. I have to admit that I share in some of this prejudice, albeit 250 years later, in that I find them too stodgy a grain for certain dishes, such as stuffings and dumplings, where wheat flour or breadcrumbs give a lighter texture. However, they are superlative in other recipes, in particular in oatcakes, biscuits, parkin and breakfast cereals. All of which leads me on to porridge.

There are few dishes that can provoke such heartfelt opinions as porridge. Most have sampled it at some time in their lives and, depending on their initial experience, either love or loathe it. References to the ordeal of eating badly made or burnt porridge are scattered throughout our literature. Its ancient pedigree has given plenty of scope for the scathing pen. From *Jane Eyre* to *Cold Comfort Farm*, porridge appears to embody the very essence of deprivation. Yet in reality a well-made dish can revive a weary body and comfort the soul. Porridge-lovers continue in the sensible Scottish tradition of eating it for breakfast, lunch or supper, depending on their needs. It has also become a popular choice in hotels, with tourists wishing to sample this peculiarly British experience.

Fortunately, 2,000 years of oat-eating have not deprived us of our taste for them. Alongside traditional recipes, for example parkin or oatcakes, new dishes are gradually being developed to suit our current tastes. Modern interpretations of brose, for instance, have been reinstated, usually sweetened, and using a wide range of fruit and dairy products from gooseberries to yoghurt. Chefs are also experimenting with oatmeal, in particular as a textured, flavoursome substitute for breadcrumbs, whether it be in ice cream or as a crisp coating for fried sweetbreads. Their high fibre and vitamin content has also led them to be commercially reinstated in mixed-grain breads, biscuits and chewy snack bars, as well as in luxury brands of porridge and muesli. In other words, the humble oat appears to be enjoying a renaissance.

Practical guide

It is important to understand the nature of oats, which unlike most other cereals have a low gluten content and are therefore less malleable as a flour. They also have a high oil and water content. In practical terms this means that oats should always be stored in a cool, dark, airtight container to prevent them from absorbing moisture or turning rancid. It also means that the drier the oat the more concentrated its flavour, which is why many recipes instruct the cook to toast their oatmeal in the oven.

Once the oats have been harvested they are sent to the miller. As they contain about 14 per cent moisture they are first dried out in a kiln. Traditional mills, which are few and far between, carefully turn the oats manually at this stage. The heat is gradually increased until only 5 per cent moisture remains and the oats have developed a deliciously sweet, nutty flavour. They are then carefully sorted to remove any weeds or undersized grains before being lightly ground. This loosens their outer casing, which is then discarded, leaving the kernel or groat, as it is known, ready for the miller to grind as he sees fit. Most shops distinguish between only three different grades – fine, medium and coarse – but some mills still grind into six grades.

Pinhead is the roughest grade. The whole kernel is cut in half and sifted to remove any floury meal. It is mainly used for haggis and oatmeal loaves. Some recipe books recommend adding it to soups and stews, although it is too gluey for my taste. It is followed by rough ground oatmeal which can be used for porridge or brose. It can also be added to rough oatcakes.

Medium rough (also sold as coarse medium) oatmeal is mainly used by butchers for mealie pudding (made from blood, oats and onion), although it can be used for sausages, stuffing and the like. Medium fine oatmeal is widely used for porridge, brose, and skirlie (pan-fried onion and oats). It is also good for baking, such as parkin or oatcakes, although it is often mixed with wheat flour.

Super-fine oatmeal looks like a coarse version of wheat flour. It can be used for oatcakes, pancakes and for baking. Some cooks recommend dusting fish such as herring with this grade of oatmeal, others prefer a rougher grade. Do not confuse oat flour with super-fine oatmeal, as the former is literally ground to a fine flour.

Rolled oats (oatflakes or porridge oats) are a relatively recent American invention. They were developed by the Quaker Oat Company in 1877 as a fast-cooking porridge oat, taking only 10 minutes to cook. They are made from pinhead oats that are then steamed and rolled, which allows them to cook very quickly. However, some of their flavour and nutrients are lost in the process. They are particularly good added to flapjacks and, of course, variations of muesli. Jumbo oatflakes are whole oat groats prepared in the same manner.

Taste notes

◊ Fine or medium rough oatmeal can be used as a crisp coating for herrings. These are normally boned and patted dry before being dusted in fine oatmeal or dipped in egg and crumbed in rough oatmeal. Wonderful fried in bacon fat.
◊ Rough or pinhead oats can be used in place of breadcrumbs in a wide variety of dishes; for example, they can be pressed in the Irish manner on to fluffy potato cakes.

◊ Pinhead oatmeal or oatflakes are excellent lightly fried (toasted) in butter and sugar before being sprinkled over stewed fruit or folded into ice creams or fools.

◊ Fine oatmeal can be added to ordinary wheat flour before being made into fluffy pancakes, shortcrust pastry or a wide variety of biscuits. It can also be used as a thickener for hearty soups. Winter vegetables, such as carrots, onions, turnips and swedes, are lightly fried with the whites of leek before the oatmeal is added in place of flour. Stock is then added, followed by cream or milk. If it is to be served as a chunky thick broth, the finely sliced green part of the leeks is added shortly before serving, otherwise purée and serve as a creamy smooth soup.

◊ Oatcakes are delicious eaten plain with butter or with a wide variety of cheeses. Lightly buttered or spread with cream cheese, they make an excellent accompaniment to smoked or cured fish. Try serving them with the marinated kippers on page 134. Alternatively eat them with heather honey or bitter marmalade.

Buttermilk oats with fruit and nuts

This is a variation of the ancient Scottish dish of brose, although to the modern eye it might appear to be closely related to muesli. Brose is an uncooked version of porridge, although it can also be made with peasemeal. Oats are mixed into a hot or cold liquid. According to the cook's taste this can be water, stock, milk or cream. Savoury variations might include greens or herbs, while sweet interpretations can include butter, fresh or dried fruit. (Serves 2)

30g/1oz rolled oats	1 apple, roughly grated
salt	30g/1oz hazelnuts
140ml/¼ pint buttermilk	1 banana, sliced
140ml/¼ pint cold water	sugar or honey to taste

Mix the oats with a pinch of salt into the buttermilk and water, cover and refrigerate overnight. When you are ready to eat, quickly grate the unpeeled apple and stir into the oats along with the nuts and banana. You can thin the mixture with more buttermilk if wished. Serve with sugar or honey.

Note: You can vary the ingredients to taste: try adding a handful of dried cherries or blueberries or a mixture of fresh raspberries and peeled and diced fresh peach.

Porridge

I am constantly amazed at the countless different ways you can make porridge. For a recipe that usually consists of three ingredients it is extraordinary that cooks have devised so many different methods. If you are using rolled oats, such as Quaker, you should follow the cooking instructions on the packet. Most recipes suggest ½ cup of oats per person, sprinkled into 1½ cups cold milk or water. This is then salted, brought to the boil and stirred for 5 minutes. However, if you decide to make porridge with medium oatmeal the following method applies for a thick, soft porridge. (Serves 1)

85g/3oz medium oatmeal	salt
565ml/1 pint water	

Have your oats, salt and wooden spoon ready before you begin. Bring the water to the boil in a saucepan. Add a pinch of salt then slowly but evenly sprinkle the oatmeal into the boiling water with one hand while stirring constantly with the other. The water must continue to boil throughout the slow but steady addition of oatmeal. Once added, keep boiling and stirring for 10 minutes, then reduce the heat and allow the mixture to simmer for 30 minutes, stirring occasionally, especially near the end of cooking time. Some recipes suggest adding the salt half-way through the cooking, claiming that otherwise it will toughen the oats. Alternatively, use a double boiler and omit some of the stirring.

Porridge is delicious accompanied by a bowl of cold, creamy milk, cream or buttermilk into which you dip your spoonful of hot porridge, thereby allowing the rest of your porridge to stay piping hot. Then, depending on your taste, you can eat it plain or with a little extra salt or with sugar (white or brown), golden syrup, treacle or honey. Some like a shot of whisky, while others enjoy a light sprinkling of cinnamon.

Note: A more textured porridge can be made by adding 55g/2oz of medium oatmeal to 285ml/½ pint of boiling salted water and cooking it for 10 minutes.

Cranachan

Cranachan, which is also known as cream crowdie, is definitely a pudding for oat-lovers, so reserve it for them and do not tempt fate by serving it to those uninitiated in oat cuisine. Although Catherine Brown in *Scottish Cookery* recommends keeping all the ingredients separate so that your guests can mix it according to their taste, I prefer to prepare it in advance as the oats have a softer texture. Traditionally, you should allow 2 parts crowdie (Scottish cream cheese) to 1 part whipped double cream. (Serves 6)

8 tablespoons pinhead
   oatmeal
225ml/½ pint double cream
400g/14oz fromage frais
6 tablespoons heather honey
   or to taste

4 tablespoons whisky
455g/1lb raspberries,
   blackberries or blueberries

If the oatmeal is quite soft, preheat the oven to 150°C/300°F/gas 2 and bake for 15 minutes or until it is evenly toasted and crisp.

Whisk the double cream gradually into the fromage frais before adding the honey and whisky to taste.

When you are ready to serve, fold the crunchy oats and the berries into the cream.

Parkin

Parkin, perkin or parken is a northern oatmeal-based variation of ginger-bread. It is widely made, from Yorkshire and Lancashire up to the Orkneys. English parkins are cooked as large cakes that are then cut apart, while Scottish parkins are baked as small cakes. Recipes vary from family to family but can use golden syrup instead of black treacle, beer or buttermilk in place of milk and can even include chopped candied peel or cooked dried figs.

170g/6oz plain flour	455g/1lb black treacle
3 teaspoons ground ginger	115g/4oz butter
2 teaspoons mixed spice	140ml/¼ pint milk
340g/12oz medium oatmeal	30g/1oz soft brown sugar
1 teaspoon bicarbonate of soda	

Preheat the oven to 180°C/350°F/gas 4 and lightly oil a 25cm/10 inch cake tin. Line this with bakewell paper or lightly oiled greaseproof paper. Begin by cutting a strip of greaseproof paper that is slightly longer than the circumference of the cake tin and 1cm/½ inch wider than the depth of the tin. Make a fold about 1cm/½ inch deep along one of the long edges and snip into this every 1cm/½ inch or so at a slight angle. Fit this inside the cake tin, so that the snipped fold lies flat on the base. Cover this with a paper circle or square that is cut to fit inside the tin.

Sift the flour and spices into a large mixing bowl. Stir in the oatmeal and bicarbonate of soda.

Place the treacle, butter, milk and sugar in a saucepan over a low heat, stirring occasionally until the butter and treacle have melted and the sugar dissolved. Immediately pour into the dry ingredients and beat thoroughly before pouring the sticky mixture into your cake tin. Spread evenly and bake in the centre of the oven for 45 minutes or until firm.

Leave to cool in its tin, then cut into squares. It tastes even better if left to mature for a day or two, well wrapped in foil.

Chocolate butter oat biscuits

These delicious biscuits were known as sinkers in my family for reasons that become obvious if you manage to eat more than two. I have slightly amended the recipe from its original, which came from my mother's 1951 edition of *The Glasgow Cookery Book*. (Makes 13 biscuits)

vegetable oil or butter for greasing baking sheets
115g/4oz softened butter
85g/3oz caster sugar
115g/4oz plain flour
1 level teaspoon bicarbonate of soda
2 level teaspoons baking powder
115g/4oz rolled oats
1 teaspoon syrup

3 teaspoons boiling water
1 teaspoon natural vanilla essence

Chocolate butter filling
115g/4oz dark chocolate
55g/2oz icing sugar or to taste
115g/4oz softened butter
a few drops natural vanilla essence

Preheat the oven to 190°C/375°F/gas 5 and grease 2 baking sheets. Beat the butter and sugar together until pale and fluffy. Sift the flour, bicarbonate of soda and baking powder into a clean bowl and stir in the oats.

Measure the syrup and hot water into a small bowl and stir until the syrup melts. Tip the dry ingredients, melted syrup and vanilla essence into the creamed butter and beat vigorously until well mixed. Turn out on to a floured board, lightly knead and divide in half. Roll out each half as thinly as possible and using a small scone cutter, stamp out as many rounds as you can. Transfer these to the baking sheets, remembering that they will spread out as they cook. Then knead together the dough and keep re-rolling until you have about 26 rounds in all. Bake for 10–15 minutes, then cool on a baking rack.

Break up the chocolate and place in a small bowl over a pan of simmering water. While it is melting, beat the icing sugar into the butter. As soon as the chocolate has melted remove from the heat and allow to cool. Once it is tepid, beat it into the butter and add the vanilla essence to taste. Cover and chill until the butter has a firmer consistency.

Spread the chocolate butter over the flat side of 13 biscuits, sandwiching them together with the remaining biscuits. Do not serve until the butter has firmly set.

PEAS

When the ducks and green peas came, we looked at each other in dismay; we had only two-pronged, black-handled forks. It is true the steel was as bright as silver; but what were we to do? Miss Matty picked up her peas, one by one, on the point of the prongs, much as Amine ate her grains of rice after her previous feast with the Ghoul. Miss Pole sighed over her delicate young peas as she left them on one side of her plate untasted, for they *would* drop between the prongs. I looked at my host: the peas were going wholesale into his capacious mouth, shovelled up by his large, round-ended knife. I saw, I imitated, I survived! My friends, in spite of my precedent, could not muster up courage enough to do an ungenteel thing; and if Mr Holdbrook had not been so heartily hungry, he would probably have seen that the good peas went away almost untouched.

The famous bachelor dinner in *Cranford*, which is believed to describe Elizabeth Gaskell's youth in the early 1800s

Fresh peas, adored by all, are an unspoken means of categorizing class in Britain. Many a small child has suffered agonies under the parental eye by having to press their peas on to the prongs of a fork or illogically balance them on top. If only it were socially permissible to shovel them into delicious piles on to an up-turned fork or spoon. Even today, peas can be a minefield for the socially unaware. It is not only how you eat your peas, it is which peas you serve. Are tinned petit pois in or out? Are frozen peas socially unacceptable? Are you a non-foodie if you happen to enjoy fresh, ready-shelled, out of season supermarket peas? And what about dried peas, split green and yellow or mushy? Naturally, the obvious answer should be that one does not care, but there are few who do not secretly flinch at the thought of judgemental guests.

Before the advent of canning at the end of the nineteenth century, life was supposed to be slightly simpler. Fresh garden peas were a seasonal luxury to be enjoyed during the summer, although gardeners of the rich strove to extend their season. Thackeray satirizes such social expectations in his article 'Dining-out Snobs' which appeared in *Punch* in 1845:

There is Guttleton, who dines at home off a shilling's-worth of beef from the cookshop, but if he is asked to dine at a house where there are not pease at the end of May, or cucumbers in March along with the turbot, thinks himself insulted by being invited. 'Good Ged!' says he, 'what the deuce do the Forkers mean by asking *me* to a family dinner? I can get mutton at home.'

Dried peas, on the other hand, were seen as a utilitarian food that many ate during the winter. They are harvested from what is commonly known as the field pea. This has been grown in Britain since the bronze age and has seen us through times of famine, with its easy growth and ability to keep. Originally they were boiled in thick and thin pottages, the ancestors of pease pudding, mushy peas and pea soup, as well as roasted and ground into a fine flour (peasemeal). This was made into a form of bread or porridge that still survives in some parts of Scotland as pease bannocks and pease brose.

The garden pea did not arrive until the sixteenth century, but it was to change our taste in peas for ever. Initially it was boiled whole before being dipped in butter and noisily sucked from its pod. Soon, however, we were experimenting with all manner of French fashions from stewing it with lettuce hearts, spring onions and butter to sautéing it with bacon and pigeon. New traditions were rapidly established; peas accompanied a spring chicken for Easter and roast duck for Whitsun – strange to think that the sixties custom of serving frozen peas with roast chicken has an ancient precedent. They were cooked with the first sprigs of mint or lightly stewed in cream. The same combinations can be found throughout the centuries, simply reworked according to the latest culinary vogue.

Today we are spoilt for choice, particularly as commercial fresh peas have greatly improved in quality. As late as the seventies it was all but impossible to buy them tender and sweet, yet now you can enjoy them throughout the summer. If you are prepared to pay a premium, you can serve imported fresh peas throughout most of the year, although I feel that this detracts somewhat from the pleasure of their brief season. Certainly dried peas are best appreciated during the winter months – there is something deliciously warming about supping a velvety pea soup on a cold November day or dipping into a buttery pile of mushy peas when the wind is howling outside.

Practical guide

Garden peas are normally divided into two categories – round and wrinkled. The former are more hardy but less sweet. Marrowfat peas are the best-known dried version of sweet, wrinkly peas and it is from these that mushy peas can be made. The British pea season begins in June and can finish as late as October.

As soon as a pea is picked it begins to convert its sugar into starch, so they should be cooked or frozen as quickly as possible to halt this process. The fresh ready-shelled peas are grown from petit pois varieties, which are a particular dwarf strain of round peas.

The majority of dried peas are sold split and are categorized by their colour. Yellow split peas are skinned green split peas. Opinions differ as to how long dried peas should be soaked, so it is sensible to follow the instructions on the packet. You should allow about 30–55g/1–2oz dried weight per person. Once soaked, whole peas will take about 1–1½ hours to cook, while split peas take 1 hour. If they are over-cooked they will turn into a pulp.

Allow 905g–1.4kg/2–3lb fresh peas in their pods to serve 4 people unless you are using shelled, in which case allow 400g/14oz for 4 people. Bring a large pan of water to the boil. Add salt and, if wished, a large sprig of mint along with the peas. Return to the boil, then simmer for 3 minutes or until tender. Drain well and serve with a knob of butter.

Taste notes

◊ The delicate tendrils and top pairs of leaves at the tip of a pea stem can be snipped and eaten as pea shoots. They taste exquisitely pea-like and can be eaten raw or briefly steamed or stir-fried.

◊ Cucumber, lettuce, sorrel, mint, parsley, spring onions and bacon are all traditional flavourings for fresh peas. However, they also taste wonderful when partnered with shellfish, light curry spices, cream and stock.

◊ Dried peas are gorgeous cooked with garlic, celery, carrots and onions. Their sweet flavour is further enhanced when cooked in a good ham stock.

Summer greens salad

The modern British green salad is becoming increasingly sophisticated, as the supermarkets sell pillow bags filled with scarlet-veined red chard, delicate leafed mizuna, peppery mustard leaves, tender young lettuces and herbs. However, the latest introduction to restaurant salads is the pretty pea shoot, whose sweet, juicy stems taste divine. Sadly, these are only available to gardeners, as their commercial value has yet to be appreciated by the larger growers. (Serves 4)

1 tablespoon lemon juice
3 tablespoons good extra
 virgin oil
salt and freshly ground black
 pepper
a handful of pea shoots,
 washed

200g/7oz mixed salad greens,
 trimmed and washed
4 young mint sprigs
a small bunch garlic chives or
 chives, roughly snipped

Whisk together the lemon juice and olive oil and season to taste. Place the pea shoots in a beautiful large salad bowl with the other leaves. Strip the mint leaves from their stems and gently fold into the greens with the garlic chives. When you are ready to serve, whisk the vinaigrette, pour over the salad and lightly toss. Serve in airy piles.

Note: Of the many different greens to choose from, consider claytonia, mizuna greens, mustard greens and flowers, nasturtium leaves and flowers, perilla, chive flowers, salad burnet, various cresses, purslane, young lettuces, for example, Lollo Rosso, Cos, Little Gem, oak leaf and so on.

Spring chicken with peas, morels and carrots

Fresh peas are delicious simmered in a creamy chicken stew. Vary your spring vegetables to taste; for example, Mrs Rundell (1853) includes sorrel in her more labour-intensive recipe for *Fowl aux Poix*. (Serves 4)

30g/1oz dried morels or
  85g/3oz fresh morels
4 corn-fed chicken breasts
2 cloves garlic, crushed
salt and freshly ground black
  pepper
3 tablespoons olive oil
6 plump salad onions,
  quartered
2 young carrots, peeled and
  sliced
1 lemon, finely grated

285ml/½ pint chicken stock
  (see page 339 or buy ready
  made)
200ml/7fl oz double cream
115g/4oz shelled peas
1 teaspoon finely chopped
  tarragon
1 tablespoon finely chopped
  chervil
2 tablespoons finely sliced
  chives

If you are using dried morels, rinse thoroughly and leave to soak for 30 minutes in a bowl of warm water. Drain when soft and cut in half. Fresh morels should be cut in half and gently brushed. If they are very gritty you will need to ignore all rules and quickly wash them in plenty of cold water just before using.

Rub the chicken breasts with garlic, salt and pepper. Heat the oil in a non-stick frying pan and fry the chicken skin side down over a moderately high heat until golden. Turn over and colour the other side before removing from the pan. Add the onions, carrots and mushrooms. Gently sauté for 2–3 minutes before stirring in the lemon zest and stock. Bring to the boil and allow to bubble for 3 minutes. Then stir in the cream, return to the boil and add the peas. Simmer for a further 3 minutes, then return the chicken and gently cook for 3–5 minutes or until it is just cooked. Adjust the seasoning to taste, stir in the herbs and serve immediately.

Lobster tagliatelle with spiced peas

The British excel at delicately spicing food, perhaps from their long love of Indian dishes. (Serves 2)

30g/1oz butter

½ small onion, finely diced

2 cloves garlic, crushed

½ small fresh red chilli, finely diced

a small pinch ground turmeric

¼ teaspoon ground cumin

½ teaspoon ground coriander

3 tomatoes, peeled, seeded and roughly chopped

140ml/¼ pint double cream

salt and freshly ground black pepper

225g/8oz fresh tagliatelle

1 teaspoon vegetable oil

85g/3oz fresh peas

2 ready cooked and shelled lobsters

lemon juice to taste

1 tablespoon fresh coriander leaves

Melt the butter in a saucepan and fry the onion and garlic until soft. Add the chilli and spices and cook for a minute before adding the tomato flesh. Cook over a moderate heat until the mixture forms a thick paste, then stir in the cream, season to taste and bring up to a simmer.

Cook the pasta in a large pan of boiling salted water to which the vegetable oil has been added. Fresh pasta will take only a few minutes to cook.

Add the peas to the simmering cream and cook gently for 3–4 minutes. Cut the lobster into attractive slices and add to the peas. Gently heat through, add a squeeze of lemon juice and season to taste. Remove from the heat while you finish the dish.

Drain the pasta thoroughly and divide between 2 plates. Spoon over the hot lobster, squeeze on a little extra lemon juice and scatter with the coriander leaves. Serve immediately.

Split pea soup

Men and women, and most especially boys, purchase their meals day after day in the streets. The coffee-stall supplies a warm breakfast; shellfish of many kinds tempt to a luncheon; hot-eels or pea-soup, flanked by a potato 'all hot', serve for a dinner; and cakes and tarts, or nuts and oranges, with many varieties of pastry, confectionery, and fruit, woo to indulgence in a dessert; while for supper there is a sandwich, a meat pudding, or a 'trotter'.

London Labour and the London Poor by Henry Mayhew (1862) describing some nineteenth-century fast food

(Serves 4)

225g/8oz split green or yellow peas	1 carrot, diced
2 tablespoons olive oil	sprig of parsley
1 large onion, diced	1.7 litres/3 pints water or ham stock
4 cloves garlic, crushed	salt and freshly ground black pepper
3 sticks celery, diced	

Spill the peas on to a clean white plate and check for stones or brown peas – discard both. Tip into a sieve and wash thoroughly under the cold tap, then leave in a large bowl covered with plenty of water. Soak overnight or according to the packet instructions.

Heat the oil in a large saucepan and gently fry the onion, garlic, celery and carrot until soft. Drain the peas and add with the parsley and water or stock. Return to the boil, then simmer gently for 2 hours or until mushy, replenishing the stock with extra water if necessary. Purée and strain into a clean pan. Reheat before thinning with water if necessary and adjusting the seasoning to taste.

Mushy peas

Mushy peas are made from dried marrowfat peas and are usually sold with an accompanying 'soaking tablet' of sodium carbonate and sodium bicarbonate. This is to ensure that the peas keep their rather weird bright green colour when cooked. If you are not bothered about the colour, omit the tablet and soak for the recommended time on the packet.

Mushy peas are believed to have originated in the north of England, where they still enjoy the greatest popularity, although you can buy them throughout the country. Traditionally, they are served plain, although they are also very good eaten as suggested below or flavoured with the juices from the roast meat. (Serves 4)

255g/9oz dried marrowfat
   peas
½ teaspoon caster sugar
½ teaspoon salt
30g/1oz butter
4 slices back bacon, trimmed
   of fat and finely diced

1 clove garlic, crushed
4 spring onions, finely
   chopped
freshly ground black pepper

Soak the dried peas according to the packet instructions.

Bring 565ml/1 pint of water to the boil and add the drained, soaked peas with the sugar and salt. Return to a gentle boil and cook over a moderate heat for 15–20 minutes or until the water has been absorbed and the peas are suitably mushy.

Meanwhile, melt the butter in a small frying pan. Fry the bacon for 3 minutes, then add the garlic and spring onions. Fry for a further minute, then remove from the heat and stir into the cooked peas. Adjust the seasoning to taste and serve.

PHEASANT

Pheasant poached. Pheasant is fairly common in England in summer, when the cock invades the cottage gardens to sneak the peas. You catch him quietly, with a paper bag and raisins.

Smear the paper cone inside with treacle or gum, put a few raisins at the bottom, and prop the bag up amongst the peas. When he sticks his head in he cannot see where to go, so he stands still till you fetch him.

Food in England by Dorothy Hartley, 1954

The pheasant, as any country dweller will tell, is an extraordinarily stupid bird. It may look exquisitely beautiful and taste delicious, but its wits are dim. This dullness only increases its charm for both shooter and poacher. Once startled by the beaters, it rises up and flies in an erratic manner that tests the skill of any shot. Poachers, on the hand, appreciate its capacity to be dazzled by torchlight, as it is too confused to resist their deft hands.

Pheasants were originally introduced into Britain by the Romans, who fattened them in pens, along with their hens, ducks and geese. Curiously, they then disappear from our records until the middle of the eleventh century. However, once reinstated on the royal menus, they made up for lost time by being bred in increasingly large quantities. By the eighteenth century ever more beautiful breeds were introduced from the Far East, much to the plague of tenant farmers and local gardeners. Unlike other types of game, pheasants were reared by landowners and small country families alike. Gamekeepers bred them for the huge shooting parties that first became popular in the nineteenth century, while local families kept them as poultry. Perhaps because of this, the pheasant has avoided the exclusivity of grouse and the over-familiarity of rabbit and has remained popular right up until today. It has not, however, escaped from its awesome reputation of being tough, a problem that many a person has had to wrestle with, including the bon vivant Dr Grant in *Mansfield Park* as described by his unsympathetic sister-in-law Mary Crawford: 'Dr Grant is ill,' said she, with mock solemnity. 'He has been ill ever since; he did not eat any of the pheasant to day. He fancied it tough – sent away his plate – and has been suffering ever since.' (Jane Austen, 1814.) The solution lies in careful hanging and even more astute cooking. No cook should risk his or her guest's good will when it comes to a chewy bird; better by far to tenderize it by chopping and potting.

Pheasants combine the best of most game birds – they come in a reasonable size with a sensible price yet taste delicious. They have a delicate gamey flavour that works equally well plainly roasted or served in a richly flavoured ragout. What is more, they are equally good served hot or cold. Who could ask for more?

Practical guide

The pheasant season stretches from 1 October to 1 February (or 31 January in Northern Ireland). Pheasant is considered to be at its best in November and December, as it becomes increasingly tough towards the end of its season. Old birds need to be slowly simmered, gently pot-roasted or finely chopped. Hen pheasants are usually slightly plumper and more juicy than the larger cock birds. One pheasant will serve 2 people generously. A brace of pheasants consists of a hen and cock bird.

All pheasants should be hung by their heads uneviscerated for up to 10–14 days if the weather is cold, dry and crisp. This will tenderize their flesh, intensify their flavour and make them easier to pluck. Unhung pheasant is supposed to taste like chicken. However, if the weather is warm, a mere 5 days will suffice. Care is needed, as if you hang your bird for too long it will literally go off. It is supposed to be ready for eating when you can easily pull out one of its tail feathers. If you are presented with a freshly shot pheasant, you can either hang it in a cool airy outhouse, out of reach of enterprising cats and foxes, or you can rush round to your local butcher. Many will not only hang your bird for you, for a small fee they will pluck, gut and prepare it as well. Having had the pleasure of the latter, I can thoroughly recommend persuading someone else to pluck and gut it – it is not a task for the squeamish.

If you are buying from a supermarket you have no means of gauging a pheasant's age, so you have to trust to the skill of their buyers. Otherwise, you are best advised to inspect your bird while still in its feathers. A young hen pheasant will be a lighter colour than an older bird. Next check its wings – when young, both sexes have soft downy feathers on the underside and rounded (as opposed to pointed) flight feathers. Finally, if you are buying a cock bird, look to see if it has short, rounded spurs, as these lengthen and sharpen with age.

Taste notes

◊ Traditionally roast pheasant is accompanied by a clear gravy, and can also be served with bread sauce, fried breadcrumbs and/or an apple, crab apple, rowan, redcurrant or red gooseberry jelly. Fresh watercress, game chips, Brussels sprouts, chicory, celery, celeriac and cabbage are also popular accompaniments.

◊ Stewed pheasant taste particularly good with bacon, button onions, wine and mushrooms or apples, cider and cream. Sweet herbs such as thyme, bay, rosemary, parsley and tarragon also complement pheasant, as do juniper berries, mace, cayenne pepper, lemon and orange zest.

◊ British recipe books cannot agree on the most effective way to roast a young pheasant. Some advocate stuffing, others insist the opposite; some recommend liberal basting, others a careful wrapping in streaky bacon, while a few maintain that pheasants need no such attention as they are fatty enough. There are no hard and fast rules so it is best to play it safe. Always make sure that your bird is regularly basted, whether it be with the pan juices or a bacon jacket. If you feel like making it go further or you just enjoy it, add stuffing, otherwise omit it and lessen the cooking time stated on pages 228–9 by 15 minutes.

Grilled juniper pheasant breast

Traditionally pheasant was never grilled, unless it had already been cooked, roughly shredded and covered in a devilled sauce. However, our tastes are changing and the current fashion for marinating meat allows even dry-fleshed young pheasant breasts to be served as a quickly seared succulent dish. (Serves 2)

2 skinned pheasant breasts	1 orange, juiced
salt and freshly ground black pepper	3 juniper berries, smashed
	1 sprig parsley, roughly chopped
Marinade	1 small clove garlic, roughly
3 tablespoons olive oil	chopped

Gently wipe clean the pheasant breasts and pick away any tiny stray feathers. Pat dry and place in a bowl with all the marinade ingredients. Cover and chill for at least 6 hours.

Preheat your ribbed cast-iron oven-top grill pan until it is very hot. Remove the pheasant breasts from their marinade and pat dry. Lightly oil and season before quickly searing for 2–3 minutes on each side. The meat should be just cooked through, otherwise it will be very chewy.

Remove and allow to rest for 5 minutes before serving with crab apple or redcurrant jelly. Gorgeous eaten with chips and a green salad.

Note: For the best results, if you do not have a ribbed cast-iron oven-top grill, either use a gas-fired grill, which will cook evenly and to a very high heat, or pan-fry.

Roast pheasant with bread sauce

Do not be discouraged by the length of this recipe; it is in fact easy to make and can be simplified even further by omitting the stuffing or the bread sauce. In *Modern Domestic Cookery*, 1853, Mrs Rundell suggests using veal and bacon as a forcemeat to add further flavour and succulence. This is a modern adaptation of her idea. Use only humanely reared British veal. (Serves 6)

Stuffing
4 slices unsmoked back bacon
225g/8oz lean (British) veal or
    pork*
1 small apple, peeled, cored
    and roughly grated
1 medium egg yolk
3 tablespoons finely chopped
    parsley
1 lemon, finely grated
salt and freshly ground black
    pepper
30g/1oz butter
1 small onion, finely diced
1 clove garlic, crushed

Roast pheasants
2 plump oven-ready hen
    pheasants
55g/2oz softened butter

Bread sauce
285ml/½ pint milk
1 peeled onion, stuck with 3
    cloves
1 small bay leaf
a pinch of ground mace
4 black peppercorns
15g/½oz butter
2 tablespoons double cream
55g/2oz fresh white
    breadcrumbs

Gravy
115ml/4fl oz dry white wine
345ml/12fl oz chicken stock
    (see page 339 or buy ready
    made)

Preheat the oven to its highest setting. Begin by making the stuffing. Roughly dice the bacon, fat and all, and place in the food processor with the roughly diced veal or pork. Process in short bursts until it is thoroughly minced but not as smooth as a paste. Transfer to a bowl with the apple, egg yolk, parsley, lemon zest and seasoning. Melt the butter in a frying pan and gently fry the onion and garlic until soft. Tip into the veal and mix together. Fry a small patty of the mixture to check the seasoning. Adjust according to your taste.

Carefully wipe each bird inside and out with a damp cloth and season. Pack the stuffing into each bird, cross its legs and tie them together with some string to prevent the stuffing from falling out. Liberally smear each breast with butter and place in a roasting tray.

Roast in the centre of the oven for an hour, basting every 10 or 15 minutes. Test the bird by inserting a skewer between its breast and thigh. If the juices run clean the pheasant is cooked.

As soon as the pheasants are in the oven you should begin the bread sauce so as to allow sufficient time for the flavourings to infuse into the milk. Place the milk, onion, bay leaf, mace and peppercorns in a small pan and scald. Remove from the heat, cover and leave to infuse for a minimum of 30 minutes.

Strain the milk into a clean pan and reheat with the butter and cream. Whisk in the breadcrumbs over a low heat and stir occasionally until the sauce has thickened. Season to taste and serve separately along with the gravy.

Once the pheasants are cooked, set them on a clean dish and leave to rest in a warm place while you make the gravy. Pour off any excess fat from the roasting tray and place over a moderate heat. Add the wine and boil vigorously while you scrape away at any encrusted debris. Once the wine has reduced by half add the stock and continue to boil until it tastes good. Adjust the seasoning and strain into a warm sauce boat. Serve with the pheasants.

See above for other serving recommendations.

Note: If you do not have a food processor buy minced veal or pork and finely dice your bacon.

Game pie

There are two forms of game pie – the cold hot-water crust pie and the hot puff or shortcrust pie. The former is undoubtedly wonderful, but many cooks have neither the equipment nor the patience to mould these pies, slowly bake them and then painstakingly fill them with almost jellified stock. Consequently, I am giving a modern recipe for the latter. Traditionally, it was an excellent way of tenderizing older, tough birds, since they were gently poached before being taken apart and used as a filling, while their stock was added to a flour-thickened sauce. This recipe cheats, in that it uses only young partridge and pheasant breasts, thereby shortening the cooking time by a couple of hours at least and imbuing the pie with a lighter flavour. (Serves 4)

2 partridges, cleaned
4 skinned pheasant breasts
salt and freshly ground black pepper
3 tablespoons olive oil
10 thin slices back bacon
1 medium onion, finely diced
2 cloves garlic, crushed
2 inner sticks celery, finely sliced
2 carrots, cut into fine half-moons
1 heaped tablespoon plain flour

285ml/½ pint dry white wine
565ml/1 pint chicken stock (see page 339 or use ready made)
1 lemon, finely grated
¼ teaspoon thyme leaves
3 sprigs parsley
225g/8oz chilled puff pastry (see page 338)
½ small egg beaten with 1 tablespoon milk

Preheat the oven to 220°C/425°F/gas 7.

Neatly remove the 2 breast fillets of each partridge by cutting along the breast bone and down around the rib cage. Pull off any skin and cut into chunks. If you are confident about boning you can remove the legs and cut the meat away from the thigh bone, before skinning and dicing. The drumsticks are too small to worry about but can be used with the carcasses for a good game stock if wished.

Cut the pheasant breasts into similar sized chunks, add to the partridge and season. Heat the oil in a large frying pan and fry the cubes in batches until they are all lightly and evenly coloured. Remove and place in the pie dish.

Remove the fat from the bacon and cut into medium-sized dice. Fry briskly in the same oil until lightly coloured. Reduce the temperature, mix in the onion, garlic, celery and carrots. Sauté gently until they begin to soften. Sprinkle with the flour, cook for a further minute, then stir in the wine. Boil vigorously until the liquid has been reduced by two-thirds. Stir in the stock, lemon zest and herbs. Continue to boil until the sauce has reduced down a little and thickened. Adjust the seasoning to taste. Pour over the diced game and mix thoroughly. If possible allow the mixture to cool before covering with pastry.

Roll out the pastry on a lightly floured surface in roughly the same shape as your pie dish only larger. Cut a ribbon from the edge of the dough and press it firmly on to the rim of the pie dish. Brush this with a mixture of beaten egg and milk and place a pie vent in the centre of the filling. Using a fork, firmly press around the rim so that the two pastries are glued together. Cut off the excess. Prick the lid with a knife, ensuring that the vent has a hole, and paint the crust with some more egg and milk. It can be chilled until needed at this stage.

Place in the centre of the preheated oven and bake for 25–30 minutes or until the pastry has puffed up and become golden. When you are serving, remember to fish out the parsley sprigs.

Potted pheasant

An excellent way to serve older birds. All forms of meat, game and fish have been potted in Britain for centuries. Delicately flavoured, they could be served as part of a cold table or picnic, but were most popular as a savoury addition to the breakfast table in the nineteenth century. Today, we tend to eat them as an appetizer or light main course with lots of hot buttered toast, although they make excellent sandwiches, especially when accompanied by crisp lettuce, sweet pickled cucumbers or roughly chopped capers. (Serves a generous 4)

2 oven-ready pheasants	ground cayenne
6 sprigs thyme	salt and freshly ground black
1 lemon, halved	pepper
115g/4oz butter	
ground mace	*Clarified butter*
ground nutmeg	340g/12oz butter

Preheat the oven to 140°C/275°F/gas 1.

Wipe the pheasants clean inside and out with a damp cloth. Place 3 sprigs of thyme along with half the lemon and some of the butter into the cavity of each pheasant. Mix together a large pinch of mace, nutmeg, cayenne, salt and pepper and rub into each bird. Arrange them in a casserole dish with a tight-fitting lid and plaster the remaining butter all over their breasts and legs. Cover and place in the centre of the oven.

Bake for 2 hours, remembering to turn the birds on to each side every 30 minutes, liberally basting with the butter as you do so.

While the birds are cooking, clarify some butter. Melt 340g/12oz of butter in a saucepan over a low heat and line a small sieve with a double layer of wet muslin or a clean, wet J-cloth. Place this over a small bowl. When the butter has thrown up a pale scum, gently pour the clear golden-coloured liquid through the muslin, carefully leaving the milky dregs in the saucepan. Set aside the strained, clarified butter and discard the rest.

Once the pheasants are cool enough to handle, pull away all the meat, discarding any skin, sinews or fat. Place in a food processor and give a few quick whizzes to chop the flesh into tiny pieces. Season to taste with some more mace, nutmeg, cayenne, salt and pepper and add two-thirds of the melted clarified butter. Process once again, until the pheasant forms a rough-textured paste. Remove and pack tightly into 4 small white ramekins. Press the meat down with the back of a spoon to eliminate any air-holes, then pour over the remaining butter, so that it forms a thin layer over the pheasant. Chill and cover once the butter is firm.

This is best left a day before eating, so that the flavours will fully mature. Keep in the fridge and eat within 4 days.

Note: If pheasant is young, it can be roasted in the ordinary way. The flavourings can be altered to taste; for example, Mrs Rundell recommends allspice mixed with mace, white pepper and salt, while Elizabeth David suggests combining grouse or partridge with a quarter of its weight in ham, but it would taste equally good with pheasant.

Pheasant and wild mushroom ragout

As pheasant invariably becomes tougher towards the end of its season in January, British cookery books are liberally sprinkled with recipes for stewed pheasant. These range from a simple pot-roasted pheasant to the more complicated French-influenced salmis, where the bird is partially roasted before being stewed in a richly flavoured sauce, made from its crushed carcass. We have fallen out of the habit of cooking such time-consuming dishes, so this recipe is for all those who enjoy instant gratification by using ready-portioned supermarket pheasant breasts. If you are using an older bird, cook as instructed below until you have added the chicken stock and herbs. At this stage return the meat to the ragout and transfer everything to a saucepan. Simmer very gently for 30 minutes or until the pheasant is tender. Finally add the cream, remove the parsley and serve. (Serves 2)

20g/¾oz dried chanterelles	140ml/¼ pint late-bottled
285ml/½ pint water	vintage port
3 tablespoons olive oil	285ml/½ pint chicken stock
salt and freshly ground black	(see page 339 or use ready
pepper	made)
2 skinned pheasant breasts,	1 sprig parsley
cut into dice	1 lemon, finely grated
10 small (pickling) onions,	¼ teaspoon fresh thyme leaves
halved	140ml/¼ pint double cream
1 clove garlic, crushed	

Wash the dried mushrooms carefully in several changes of water to remove any grit. Leave to soak for 20 minutes in the 285ml/½ pint water.

Heat the oil in a frying pan, season the diced pheasant breasts and quickly colour over a high heat. Remove and set aside. Turn your attention to the mushrooms. Strain and save their water, then trim off any very tough mushroom stalks. Do not worry if they are a little chewy.

Add the onions to the frying pan and reduce the heat. Allow them to fry gently for 5 minutes before adding the garlic and mushrooms. Continue to fry for a couple of minutes then add the port, mushroom water and chicken stock along with the parsley, lemon zest and thyme. Boil vigorously for about 10 minutes or until the broth has reduced by two-thirds. Pour in the cream and continue to boil for a further 4 minutes or until the cream has thickened. Stir in the pheasant pieces, reduce to a gentle simmer, and cook for 5 minutes or until they are just tender.

Remove the parsley, adjust the seasoning to taste and serve.

RASPBERRIES

The Barberry, respis and gooseberry too
look now to be planted, as other things do,
The gooseberry, respis, and roses, all three,
With strawberries under them, trimley agree.

September's *Five Hundred Pointes of Good Husbandry*
by Thomas Tusser, 1573

The raspberry is a fruit that has been woven into the British diet since time immemorial. An indigenous plant whose seeds can be traced back to the late glacial period in both Scotland and southern England, it has always been regarded with deep affection rather than adulation. Perhaps this is partly because, unlike the elusive strawberry, it keeps its delicious flavour when preserved. Yet I suspect that it is also due to the fact that for centuries it has been seen as a useful medication as well as a delectable food. Culpeper, in the mid-seventeenth century, neatly describes its medicinal virtues with the following entry in his *Complete Herbal*:

Government and Virtues – Venus owns this shrub. The fruit, which is the only part used, has a pleasant grateful smell and taste, is cordial and strengthens the stomach, stays vomiting, is somewhat astringent, and good to prevent miscarriage. The fruit is very grateful as nature presents it, but made into a sweetmeat with sugar, or fermented with wine, the flavour is improved. It is fragrant, a little acid, and of a cooling nature. . . The juice of the ripe fruit boiled into a syrup with refined sugar, is pleasant and agreeable to the stomach, and prevents sickness and retchings.

In 1629 John Parkinson was recommending that 'The berries are eaten in the Summer time, as an afternoon dish, to please the taste of the sicke as well as the sound. The juyce and the distilled water of the berries are verie comfortable and cordiall.' From then on the course of British raspberry recipes was set. The finest fruit was served fresh, while large quantities were preserved as wines, liqueurs, syrups, vinegars, jams and jellies. As cooking techniques developed so the raspberry was incorporated into new recipes. The nineteenth century, for example, saw the rising popularity of raspberry ice creams and jellies, while the advent of refrigerators in the twentieth century triggered a wide variety of raspberry mousses and creams. Unfortunately, its popularity as a jam was somewhat marred for many schoolchildren, by cheap pappy versions being served with horrid bowls of tapioca, semolina and rice pudding. The arrival of the frozen raspberry in the 1970s appeared to demote the poor raspberry even further, as watery raspberry syllabubs and pavlovas appeared on menus across the land.

Fortunately the culinary renaissance that has swept Britain in the 1990s has diverted the raspberry from its downward spiral into dullness. Today if you walk into a supermarket you will find punnets of raspberries identified by place and name. Scottish-grown Glen Moy or Glen Clover in early July, for example, or the small-fruited English-grown Autumn Bliss in September. Once more raspberries are grown predominantly for flavour. Some supermarkets have even tentatively started selling golden varieties. Town cooks can at last enjoy the simple pleasure of eating a plate of raspberries, sprinkled with caster sugar and served with thick double cream. It almost seems like a crime to accompany them with crisp pain perdu or fold them into cream as a gorgeous filling for a sponge cake.

The popularity of the pick-your-own farms has also allowed many urban cooks to become more experimental in their preserve-making, as they can buy large quantities of fruit quite cheaply. Traditional recipes are now enjoying a healthy revival with the likes of the old-fashioned sweet fruit vinegars reappearing alongside delectable pots of raspberry redcurrant jam.

Practical guide

The British raspberry season is gradually being extended by commercial growers to stretch from May until November. New varieties have been developed to fruit late into the year, and rows of slender canes can now be found fruiting under polythene tunnels in the colder months. These days the supermarkets often name the raspberry variety on the label, although most experts agree that it is hard to distinguish different flavours between breeds. Far more important is the weather – too cloudy and they can taste sharp, too dry and they will be small and pippy. Scottish raspberries in particular are famed for their intense flavour, which is said to be caused by their slow growth in a cool, damp climate with long daylight hours. However, larger-fruited strains are now beginning to be sold, the most recent of which is Terri-Louise, which was developed for Marks and Spencer.

Although the majority of British cooks only buy their raspberries during their traditional season, shops are increasingly selling foreign imports throughout the rest of the year. These tend to be dull, dry and expensive in comparison to our native varieties, so it is more sensible to buy good-quality frozen raspberries out of season and restrict their use to hot puddings.

Raspberries are a delicate fruit and should always be treated as gently as possible. If you are picking them yourself, never place too many in one bowl or bag as their weight will crush the fruit at the bottom. Bought raspberries should always be inspected for damaged or mouldy fruit. Once home they should be kept in the fridge, but brought up to room temperature before serving. They should never be washed, as they will disintegrate into a mush; instead tip the fruit out in small batches on to a white plate and inspect and remove any tiny insects such as little black beetles and tiny caterpillars. However, if caught out, you can remind your guests that wildlife is a healthy indication that the fruit has not been sprayed with insecticide.

Taste notes

◊ There is little difference in taste between yellow and red raspberries, although combining either with redcurrants will enhance their natural raspberry flavour as well as improve their ability to set as jam or jelly.

◊ Strawberries, blackberries, apples, peaches, nectarines, passion fruit and rhubarb have a natural affinity to raspberries, as do blackcurrants, red-currants, whitecurrants, cherries and blueberries.

◊ Hazelnuts or almonds are often used to accompany raspberries, for ex-ample, in the form of a nutty meringue or a delicious crumble (see bramble hazelnut crumble, page 72).

◊ The British have never developed much of a taste for savoury raspberry dishes, the only exception appearing to be roast grouse stuffed with raspberries. The rationale for this rather odd recipe appears to be that they can both be found in Scotland – so too can salmon, but that is not partnered with these tart berries.

Raspberry pie

This is a wonderful pudding, perfect for a chilly wet summer day. In the eighteenth century, cooks would enrich their fruit pies by pouring a caudle of cream beaten with egg yolks and flower water through a small hole in the cooked pie-crust. This is a simpler modern interpretation that never splits or curdles, as there are no egg yolks and the cream has been thickened by reduction. (Serves 4)

285ml/½ pint double cream	1 tablespoon orange-flower
140g/5oz caster sugar	water
225g/8oz puff pastry (see	1 small egg white, beaten
page 338)	1 tablespoon granulated sugar
455g/1lb raspberries	

Preheat the oven to 190°C/375°F/gas 5. Place the cream in a heavy-bottomed saucepan and simmer gently until it has thickened and reduced by almost half. Stir in the caster sugar and leave to cool.

Roll out the pastry on a lightly floured surface in roughly the same shape as your pie dish only larger. Cut a ribbon from the edge of the dough and press it firmly on to the rim of a deep pie dish. Gently mix the raspberries and orange-flower water into the cold cream and carefully spoon into the pie dish.

Brush the pastry rim with some of the beaten egg white. Then loosely roll the pastry on to the rolling pin and lift on to the pie dish. Using a fork or spoon, firmly press around the rim so that the two pastries are glued together in a pretty manner. Cut off the excess pastry. Prick the lid with a knife and paint with the egg white before sprinkling with the granulated sugar.

Place the pie in the centre of the preheated oven and bake for 35 minutes or until the pastry has puffed up and turned golden.

Raspberry jelly

I could not write a book about British food without including one recipe for jelly. This makes a superb, intensely flavoured, ruby red jelly. If you want to serve it as a luxurious pudding, try accompanying it with a softly whipped syllabub rather than plain cream. Mix 4 tablespoons of dry cider, 2 tablespoons of Calvados and 55g/2oz of caster sugar in a bowl. Add the finely grated zest and juice of ½ a lemon and 140ml/¼ pint of double cream. Whisk briskly until it forms soft peaks, then serve chilled with the jelly. This recipe can be made with fresh or frozen raspberries, depending on the time of year. (Serves 4)

905g/2lb raspberries	1 sachet (1 tablespoon)
115g/4oz granulated sugar	powdered gelatine
3 tablespoons Kirsch	

Place the raspberries in a non-corrosive saucepan with 140ml/¼ pint of water. Set over a low heat until the raspberries have released lots of juice. Add the sugar and stir until dissolved, then remove from the heat and strain through a fine sieve or jelly bag. Do not force any pulp through, as the clearer the liquid the more beautiful the jelly. Pour the kirsch into a measuring jug and add enough raspberry juice to make up 565ml/1 pint. If necessary, add a little water.

Pour 3 tablespoons of boiling water into a small bowl and evenly sprinkle with the gelatine. Leave for 5 minutes, then stir. If the gelatine has not completely melted, place the bowl in a shallow pan of simmering water and heat very gently until the gelatine has dissolved. Then slowly mix a small amount of the raspberry juice into the melted gelatine. As soon as it is tepid mix the gelatine into the rest of the raspberry juice and pour into an attractive bowl or 4 pretty glasses. Chill for a good 4 hours before serving.

Peaches with raspberry granita

Escoffier's pêche Melba – a delicate poached peach served on vanilla ice cream and drizzled in a fresh raspberry sauce – has been the inspiration for countless British recipes, ranging from fresh slices of peach macerated in Grand Marnier and served with a raspberry purée, to lurid burger-bar interpretations of synthetic vanilla ice topped with canned peaches and a squirt of shocking pink sauce. (Serves 6)

425ml/¾ pint dry champagne
or white wine
140ml/¼ pint water
1 vanilla pod, split
225g/8oz granulated sugar
3 strips lemon peel

4 white peaches, ripe
½ lemon, juiced
340g/12oz raspberries
3 tablespoons Grand Marnier
or Cointreau

Place the wine, water, vanilla pod, sugar and lemon peel in a non-corrosive saucepan. Dissolve the sugar over a moderate heat. Quarter and stone the peaches. Add to the hot syrup and simmer very gently for 10 minutes or until they are tender. Add the lemon juice and leave to cool in their syrup.

Once cold, peel and halve the peach quarters. Arrange in a clean container. Remove the vanilla pod and discard the lemon peel from the syrup, and add a ladleful to the peaches. Cover and chill.

Roughly crush the raspberries while you reheat the remaining syrup. As soon as it comes to the boil, tip over the raspberries and leave to cool. Once cold, liquidize and strain the raspberry liquid. Add most of the remaining peach juice and stir in the Grand Marnier or Cointreau. Pour the liquid into 2 shallow containers. Cover and freeze in the coldest section of the freezer.

Leave for 1 hour, then, using a fork, mix any ice crystals that have formed around the edge and bottom back into the main liquid. Repeat every hour for a further 3 hours until smooth ice crystals have formed throughout the whole mixture. As this granita is predominantly made from alcohol, it will not freeze as hard as a normal granita and consequently can be stored in the freezer for several days.

To serve, alternate layers of the raspberry granita with the peach slices in 6 tall glasses or glass bowls.

Pain perdu with raspberries and cream

Pain perdu appears to have been introduced into Britain by the Normans. Fine white bread (pandemain or manchet) was soaked in egg yolk before being fried in butter and sweetened. Over the following centuries the same idea was adapted to using alcohol, spices and/or cream. Such dishes went under various names including Poor Knights of Windsor, Cream Toast, Pan Perdy, etc. Too good to be forgotten for long, pain perdu is currently enjoying a revival with modern cooks who have taken to using packets of supermarket brioche buns in place of pandemain. (Serves 4)

85g/3oz butter	8 slices brioche buns
4 medium egg yolks	340g/12oz raspberries
2 tablespoons dry sherry	4 tablespoons thick double
caster sugar	cream

Melt the butter in a small saucepan over a low heat. Once it is bubbling pour slowly through a sieve that has been lined with a wet double layer of clean muslin or J-cloth into a non-stick frying pan.

Beat together the egg yolks and sherry and strain into a mixing bowl. Beat in a heaped tablespoon of caster sugar.

Heat the butter over a moderately high heat. Dip the sliced brioche into the egg mix, so that it is well soaked, then fry until it is crisp and golden on both sides. Remove and place on individual plates. Liberally dust with more sugar before topping with the fresh raspberries and cream. Sprinkle the raspberries with some more sugar and eat immediately.

Raspberry vinegar

Raspberry vinegar has been used for centuries in Britain as both a refreshing drink and a tonic for the sick. Unlike its pert French cousin, which was introduced in the 1980s on the coat-tails of Nouvelle Cuisine, it has an intense sweet raspberry flavour with just a hint of vinegar. It is delicious added to summer fruit or splashed on to lacy pancakes. It also makes an exquisitely cool summer drink when poured on to ice and diluted with soda water. Originally, the strained raspberry vinegar syrup was boiled for a good 10 minutes, but I find that this kills the delicate fresh raspberry flavour so I have amended the recipe accordingly. (Makes 850ml/1½ pints)

905g/2lb raspberries (only buy 455g/1lb at a time)	granulated sugar
635ml/1⅛ pint white wine vinegar	

Place 455g/1lb raspberries in a bowl, roughly crush and cover with the vinegar. Transfer to a large clean Kilner jar. Seal and leave to sit for 4 days, giving an occasional shake.

On the fourth day gently tip the raspberries and vinegar into a jelly bag or muslin-lined sieve, set over a large bowl containing a further 455g/1lb fresh, roughly crushed raspberries. Leave the old vinegary raspberries to drip through the sieve for a couple of hours. You must not push them through, as this will turn the vinegar cloudy. Discard the old raspberries and transfer the new to another clean Kilner jar. Leave for a further 4 days.

Finally strain the vinegar once again through a jelly bag and measure the liquid. Allow 455g/1lb of granulated sugar for every 565ml/1 pint of liquid and place the two together in a non-corrosive saucepan. Dissolve the sugar over a moderate heat. Bring to a full boil, skim off any pale scum and remove from the heat. Allow to cool before pouring to just under 2.5cm/1 inch below the top of sterilized bottles or Kilner jars (see page 179). Make sure that the top is plastic-coated and therefore vinegar-proof. Date, label and store in a cool, dark place.

RHUBARB

Saturday 29th. I was much better. I made bread and a wee Rhubarb Tart and batter pudding for William. We sate in the orchard after dinner. William finished his poem on Going for Mary. I wrote it out. I wrote to Mary H., having received a letter from her in the evening. A sweet day. We nailed up the honeysuckles, and hoed the scarlet beans.

Dorothy Wordsworth's 1802 *Grasmere Journal*

The Europeans have regarded rhubarb as a quintessentially British food, no doubt due to our obsession with it during the last century. As with so many typically British ingredients, opinions are widely divided between love and loathing for this curious plant. 'Nanny-food. Governess-food. School-meal-food (cold porridge with rhubarb for breakfast),' writes Jane Grigson in her *Fruit Book*, a far cry from the words of Margaret Costa in her *Four Seasons Cookery Book*: 'shrilly pink and pretty, the crisp slender stems of forced rhubarb are one of the consolations of late winter and early spring. I have seen children suck them like lollipops.' There is little room for middle ground when it comes to rhubarb, so I will immediately admit to loving it.

Garden rhubarb, otherwise known as *Rheum Rhabarbarum*, was first introduced into Britain in the seventeenth century, although it only became fashionable to cook it in tarts in the late eighteenth century. References to it are scattered and it seems that it only began to be grown commercially in the nineteenth century when rhubarb mania gripped the nation, as Mrs Beeton calmly explains in 1861, in her *Book of Household Management*:

It is one of the most useful of all garden productions that are put into pies and puddings. It was comparatively little known till within the last twenty or thirty years, but it is now cultivated in almost every British garden. The part used is the footstalks of the leaves, which, peeled and cut into small pieces, are put into tarts, either mixed with apples or alone. When quite young, they are much better not peeled. Rhubarb comes in season when apples are going out. The common rhubarb is a native of Asia; the scarlet variety has the finest flavour. Turkey rhubarb, the well-known medicinal drug, is the root of a very elegant plant (*Rheum palmatum*), coming to greatest perfection in Tartary. For culinary purposes, all kinds of rhubarb are the better for being blanched.

Ironically, its success caused its downfall, as it undermined its status as a luxury item and exposed it to the very best of our bad cooks in our schools, homes and hospitals. As Mrs Beeton points out, rhubarb was used in place of apples as a bulking agent. It was thrown into pies, puddings, jams and jellies. Our obsession for adding it to pies and tarts led to it being referred to as the pie plant on the continent. Perhaps its reputation might have survived intact despite all this abuse, if it were not for the widespread confusion between culinary rhubarb and the imported medicinal rhubarb root that was widely sold as a purgative. Sadly, many children were brought up with the idea that they had to eat rhubarb because it was good for them. There are few things more dissuasive than the idea of something being good for one.

After nearly a hundred years, rhubarb is finally shedding its image of badly cooked institutional food. It has been reinstated as an elegant and stylish ingredient. Refreshing rhubarb sorbets, creamy fools and pretty tarts once again grace enlightened tables. Children no longer have unappetizing preconceptions of stewed rhubarb and can instead appreciate its excitingly sharp flavour, offset with sugar, that is so perfectly adapted to our British taste.

Practical guide

From the culinary viewpoint, there are two types of rhubarb – forced and garden. Forced rhubarb appears in January and is sold throughout the spring. Its beautiful pink stems are tipped with bright yellow crinkly leaves and it has a delicate sharp flavour. Garden rhubarb can grow to vast proportions. Its stems are usually flushed deep red and green, while its leaves form giant dimpled green umbrellas. Shop-bought varieties are normally picked while still young and tender. It has a stronger, more acidic taste and holds its shape better when cooked. Greengrocers still sell rhubarb with its leaves attached to prevent it from wilting. Never buy discoloured or scarred stems and always choose the perkiest-looking stalks you can find. Home-grown rhubarb is favoured by slugs, so be mindful when washing.

Technically rhubarb is a vegetable, although in British cooking it is always treated as a fruit. Its leaves are poisonous, containing toxic amounts of oxalic acid, so never even contemplate eating them. It is easily prepared by trimming off the leaves and slicing off the brownish cut end. Wash thoroughly, removing any excess strings from the stems, and cut to the required size. It can then be dried and stored in plastic bags in the fridge for up to 4 days. If you have a mad urge to cook the tough fat stalks of well-matured rhubarb you will need to peel the outer stringy layer, leaving you with a bundle of green stems. However, if they are really large, remember that their flavour and texture may be somewhat coarse and may therefore need some help.

Forced rhubarb is cooked in a slightly different way from garden rhubarb. When poaching for a compote you will need to make a thicker sugar syrup than you would for garden rhubarb, as it releases lots of juice. In the same way, if it is baked in the oven, try to avoid stirring it as it disintegrates easily. Garden rhubarb, being more robust, can be baked in a moderate oven, tightly covered and layered with plenty of sugar or sieved gooseberry or raspberry jam for about 30–35 minutes. Cooking times will vary according to the type and quantity of rhubarb. Forced rhubarb is usually lightly cooked, so that it holds its shape, while young garden rhubarb is delicious cooked down to a frothy mess. Either type can be lightly cooked and frozen.

Taste notes

◊ Freshly picked young rhubarb sticks taste lovely dipped in the sugar bowl.
◊ Rhubarb has been used as a bulking agent with gooseberries, raspberries, blackberries and blackcurrants. It also tastes surprisingly good with strawberries (see summer fruit cobbler, below). Alternatively, try flavouring some home-made jam or jelly with rose petals or fresh lavender.
◊ Although orange and stem ginger (with its syrup) are popular British seasonings for rhubarb, lemon, cinnamon, nutmeg, allspice and Demerara sugar are also good. Grapefruit is occasionally used in rhubarb jam, while Margaret Costa suggests adding a few drops of Pernod to a creamy rhubarb fool. Perfect for winter. My favourite flavourings are elderflowers or lavender in summer and Cointreau in winter.

Rhubarb elderflower fool

There are few dishes so delightful as a fool. Opinion differs as to whether custard should be folded in with the cream, but I prefer the pure taste of rhubarb and cream. (Serves 6)

455g/1lb (prepared weight) rhubarb	granulated sugar, to taste
3 elderflower heads	285ml/½ pint double cream

Trim the rhubarb, discarding the tops and bottoms. Wash and cut into medium chunks. Place in a non-corrosive pan with the elderflowers, 4 tablespoons of sugar and 2 tablespoons of water. Cook gently over a low heat until the rhubarb is tender but not completely disintegrated. Add about 85g/3oz of sugar to taste and leave to cool.

Once the rhubarb is cold, whisk the cream into very soft peaks. Remove the elderflowers from the fruit and gradually fold the rhubarb with its juice into the cream. Spoon into delicate glasses and serve with sponge fingers or macaroons. The uninhibited can dip these into the creamy fool.

Summer fruit cobbler

Strawberries, raspberries and rhubarb might sound peculiar, but are a delicious way to use up the ever-rampant rhubarb. (Serves 4)

340g/12oz rhubarb, trimmed
  weight
55g/2oz caster sugar
225g/8oz strawberries
115g/4oz raspberries

Scone topping
225g/8oz self-raising flour
salt

85g/3oz cold butter, diced
55g/2oz caster sugar
1 medium egg
4 tablespoons milk
1 tablespoon granulated sugar

Preheat the oven to 200°C/400°F/gas 6.

Wash the rhubarb and cut into medium-sized even chunks. Mix the rhubarb and sugar in the pie dish and place in the oven for 10 minutes. Wash and hull the strawberries and gently mix into the warm rhubarb with the raspberries. Set aside while you prepare the topping.

Sift the flour and salt into a bowl and rub in the butter until it forms fine crumbs. Stir in the sugar. Beat the egg and place in a measuring jug. Add enough milk to reach 140ml/¼ pint. Then pour into the flour and roughly mix with a fork until it forms a lumpy dough.

Transfer to a floured surface and lightly knead until it becomes smooth. Quickly roll out to 1cm/½ inch depth, then stamp out about 9 scones using a floured pastry-cutter. Arrange these in neatly overlapping circles on top of the fruit. Brush with milk and scatter with sugar.

Place in the centre of the preheated oven and bake for 15 minutes. Then reduce the temperature to 190°C/375°F/gas 5 and bake for a further 10–15 minutes. Serve warm with lots of thick double cream.

Rhubarb tart

Food fit for the gods. (Makes 6 tartlets)

225g/8oz shortcrust pastry	200g/7oz granulated sugar
(see page 335)	455g/1lb trimmed, forced
200ml/7fl oz water	rhubarb

Roll out the pastry on a lightly floured surface and line 6 x 9cm/3½ inch greased tart tins. Prick their bottoms with a fork then line with scrunched-up foil and chill for 30 minutes.

Preheat the oven to 200°C/400°F/gas 6 and bake the tartlets blind for 10–15 minutes, until the pastry begins to colour. Remove the foil and return to the oven to dry out for a further 5 minutes.

In the meantime place the water and sugar in a non-corrosive saucepan and dissolve over a moderate heat. Wash the rhubarb and cut into 2.5cm/1 inch lengths. Place a single layer of rhubarb in the syrup and simmer gently for 2–3 minutes or until it begins to soften. Carefully remove from the syrup with a slotted spoon and spread in a single layer on a large plate. Repeat with the remaining rhubarb. Once you have finished the rhubarb, vigorously boil the remaining syrup until very thick and syrupy. Do not let it caramelize.

Arrange the half-cooked rhubarb in an attractive manner in the pastry cases and spoon over some of the thickened syrup. Return to the oven and bake for a further 8 minutes.

Serve warm or cold for pudding or tea but preferably with lots of thick double cream.

Note: As this recipe makes more syrup than you need, store the remainder in a clean covered container in the fridge for 2 days or freeze until needed.

Rhubarb sorbet

This refreshing sorbet is usually served on cold, frosty days when the first of the forced rhubarb arrives. It carries the promise of spring. (Serves 4)

905g/2lb (prepared weight) rhubarb	340g/12oz granulated sugar
	1 tablespoon lime juice
285ml/½ pint water	4 tablespoons vodka (optional)

Trim the rhubarb, discarding the tops and bottoms. Wash and cut into small chunks. Place in a non-corrosive pan with the water. Cover and bring up to the boil before simmering for 10 minutes or until the rhubarb is meltingly soft. Add the sugar and stir until it has dissolved.

Strain the rhubarb in batches, allowing it to drip slowly over a large bowl. The pulp can be used to make a fool later. Taste the liquid and adjust the sweetness to taste. Cover and chill.

Once the rhubarb juice is cold, stir in the lime juice and vodka. If you have an ice cream maker, churn the rhubarb juice in the usual manner, before freezing for a further hour. Otherwise pour the liquid into a shallow plastic container, cover and place in the fast-freeze compartment of your freezer. Every 30–40 minutes, mash up the ice crystals with a fork until the mixture has set into a sorbet.

If you have made the sorbet in advance, allow it to soften slightly for about 30 minutes in your fridge before serving.

Note: This is also an excellent way of using up excess summer rhubarb, although you may have to discard the pulp if it is too fibrous.

SHRIMP

Shrimp – There are several varieties of shrimps, and amongst these the best known are the brown shrimp and the red shrimp. The brown shrimp is the more highly flavoured of the two. It keeps close to the shore, and even affects brackish waters. It is mostly caught by fishermen or women, who wade into the sea, and push a shrimp-net before them.

Cassell's Dictionary of Cookery, 1899

It is an odd thought that such a delicacy as the British brown shrimp should be gradually slipping from the nation's consciousness. For centuries, every summer, this sweet-fleshed crustacean was sold by fishmonger and seaside stall-owner as a tasty treat. No seaside holiday was complete without a bag of freshly boiled shrimp or a shrimp tea. No self-respecting cook would serve a formal dish of turbot without its accompanying shrimp sauce or arrange a breakfast table without some cold shrimp set in a white napkin, perhaps with a wreath of curled parsley or a few leaves of purple endive. Yet today the common prawn (*Palaemon serratus*), along with innumerable other varieties, is now sold in place of our indigenous brown shrimp (*Crangon crangon*). The reason is simple – it is purely a matter of cost, size and convenience. The brown shrimp may taste better than any other prawn sold in Britain, but these days most cooks prefer to buy the plumper, ready-shelled prawns (*Pandalus borealis*) that are caught in vast quantities from the icy depths of the Atlantic. The brown shrimp is simply too small to be worth much commercial investment in shelling plants and the like. Few shoppers can be bothered with such a fuss over so little meat, so naturally they turn to their cheaper, larger cousins. Gone are the days as described by Eliza Acton in 1845 when 'prawns, though superior to shrimps only in *size*, are always much higher in price'.

Nevertheless, the humble shrimp can still be bought from any good fishmonger and it is well worth the effort of picking or shelling. Such a task can become a pleasure if one is settled with the radio or some pleasant company. Alternatively, gullible children can usually be temporarily enlisted in the task. So as this is a book about British food I shall dedicate a whole chapter to the pleasures of eating shrimp, mindful of the fact that all independently minded cooks will, of course, adapt the following recipes to prawns when they are nowhere near a shrimp-selling fishmonger.

For those who have been brought up on ready-shelled frozen prawns, the intense yet perfect flavour of a small freshly boiled shrimp will come as a surprise. In true British fashion they should be enjoyed simply: with fresh watercress, lemon and brown bread and butter or potted in lightly spiced butter. The former allows the eater to indulge in the leisurely activity of making their own sandwiches while the latter is the ultimate fishy treat – no fuss and lots of gustatory pleasure. A slightly more economical but equally delicious compromise is to make a shrimp butter with equal quantities of shrimp and butter, seasoned to taste. This will make excellent sandwiches without any of the usual embarrassment of small shrimps falling out as you munch.

Naturally, shrimp can be used in any dish that requires prawns, although, in my opinion, they are best enjoyed cold or barely warmed as they tend to shrink too much when heated. Thus they can be added to all manner of salads, from rice mayonnaise to oriental noodle. Although many of the classic shrimp dishes, such as shrimp sauce or shrimp pies, have virtually disappeared, they have been replaced by lighter new recipes that are more suited to our current taste.

Practical guide

The British brown shrimp is a tiny chameleon-like creature that changes from brown to grey to match the sandy ground it lives and scavenges on. Unlike our common pink prawn (known as white in Norfolk) it lives in the shallow waters. Despite its unsavoury diet it has an exquisitely delicate fish flavour. Brown shrimp (known as grey in Norfolk) are usually sold whole and already boiled. When buying them make sure that their shells are brightly coloured, crisp and springy, and avoid any that look limp or smell of ammonia. If you are buying whole prawns, you will need to buy nearly double the prepared weight listed in your recipe. Always try and sample any ready-shelled brown shrimp before buying, as their flavour quickly fades once peeled.

To 'pick' or shell a shrimp, gently straighten out the tail and pull it away from the head, twisting it slightly as you do so. Discard the head (or use as a base for shrimp stock) and carefully unwrap the hard casing from the shrimp's tail. The legs should come away as you do this.

If you are lucky enough to be offered some live shrimp, check that they are still quite lively then take them home and keep them in the bottom of the fridge, covered in damp newspaper or seaweed, until you are ready to cook them. You can, provided you are sufficiently hard-hearted, prepare them in one of two ways. You can either boil them in salty water or cook them as you would mussels. In either case you should cook them in small batches to ensure that they die very quickly. If you wish to boil your shrimp, make up a pan of very salty water, roughly about 170g/6oz of sea salt to 2 litres/3½ pints of water. It has to be sufficiently salty to float a *clean* egg in – remember to wash the egg before testing. Bring the brine to the boil and drop in some of the shrimp – not too many – so that the water quickly returns to the boil. As soon as they change colour to a brownish pink remove with a slotted spoon. Return the water to the boil and repeat until all the shrimp are cooked. Do not use sea water – apart from the fact that it is thought to imbue the shrimp with an inferior flavour, it is not always clean. Otherwise place some finely chopped shallots, garlic, white wine and a few sprigs of parsley in a wide saucepan, then cook the shrimp in small batches. The resulting juice can be strained and added to a simple white or cream sauce. Remember that shrimp become tough if overcooked, so always add them at the last minute to a hot dish and warm gently.

Taste notes

◊ The sweet flavour of shrimp is delicious combined with cream, butter or eggs. The classic British shrimp sauce can be made either as a form of butter sauce, made with water and a butter-enriched roux, or as a variation of a béchamel or velouté sauce. In essence the shrimp are added at the last minute to any one of these sauces, either whole or chopped, before the flavour is adjusted to taste with the help of anchovy essence, lemon juice or a spot of cayenne or mace. Potted shrimp can be used, provided their excess butter is removed.

◊ Shrimp taste surprisingly good with all manner of egg dishes. These can range from a lightly curried stuffing for hard-boiled eggs to a delicate herb and egg mousse.

◊ They are excellent added to creamy scrambled eggs or oeufs en cocotte (baked eggs).

◊ A wide variety of mayonnaises are served with shrimp. Perhaps the most popular are plain, lemon or rose. The first two can be further enhanced by the subtle addition of tarragon, chives or chervil, while the latter is always made with tomato ketchup, Worcestershire sauce, lemon juice and Tabasco.

◊ Dressed with mayonnaise shrimp can be added to sandwiches or tossed in salads with rice, cucumber, radishes and spring onions.

◊ Shrimp make delicious appetizers, in particular when combined with bitter or peppery lettuces such as curly endive, trevisse, rocket or watercress. They also taste wonderful eaten with bacon, avocados, peppers, blanched leeks, asparagus and artichokes, both globe and Jerusalem.

◊ Other favoured seasonings include mace, cayenne pepper, ground cloves, curry powder, lemon or lime juice, a wide variety of herbs, anchovies (chopped or essence), soy sauce, honey, sesame oil, fresh ginger, lemon grass and garlic.

◊ Lastly, shrimp are often used with other fish and shellfish from kedgeree to fish pie.

All of the following recipes can be adapted to prawns when brown shrimp are not available.

Potted brown shrimp

Like all potted dishes this benefits from being allowed to sit in the fridge for a day or two, so that its flavours can develop and merge into one another in the most delicious way. It can be served for breakfast, lunch or tea but is best enjoyed with lots of hot buttered toast and a squeeze of lemon. Formal culinary teaching recommends that the toast is served unbuttered so that guests can add their butter to taste, but I always find that the toast cools too quickly to make this method enjoyable. (Serves 6)

455g/1lb butter	large pinch of ground mace
455g/1lb shelled cooked	large pinch of cayenne pepper
brown shrimp or about	a few drops anchovy essence
905g/2lb unshelled shrimp	(optional)

Set aside a quiet moment to shell your shrimp (as described above). If they are already shelled, lightly pat them dry with some paper towelling and check for any small pieces of debris.

Melt the butter over a low heat and simmer gently for 15 minutes, allowing it slowly to throw up a pale froth. Skim this off before pouring the clear golden butter through a clean, damp muslin- or J-cloth-lined sieve. Discard the milky dregs at the bottom of the pan.

Set aside 6 tablespoons of the clarified butter before returning the remainder to a small saucepan. Add the shelled prawns and spices. Cook over a very low heat for 5 minutes, stirring occasionally, then mix in a tiny amount of anchovy essence and carefully spoon the prawns into 6 small soufflé dishes. Cover with a thin layer of the reserved melted butter and chill immediately.

Serve with hot buttered toast and a wedge of lemon.

Shrimp canapés

There is no disputing the fact that shrimps and prawns rival cocktail sausages as our favourite drinks party nibble. A brief inspection of any party's canapés will reveal prawns tossed in mayonnaise in vol-au-vents, pressed on to herb cheese Ritz biscuits or encased in little won-tons or spring rolls. Here is an Eastern-inspired variation. (Makes 32 canapés)

4 baguette rolls
340g/12oz shelled shrimp
1 red chilli, finely diced
1 clove garlic, crushed
1½ tablespoons finely sliced
    chives
1 tablespoon finely chopped
    mint, lemon balm or
    coriander

2 limes, juiced
6 tablespoons olive oil
salt and freshly ground black
    pepper

Garnish
coriander leaves, twists of
    lemon zest or finely diced
    red pepper

Preheat the oven to its highest setting. Cut the bread rolls into neat round slices. Each roll should yield about 8 medium-thin slices. Arrange these in a single layer on 2 baking sheets and bake for 5 minutes or until lightly toasted and dry. Remove and leave to cool. These can be made a day or two ahead, provided they are stored in an airtight container.

Shell the shrimp, if necessary, and place in a food processor with the red chilli, garlic, chives and mint or other herbs, lime juice and olive oil. Process in quick, short bursts until the shrimp are chopped into a rough paste. You must not over-process or they will turn into an unpleasantly sticky paste.

Transfer to a bowl and adjust the seasoning to your taste. You can add more of any one of the ingredients if you wish. When you are ready, spoon the shrimp relish on to your croûtons. If you are in the mood to garnish, add a tiny coriander leaf, a twist of lemon zest or a sprinkling of diced red pepper.

Avocado, bacon and shrimp salad

A wonderfully light yet peppery shrimp salad. (Serves 6)

6 little gem lettuces	1 lemon, juiced
115g/4oz ready prepared	a few drops Worcestershire
watercress	sauce
285g/10oz sliced back bacon	salt and freshly ground black
3 tablespoons vegetable oil	pepper
200g/7oz Hellmann's real	400g/14oz cooked peeled
mayonnaise	shrimp
1 tablespoon finely chopped	3 ripe avocados
tarragon	

Wash, trim and dry the lettuce and watercress. Place in a mixing bowl and set aside.

Trim the bacon of any fat and cut into 2.5cm/½ inch dice. Heat the vegetable oil in a frying pan and fry the bacon until crispy. Remove with a slotted spoon and leave to drain in some kitchen paper.

Mix together the mayonnaise and tarragon. Add the lemon juice, Worcestershire sauce and seasoning to taste, then dress the shrimp.

When you are ready to serve, halve, stone and peel the avocados and cut into long slices. Mix these into the lettuces and arrange in a pretty manner on 6 appetizer plates. Finally spoon on the shrimp and scatter with the bacon. Serve immediately.

Brill with shrimp sauce

Shrimps have been served in the form of a sauce with white fish since at least the eighteenth century. Here is a healthy modern alternative. (Serves 4)

1 lemon	1 teaspoon finely chopped
7 tablespoons extra virgin	tarragon
olive oil	2 tablespoons small capers
2 tablespoons finely chopped	115g/4oz shelled shrimp
parsley	salt and freshly ground black
2 tablespoons finely sliced	pepper
chives	4 medium, skinned fillets brill

Preheat the grill to its highest setting or preheat a ribbed cast-iron oven-top grill pan.

Finely grate the lemon and place in a mixing bowl with 3 tablespoons of lemon juice. Whisk in 6 tablespoons of olive oil and the herbs. Rinse the capers and squeeze out any excess water before roughly chopping. Stir into the lemon vinaigrette. Finally add the shrimp and season to taste. Set aside while you cook the brill.

Lightly brush the fish fillets with the remaining olive oil, season and place best side up under the grill, or best side down if cooking on a cast-iron oven-top grilling pan. Cook for 2–3 minutes on each side, depending on the thickness of the fish. Serve immediately, accompanied by the shrimp sauce.

SMOKED HADDOCK

The people I give up – they are dirty and greedy – the country, too, is a perfect mass of rubbish – and the dinners not fit for dogs – the cookery, I mean; as to the materials, they are admirable – But the breakfasts! that's what redeems the land and every county has its own peculiar excellence. In Argyleshire you have the Lochfine herring, fat, luscious, and delicious, just out of the water, falling to pieces with its own richness melting away like butter in your mouth. In Aberdeenshire, you have the Finnan haddo' with a flavour all its own, vastly relishing – just salt enough to be *piquant*, without parching you up with thirst.

Dr Redgill, the extraordinary epicure, expressing some of his views on the pleasures of a Scottish breakfast in Susan Ferrier's novel *Marriage* (1818)

The haddock has a strange past. For centuries it was barely noticed by discerning cooks, as its soft white flesh and low fat content made it difficult to cure well. Then suddenly, in the eighteenth century, an anonymous Scottish genius transformed it from a workaday white fish into a superb smoked one. Its piquant nature, so much admired by Dr Redgill, ensured its establishment as an excellent nineteenth-century breakfast or supper dish, usually plainly grilled with fresh butter. However, as with all new foods, it was not long before cooks across the land began to experiment, particularly as the advent of the railways and the widespread use of ice ensured its availability from every local fishmonger. By the 1930s smoked haddock could be found on smart breakfast tables in the form of kedgeree or lightly poached with eggs in milk. Rustic lunches served Cullen Skink, a creamy Scottish soup made from milk, onions, haddock and mashed potatoes; while artistic suppers included the Savoy's omelette Arnold Bennett.

The modern smoked haddock has suffered from mass production, losing much of the fragrance that is so noticeable in one traditionally smoked. Fortunately, in recent years there has been a revival in these older methods and it is once again possible to buy such delicacies as Arbroath smokies and Finnan haddies from good fishmongers. Certainly our taste for smoked haddock has not diminished and if anything our repertoire has increased. These days British cooks think nothing of finely slicing the delicately cured London fillets and serving them in a simple salad with a blob of peppery horseradish cream, just as they will happily transform their smoked haddock into pretty fishcakes and sumptuous pies.

Practical guide

The term smoked haddock refers to a number of different cures. The most famous of these are Finnan haddock and Arbroath smokies, although there are many other variations. True Finnan haddocks, or haddies as they are sometimes known, are pale gold and come only from Scotland. They were originally developed in the village of Findon, a few miles south of Aberdeen. The fish is beheaded and split open before being dipped in brine and cold smoked at a temperature of 24°C/75°F. Glasgow Pales, Pales and Eyemouth cures are prepared in the same way, but with smaller fish and quicker brining and smoking. This imbues them with the lightest of salty smoky flavours.

The London version uses haddock fillets and employs a lighter smoke. When produced in Scotland it is known as an Aberdeen fillet.

Arbroath smokies are very different, as they are hot smoked, just like smoked trout, and require no further cooking. They originated in the tiny fishing village of Auchmithie then spread to the nearby town of Arbroath. Unlike Finnan haddocks they are not split open; instead they are beheaded, gutted and dry salted for a couple of hours before being tied into equal-sized pairs and hot smoked at 82°C/180°F. Their skin becomes darkly burnished while their flesh turns from pale gold to creamy white near the backbone. Aberdeen smokies and Pinwiddies are regional variations of the same method. They should be gently reheated if served warm.

Any smoked haddock coloured bright yellow has been dyed. For some strange reason the manufacturers believe that this makes it more appealing, although there are few fish so beautiful as a naturally smoked silvery gold haddock. Perhaps with positive discrimination, commercial producers might learn to renounce their unnecessary dyes and let the quality of their fish shine through. Incidentally, it is worth experimenting with different producers as their haddock will vary in taste according to their curing process.

Any fresh smoked haddock must be kept refrigerated and eaten within a couple of days of purchase, as its cure is too light to act as a preservative. Keep well wrapped in paper, otherwise its smoky aroma will permeate everything else and no one appreciates haddock-flavoured milk in their tea. Although commercially fresh haddock is available for much of the year, it is considered to be at its best from November until February. This is because the haddock spawn from March onwards and their flesh can be softer and of a poorer quality until the following September, when it begins to improve.

Taste notes

◊ The delicate flavour of haddock is enhanced by being cooked in milk or cream, perhaps with a touch of butter and black pepper. This simple combination has endless variations, ranging from a plain poached dish to richly flavoured haddock cakes. Try flaking Arbroath smokies into double cream and baking, perhaps with some lightly fried fennel or seeded and diced fresh tomatoes.

◊ Lemon, parsley, chives, bay leaves, black or cayenne pepper, prawns, cheese, bacon and horseradish are all popular flavourings of smoked haddock.

◊ Potatoes are a traditional accompaniment. They can also be used as a thickener, as in Cullen Skink, or as a creamy topping as with fish pie. Try making potato pancakes to accompany thinly sliced London smoked haddock with crème fraîche.

◊ Smoked haddock is often cooked with eggs, for example, in the form of a soufflé, roulade, kedgeree or omelette. Omelette Arnold Bennett is made by filling the half-cooked omelette with flaked Finnan haddock, cream and Parmesan.

Curly endive, smoked haddock and horseradish salad

This recipe needs the superior flavour of a properly smoked London (or Aberdeen) haddock fillet. Serve as an appetizer with lemon wedges and finely sliced, buttered brown bread. (Serves 6)

Horseradish cream
40g/1½oz grated horseradish
1 tablespoon white wine
  vinegar
½ teaspoon made-up English
  mustard
½ tablespoon caster sugar
salt and freshly ground black
  pepper
140ml/¼ pint double cream

Salad dressing
1 tablespoon white wine
  vinegar

½ teaspoon whole-grain
  mustard
3 tablespoons extra virgin
  olive oil

Salad
1 curly endive, trimmed
2 tablespoons whole flat-
  leaved parsley leaves
a small bunch of chives,
  snipped into 5cm/2 inch
  lengths
2 medium London smoked
  haddock fillets

Mix together the horseradish, vinegar, mustard, sugar, salt and pepper, then stir in the runny double cream. Set aside while you finish the salad.

Make the salad dressing by whisking together the vinegar, mustard and olive oil in a small bowl. Season to taste. Then using a pair of scissors, trim the head of the curly endive as if it were a mop of hair, removing all the dark green ends and the tough outer leaves. Cut through the root and wash and dry the remaining leaves. Place in a large mixing bowl with the herbs.

Place the smoked haddock fillet flesh side up on a chopping board. Run your fingers gently over it and if you feel the tips of any tiny bones, pull them out with the help of a pair of tweezers. Using a sharp knife, preferably a smoked salmon knife, cut broad paper-thin slices of haddock, beginning at the tail end and working up towards its head.

Once you are ready to serve, toss the salad leaves in the dressing and divide in an attractive manner between 6 plates. Arrange the sliced haddock on each plate and drizzle it with the horseradish sauce.

Arbroath smokies with parsley butter

Arbroath smokies are surprisingly and deliciously salty, which means that it is essential to be light-handed when seasoning the butter. Ideally, use unsalted butter. They make perfect supper food, eaten with fluffy mashed potatoes or a crisp-skinned jacket potato. (Serves 4)

140g/5oz softened unsalted butter	salt, cayenne and freshly ground black pepper
3 tablespoons finely chopped parsley	4 Arbroath smokies
lemon juice to taste	1–2 lemons, cut into wedges

Preheat the oven to 180°C/350°F/gas 4.

Place 85g/3oz of butter in a small bowl and beat in the parsley, before seasoning to taste with lemon juice, salt, cayenne and black pepper. If you are not using immediately, roughly shape the butter into a sausage on some wet greaseproof paper and roll it into a smooth cylinder. Chill until needed.

Tear off 4 sheets of aluminium foil, each large enough to comfortably wrap one fish. Divide the remaining butter between the 4 fish, placing a small nugget inside their tummies and liberally buttering the foil sheets. Bake in the centre of the oven for 20 minutes.

When they are hot through, carefully remove their skin, split each fish along its backbone and remove the bone. Place a generous pat of parsley butter on each fish before replacing the top fillet. Keep the fish warm until all are ready then serve with the lemon wedges.

Finnan haddock cakes

The ever-stylish Constance Spry recommends serving tiny smoked haddock fish cakes as an elegant after-dinner savoury. Here is a modern variation, designed for brunch or as a robust first course. Both the fish cakes and their relish can be made the day before if needed. (Serves 6)

Fish cakes
1kg/2lb 3oz Finnan haddock
425ml/¾ pint milk
4 black peppercorns
1 bay leaf
1 sprig parsley
55g/2oz butter
55g/2oz plain flour
4 tablespoons grated
    Parmesan
4 tablespoons finely chopped
    parsley
salt and freshly ground black
    pepper
a pinch of cayenne pepper
    (optional)

115g/4oz dried white
    breadcrumbs (see method)
1 large egg, beaten
4–6 tablespoons vegetable oil

Roasted pepper relish
2 red peppers, quartered and
    seeded
2 teaspoons wholegrain
    mustard
2 tablespoons white wine
    vinegar
6 tablespoons extra virgin
    olive oil
3 tablespoons whole flat-leaf
    parsley leaves

Arrange half the fish in a wide saucepan. Add the milk, peppercorns, bay leaf and parsley sprig. Place over a low heat and bring up to a simmer. Cover, remove from the heat and leave to cool. Then carefully remove the cooked fish to a plate and add the remaining haddock to the saucepan. Cook as above, saving both the fish and the milk.

Strain the milk and measure out 285ml/½ pint for the white sauce. Melt the butter in a small saucepan. Stir in the flour and cook over a low heat for 2 minutes before gradually stirring in the milk. Keep stirring until it forms a smooth sauce, then simmer gently for 3–4 minutes. Stir in the cheese and set aside.

Meanwhile, flake the haddock flesh, discarding the skin and bones as you do so. Mix together the fish flakes, parsley and cheese sauce. You may need to use your hands at this stage. Adjust the seasoning to taste, adding a touch of cayenne if wished. Cover and chill.

To make the breadcrumbs you will need about 170g/6oz white sliced bread. Spread this out on your oven racks and set the oven to 150°C/300°F/

gas 2. Leave until they have dried out and are crisp but not coloured. The time will vary according to the freshness of your bread. Once dry, remove and process into fine breadcrumbs.

When the fish mixture is cold, sprinkle your work surface and hands with extra flour and divide the mixture into 12 evenly sized lumps. Gently shape these into small cakes, patting them with a palette knife as you do so to give them an attractive shape. Finally, dip them in the beaten egg before tipping them, one at a time, on to a generous plate of home-made breadcrumbs. Lightly but firmly pat these on to all sides of each cake, before setting on a clean plate or tray and chilling.

Make the relish by preheating the grill to its highest setting and placing the peppers skin side up underneath. As soon as their skin blisters, remove to a covered bowl. Meanwhile whisk together the mustard, vinegar, olive oil and seasoning. Once the peppers are cold enough to handle, peel and cut into diamonds or squares, about the same size as the parsley leaves. Mix these into the vinaigrette and shortly before serving add the parsley leaves.

When you are ready to serve, heat the vegetable oil in a frying pan over a moderately high heat and fry the fish cakes until golden on both sides. Drain them on kitchen paper and serve piping hot with the relish. If you are serving them as a starter, dress a few leaves of curly endive in a lemon or wholegrain mustard vinaigrette and arrange around the cakes.

Fish pie

A classic British dish that arrived in the nineteenth century. This is an updated and luxuriously creamy version. You can replace the potatoes with puff pastry if wished. (Serves 4)

680g/1½lb potatoes, peeled
   and quartered
salt
680g/1½lb smoked haddock
   fillet or 4 whole Finnan
   haddocks
90g/3½oz butter
1 small onion, finely diced
115g/4oz button mushrooms,
   trimmed

1 tablespoon lemon juice
salt and freshly ground black
   pepper
115g/4oz peeled prawns
285ml/½ pint double cream
3 tablespoons finely chopped
   parsley
4 tablespoons milk

Put the potatoes in a large pan of salted cold water and bring to the boil over a moderately high heat. Continue to boil for 20–30 minutes until they are tender, but not falling apart. Drain and leave to steam dry in a colander for 5 minutes.

Meanwhile place the haddock in a saucepan and cover with cold water. Simmer gently for 3 minutes, then remove the fish and discard the water. As soon as the fish is cool, remove its flesh in large flakes and place in a bowl, ensuring that there are no bones or skin remaining.

Melt 30g/1oz butter in a non-stick frying pan over a moderate heat. Fry the onion until it is soft, then increase the heat slightly and add the mushrooms. As soon as they begin to colour, season with lemon juice, salt and pepper and tip into the fish. Add the peeled prawns, cream and parsley. Mix thoroughly, season to taste and transfer to a pie dish.

Return the potatoes to their pan and mash energetically until they are soft and fluffy. Gradually beat in the remaining butter, followed by the milk. Season to taste with salt and freshly ground black pepper and spread over the fish with a fork. The pie can be covered and chilled until needed at this stage if wished.

Preheat the oven to 200°C/400°F/gas 6 and bake for 30–35 minutes (if cold) or 15–20 minutes (if warm), until golden and bubbling hot.

STRAWBERRIES

**Doubtless God could have made a better berry but doubtless God
never did.**

William Butler (1535–1618)

The tiny wood strawberry, *Fragaria vesca*, has always grown in Britain's woods and shady banks. For many centuries its roots were gathered up and replanted in gardens, alongside violets and primroses, where, if the gardener was lucky, the fruit might grow slightly fatter than in the wild. Every summer London echoed with the cries of strawberry sellers, while country children gathered wild berries by threading them on to lengths of straw for the local markets. It was a fruit that caught the British imagination, it conformed so perfectly to our national sense of what constitutes good food. Beautiful to behold, its texture and flavour are so fine that it requires the minimum amount of work to enjoy it at its best.

Inevitably new cultivated varieties were developed and by the seventeenth century fashionable tables were graced by the latest introductions – Hautbois and the Virginian strawberry – while discerning eighteenth-century diners compared the merits of the Alpine, Chilean and Pine strawberries. The Virginian was admired for its ability to fruit under glass as early as February, while the Alpine was relished for its astonishing late October crop. However, it was Michael Keens, a market gardener in Isleworth, who was to change the size and taste of future strawberries for ever. He created Keens' Imperial in 1817 and Keens' Seedling in 1821, both large, flavoursome strawberry hybrids. The latter caused such a sensation that the French began to refer to all large strawberries as *les fraises anglaises*, despite the fact that it was their accidental cross-fertilization of a large-fruited Chilean and a sweet-flavoured Virginian that had made it all possible.

Since then the strawberry has had to endure the indignity of being the first fruit to be canned in Britain, just as it has had to survive the horror of being frozen for the newly invented freezer and later freeze-dried for the benefit of astronauts and muesli eaters. Despite all of which, it is still best loved served in the simplest of manners, or as Thomas Hill wrote in 1577:

The Berries in the Summer tyme, eaten with Creame and Sugar, is accompted by a greate refreshing to Man, but more commended beying eaten with Wine and Sugar, for on suche use these marvellously coole and moisten Chollericke stomaches or such beyng of a cholericke complexion.

It is late in the season before we can bear to crush them into fools, ice creams or water ices, let alone turn them into jam. And we have to be heartily sick of them before we will add them to tarts or bake them in pies with rhubarb or peaches. Yet there are countless delicious dishes to be made. The flavour of a strawberry sorbet, made from berries that have been macerated overnight in Cointreau and port, is heavenly, while the taste of a vanilla-flavoured rhubarb and strawberry cobbler is gorgeous on a rainy day. Yet when all is said and done, nothing can diminish the initial delight in savouring your first strawberry of the season, warm from the sun and dipped in the sugar bowl. And no Wimbledon, Ascot, Henley or summer ball could possibly be perfect without the mandatory bowl of strawberries and cream.

Practical guide

These days, if you buy your strawberries from a supermarket, you will probably buy a relatively new variety called Elsanta. Firm-fleshed with a good flavour, it has proved to be the ideal modern strawberry for the supermarkets. With careful management it can be persuaded to fruit from May through to the autumn. Yet as I write many of the supermarkets are now considering extending their policy of 'product differentiation' to strawberries. In plain English, this will mean that several different varieties are sold at any one time, which has the effect of increasing their sales while giving us a greater choice.

Currently the latest varieties are Emily, Eros, Tango and Bolero. Emily appears first and is slightly more acidic in flavour than Elsanta. Eros follows, along with Elsanta, and has large, firm fruit with a subtle peach taste. Tango follows and fills a natural lull between mid July and mid August. Finally, there is Bolero which produces sweet, glossy red fruit until mid November. If the supermarkets pursue this new strategy we may even be able to buy the delicious, albeit expensive, British-grown Fraises des Bois, a domesticated strain of the European wild strawberry.

Wild strawberries are still common throughout the British Isles and are worth collecting if you happen upon a good patch. They flower from April to July and fruit from late June to August.

Strawberries, like all soft fruit, benefit from being eaten as soon as possible after picking. If you need to buy in bulk, it is worth visiting a pick-your-own farm as this is not only cheaper, but also offers you a different range of strawberries from those on sale in the supermarkets, some of which may well be better suited to jam making. Take shallow containers for picking to prevent the weight of the fruit crushing the strawberries at the bottom.

If buying from shops, inspect each punnet for stains, as this will indicate hidden bruising, then carefully sniff the fruit. The stronger the fragrance the better the flavour of the fruit. Try to avoid buying loose berries as these are more likely to suffer from bruising. Once home, store them at the bottom of the fridge in the salad drawer, otherwise everything will smell of strawberries. Never hull your strawberries until just before you need them. They keep far better if left intact. Finally, there is the matter of washing strawberries. Some writers are firmly against this practice, but as it is rare to find berries without a little dust or mud clinging to them, I would always recommend that you briefly rinse them before hulling.

Taste notes

◊ Small strawberries do not necessarily have more flavour than large ones. The taste of strawberries will vary throughout their season, but, depending on the weather and variety, they should be at their best at midsummer.

◊ The best way to freeze strawberries is to follow Jane Grigson's sensible advice and purée the fruit with a little sugar. This can then be used for winter fools, soufflés and sauces. Otherwise you can preserve their flavour by making strawberry gin or a strawberry cordial.

◊ There are countless complementary flavours for strawberries, but here are a few of my favourites: distilled orange-flower or rose water, raspberries, cream, crushed macaroons, Grand Marnier, Cointreau, peaches, Champagne, elderflower syrup and rhubarb. However, you should also consider port, Beaujolais, claret, kirsch, Madeira, Marsala or even sherry. Many enjoy a well-matured balsamic vinegar lightly sprinkled over their strawberries.

Strawberry mess

There are only two ways of eating strawberries. One is neat in the strawberry bed, and the other is mashed on the plate. The first method generally requires us to take up a bent position under a net – in a hot sun very uncomfortable, and at any time fatal to the hair. The second method takes us into the privacy of the home, for it demands a dressing-gown and no spectators.

A.A. Milne, *Not That It Matters*

No childhood would be complete without strawberry sandwiches or mashed-up strawberries. The former are made by filling thin slices of buttered white bread with sliced, sugared strawberries. The second, which is more poetically known as strawberry mess, is so simple it does not really need a recipe. It instils a deep sense of comfort in adults. (Serves 2)

| 340g/12oz strawberries | thick double cream to taste |
| caster sugar to taste | |

Wash and hull the strawberries. If large cut in half, then divide between 2 bowls. Supply each eater with a spoon and fork, sugar and cream. Let them mash up their strawberries to a chunky mess. Juice will squirt everywhere. Then sweeten to taste and add the cream. Mash once more and eat immediately.

Variations
Single cream or even milk can be used in place of the double cream. Alternatively no cream is added and a small amount of orange-flower water is sprinkled over the berries before mashing. It is all a matter of taste.

Summer fruit salad

This is no ordinary summer fruit salad. It follows the honourable tradition of serving sugared strawberries in champagne, but with a difference. You can vary the fruit to your taste, but the Grand Marnier and a good dry champagne are essential for a successful dish. (Serves 6)

455g/1lb strawberries	225g/8oz raspberries
4 tablespoons Grand Marnier	1 bottle chilled dry
4–6 tablespoons caster sugar	champagne, such as
or to taste	Taittinger
3 ripe nectarines	
225g/8oz red or white	
currants	

Wash, hull and slice the strawberries. Place in a non-corrosive bowl with the Grand Marnier and sugar. Cut the nectarines into thin slices, discarding their stones, and mix in with the strawberries. Wash the currants and pluck them from their stems. Stir into the strawberry salad. Cover and set aside until you are ready to eat.

Just before you are about to serve, gently fold the raspberries into the fruit and spoon the mixture into 6 wine flutes. Fill each glass two-thirds full, making sure that you add plenty of the alcoholic juices. Open the champagne and cautiously pour a little into each glass. If you add it too quickly it will erupt everywhere, as it will react with the sugar. As soon as each glass is sufficiently topped up with champagne, serve and enjoy.

Strawberry ice

The British are very partial to strawberries macerated in fortified wines, so here is a late summer variation. The key to producing a truly breathtaking dish is to allow the strawberries sufficient time to macerate – up to 24 hours if possible. (Serves 4)

455g/1lb strawberries	115g/4oz icing sugar or to
55ml/2fl oz vintage port	taste
55ml/2fl oz Cointreau	3 tablespoons lemon juice

Wash and hull the strawberries. Place in a non-corrosive bowl and vigorously crush with a potato masher. Stir in the port, Cointreau and sugar. Cover and refrigerate for 12 hours.

Strain the alcoholic strawberry juice through a fine sieve. Add the lemon juice and sweeten, if necessary, to taste. If you have an ice cream maker, churn the strawberry juice in the usual manner before freezing for a further hour. Otherwise pour the liquid into a shallow plastic container, cover, and place in the fast-freeze compartment of your freezer. Every 40 minutes, mash up the ice crystals with a fork until the mixture has set into a sorbet.

If you have made the recipe in advance, allow the ice to soften slightly for about 30 minutes in your fridge before serving. Serve in pretty glass dishes with silver teaspoons and traditional ice cream wafers.

Strawberry jam

Strawberry jam is still the most popular jam in Britain, despite the fact that it is often fraught with difficulties for domestic cooks as strawberries are low in pectin and acid and consequently resist setting. In the past, British cooks used redcurrant juice to help set it, but today most people tend to use either sugar with pectin or bottled pectin such as Certo. Resist the temptation to overboil it – it is far better to retain a fresh strawberry flavour with a slightly softer set. Once made, it tastes gorgeous in jam tartlets, steamed puddings and pancakes as well as spread on to hot buttered toast. (Makes 1.1kg/2½lb jam)

905g/2lb small strawberries	1 lemon, juiced
1kg/2lb 3oz sugar with pectin	

Preheat the oven to low. Wash the jam jars in hot soapy water, then rinse thoroughly under the hot water tap and arrange on a baking sheet in the oven. Once they are completely dry they should be sterile.

Briefly wash the strawberries before hulling. Clip a thermometer on to the rim of a jam pan before adding the strawberries, sugar and lemon juice. Set the pan over a low heat and stir occasionally until the sugar has dissolved. Then increase the heat to high and bring up to a full rolling boil. Boil for 3–4 minutes or until setting point is reached, which is when the thermometer registers 106°C/220°F.

Immediately remove from the heat and skim off any pale scum, using a slotted spoon. Leave to settle for 15–20 minutes to try to prevent the strawberries from all floating up to the top of your jam jars! Then give a gentle stir and pour into the warm jars. Cover with small waxed discs (wax side down) and, once cool, seal with cellophane discs. Label, date and store in a dark, cool place.

Note: If you do not have a thermometer, chill a saucer in the fridge and as soon as the jam has boiled for 4 minutes, remove from the heat and drop a tiny amount of liquid on to the saucer. As it cools a skin will form. If this wrinkles when gently pushed, the setting point has been reached. If not, return the pan to the heat, return to the boil and boil vigorously for a couple of minutes before repeating the exercise.

Strawberry gin

Home-made fruit liqueurs are not as fashionable as they were, despite the fact that they are very easy to make and taste sublime. A good strawberry gin can imbue countless dishes with the taste of summer. Syllabubs, jellies, sweet sauces, fruit salads and pies can all be transformed with the odd splash. Alternatively, enjoy neat or as a shocking pink champagne cocktail.

After you have made your first fruit gin, you can indulge your instincts by adding each ingredient according to your taste. Extra strawberries can be added, along with more or less sugar and gin. You can even alter the seasonings to taste.

680g/1½lb strawberries
115g/4oz caster sugar
2 strips finely pared lemon
rind

850ml/1½ pints gin or as
needed

You will need 1 or 2 bottling jars, such as Kilner jars with non-corrosive seals. Wash them in hot soapy water, then rinse thoroughly and dry in a very low oven to sterilize them. Alternatively, use them hot but dry out of the dishwasher.

Once your jars are ready, wash the strawberries and very gently pat dry before hulling. Cut them in half and slip into the jars with the sugar and lemon peel. Cover with the gin – adding extra if necessary. Seal the bottles and leave in a cook dark place. Give them a vigorous shake each day for a month, then leave to mature for a further 2 months. Finally, strain the liquid through a muslin-lined sieve and pour into a sterilized bottle or jar. It is now ready to be enjoyed, but will keep indefinitely.

See also
Strawberry, cherry and elderflower salad (page 92)
Summer fruit cobbler (page 250)

TREACLE

Mrs Squeers stood at one of the desks, presiding over an immense basin of brimstone and treacle, of which delicious compound she administered a large instalment to each boy in succession: using for the purpose a common spoon, which might have been originally manufactured for some gigantic top, and which widened every young gentleman's mouth considerably; they being all obliged, under heavy corporal penalties, to take the whole of the bowl at a gasp.

The horrors of Dotheboys Hall as described by Charles Dickens in *Nicholas Nickleby* (1839). Treacle mixed with sulphur was commonly administered as a nursery medicine but had the additional advantage of ruining any appetite for breakfast and dinner.

As a child, ignorant as to the nature of brimstone, I never quite understood why the boys at Dotheboys Hall objected to eating treacle, since I loved to sneak illicit spoonfuls whenever I felt peckish. Like many British children I developed a passion for its bitter-sweet flavour early in life, through the medium of treacle toffees and gooey gingerbread. However, in true British style, the word treacle can also refer to molasses or golden syrup. So in the interests of clarity and *treacle* tart and sponge lovers I shall deal with all three in this chapter.

Curiously, the purpose to which Mrs Squeers used her treacle is far closer to its original use in Britain than one might suppose. The term treacle comes from the Greek *theriaca antidotos* (antidote for the bite of wild beasts). It seems that in the ancient world honey was mixed with various drugs and spices as a cure for numerous poisons. By the Middle Ages British apothecaries sold it under the name of theriaca or triacle. The honey was gradually replaced by imported molasses, the dark sugar syrup that is a by-product of sugar cane refining. In the sixteenth century we began to refine our own sugar and produced more molasses than the apothecaries could possibly sell. The excess was sold as a cheap sweetener, initially as 'molasses' and later as 'common treacle' until it was finally shortened to 'treacle'. Such is the odd way that new foods can find their way into our diet. Golden syrup arrived only late in the nineteenth century, created by the sugar refiner Abram Lyle and his sons, as a response to the threat of cheap imported white sugar beet. Sugar beet cannot be made into golden syrup. Its success was immediate.

Although all forms of treacle were originally intended to be a honey or sugar substitute, cooks soon took advantage of its unique qualities. The rich, liquorice-like flavour of black treacle enhanced the sharp heat of ginger in gingerbread and parkin, while its sticky nature improved the keeping qualities of a wide variety of tea breads by keeping them wonderfully soft and moist. From Aberdeenshire to Devon it was added to everything from bacon cures to biscuits. Golden syrup, with its lighter flavour and higher sugar content, was used even more widely in baking, from flapjacks to roly-poly puddings. Today, British cooks appear content to restrict themselves to tried and tested treacle recipes, whether they be for toffee apples or fruit cake.

Practical guide

Technically molasses, treacle and golden syrup are different by-products of refined cane sugar. Molasses is not widely available to the domestic cook, although it is still used in the making of treacle beer. It can occasionally be found in some health food shops and is the darkest and least sweet of all three substances. It is separated from initial raw cane sugar crystals and is mainly used in commercial foods such as rum or baker's yeast.

Black treacle is sweeter and contains about 65 per cent sugar, along with a large amount of calcium, iron and potassium. It is made by blending, evaporating and filtering a proportion of the bitter molasses with other sweeter sugar syrups; all of which are released at a later stage in the refining process.

Golden syrup is also made from some of the excess refining syrups. However, unlike black treacle and molasses it is subjected to its own refining process, which gives it a clear golden colour and pleasing flavour. It is often combined with sugar in baking recipes as it only contains about 80 per cent sugar.

All three have a long life expectancy and can be stored up until their sell-by date. Once opened, try to keep the outside of the tins clean from drips. Treacle is usually measured by weight, which makes for a sticky mess. Try warming a bowl before placing it on the weighing scales. Then set the scale to zero and pour in your treacle. It should allow you to transfer your treacle from container to mixing bowl with ease. Alternatively, flour the weighing-scale pan in a bid to prevent the treacle from sticking.

Taste notes

◊ Black treacle or a small amount of molasses added to malt breads will imbue them with their own particular sticky moistness. In the same way black treacle makes a good addition to rich fruit cakes, gingerbreads and parkins, all of which will improve with age.

◊ Black treacle makes wonderful toffee, while no fudge is complete without some golden syrup.

◊ Treacle pudding was originally made with black treacle, but this was soon ousted with the arrival of golden syrup. It sometimes went under the name of Rochester, Patriotic or Syrup pudding. Roly-poly fans can make black treacle or golden syrup variations – these can be further flavoured with citrus peel, mixed dried fruits and spices.

Sweet spiced ham

Flora had arranged two kinds of food for the two kinds of guests she was expecting. For the Starkadders and such of the local thorny peasantry as would attend there were syllabubs, ice-pudding, caviar sandwiches, crab patties, trifle, and champagne. For the County there was cider, cold home-cured ham, home-made bread, and salads made from local fruit.

Elfine's wedding feast in *Cold Comfort Farm* by Stella Gibbons, 1932

A beautiful joint of ham has always been popular with the landed gentry, and until quite recently many a farmer would use treacle in his cure along with ale and juniper berries. Few go to such trouble today, although many will still boil and roast a gammon for a special occasion. (Serves 8–10)

leg of gammon, about 3.6kg/8lb	8 lightly crushed juniper berries
225g/8oz black treacle	
285ml/½ pint beer	*Glaze*
285ml/½ pint sherry or Marsala	4 tablespoons soft brown sugar
115g/4oz Demerara sugar	2 teaspoons English mustard powder
1 large onion, quartered	1 teaspoon ground allspice
2 carrots, halved	cloves for decoration
3 sticks celery, halved	
4 lightly crushed allspice berries	

Place the gammon in a large saucepan. Add the treacle, alcohol, sugar, onion, carrots, celery and spices, then cover with plenty of cold water. Bring up to the boil, skim and reduce the temperature to a lively simmer. If you are unable to cover your joint completely with liquid, roughly cover the saucepan with a large sheet of foil and turn the gammon half-way through cooking. Cook for 2 hours, replenishing with water as the broth evaporates.

Meanwhile, preheat the oven to 200°C/400°F/gas 6 and mix together the brown sugar, mustard powder and ground allspice. After the gammon has cooked for 2 hours, remove from its stock and set in a roasting tray. Cut away its tough brown skin leaving about 5mm/¼ inch of white fat. Neatly score this into an attractive diamond pattern. Stud the diamond corners with cloves and rub the warm joint with the mustard sugar. Place in the centre of the oven and bake for a further 50–60 minutes. The sugar will turn into a deep mahogany glaze. Transfer the ham to a clean plate and either serve immediately or set in a cool airy place until cold. Wrap and keep chilled.

Red cabbage salad

It seems that in Yorkshire they have a particular taste for piquant salads, which can range from shredded lettuce, dressed with mint, onion, vinegar and treacle, to shredded cabbage and onion seasoned with a well-peppered treacle vinegar dressing. According to Dorothy Hartley in *Food in England*, the latter was also known as Yorkshire ploughboy. Here is a modern variation. It is surprisingly good and should be served with cold meat and jacket potatoes. (Serves 4)

½ large red cabbage, finely
  sliced
1 red onion, halved and finely
  sliced
3 tablespoons dried sour
  cherries or cranberries

2 tablespoons black treacle
4 tablespoons white wine
  vinegar
salt and freshly ground black
  pepper
a pinch of cayenne pepper

Place the cabbage, onion and dried fruit in a mixing bowl. Measure the treacle and vinegar into a small mixing bowl and stir until the treacle has dissolved. Pour over the salad, mix thoroughly and season to taste. Allow to sit for 10 minutes before serving.

Note: This can also be made into a warm red cabbage salad by lightly frying the cabbage with finely sliced spring onions, a little garlic and the dried fruit before tipping in the dressing.

Norfolk treacle tart

Treacle tart has a somewhat misleading name, as it is more commonly made with the more delicately flavoured golden syrup rather than black treacle. Naturally, any pudding that includes golden syrup has to have been invented after its introduction in 1883. However, instead of giving a recipe for the usual treacle tart – filled with lightly spiced breadcrumbs, soaked in golden syrup, I will give an adaptation of this wonderful recipe from Mary Norwak's lovely book *English Puddings, Sweet & Savoury*. (Serves 6)

225g/8oz shortcrust pastry (see page 335)	2 lemons, finely grated
12 tablespoons golden syrup	6 tablespoons single cream
30g/1oz butter	4 medium eggs, beaten

Preheat the oven to 220°C/425°F/gas 7.

Roll out the pastry on a lightly floured surface into a 30cm/12 inch circle and loosely wrap around the rolling pin. Hold the pin over a 23cm/9 inch tart dish and carefully unroll, gently pressing the pastry into place. Prick the bottom with a fork, press some aluminium foil or greaseproof paper into the middle, and fill with rice or old dried beans before chilling for 30 minutes.

Place the tart in the centre of the preheated oven and bake blind for 15 minutes. Remove the covering and continue to bake for another 5 minutes, until the pastry has become dry but not coloured and has lost that raw sweaty look. As soon as you have removed the pastry case reduce the oven temperature to 180°C/350°F/gas 4.

Meanwhile place the syrup and butter in a small pan over a low heat. Melt the butter, but do not let the syrup get too hot. Allow to cool while you beat together the lemon zest and cream. Gradually beat the tepid syrup into the cream, then whisk this into the beaten eggs until well amalgamated. Pour into the pastry case and bake for 35 minutes or until the filling is set and golden. Serve warm or cold.

Treacle sponge

Treacle sponge, or pudding as it is sometimes known, is the ultimate weapon against the misery of the winter glooms. (Serves 4–6)

extra butter for greasing basin	1 small orange, finely grated
12 tablespoons golden syrup	and juiced
115g/4oz softened butter	2 medium eggs
115g/4oz caster sugar	115g/4oz self-raising flour,
1 lemon, finely grated and	sifted
juice	

Place an 850ml/1½ pint pudding basin in a large saucepan. Pour enough water into the pan to come half-way up the basin's sides. Remove, cover the pan, and bring the water up to the boil.

Liberally butter the inside of the basin before pouring 6 tablespoons of syrup into the bottom. Cut a circle of greaseproof paper to fit the top of the bowl.

Beat together the butter, sugar and citrus zest until pale and fluffy, then gradually beat in the eggs. Add half the orange juice with half the lemon juice. Finally fold in the flour and spoon evenly into the pudding basin. Gently press the greaseproof paper on to the sponge mix before pleating a sheet of foil and tightly covering the bowl. Lower it into the boiling water, cover and return to a moderate boil.

Steam in the covered saucepan for 1½–2 hours, replenishing the water regularly so that it never becomes too low. The pudding is ready when well risen and firm to touch. Allow to sit for a minute or two, then loosen with a palette knife and turn out on to a warm dish.

Just before you are ready to serve, place the remaining orange and lemon juice in a small saucepan with 6 tablespoons golden syrup. Gently heat and mix together and serve warm with the hot pudding.

Gingerbread

Although gingerbread has been made in Britain since at least the fifteenth century, it has changed substantially over the centuries. The early forms were brightly coloured, chewy, flat cakes, made with honey, spices and breadcrumbs. Gradually flour or oats replaced the breadcrumbs, treacle and sugar replaced the honey, and eggs and fat were added until gingerbread diverged into two forms: hard ginger biscuits (nuts) and soft moist gingerbread or parkin. The introduction of bicarbonate of soda in the nineteenth century completed the transition from old to modern gingerbread. (Serves 6)

225g/8oz plain flour	½ level teaspoon salt
1 teaspoon mixed spice	1 medium egg
3 teaspoons ground ginger	285ml/½ pint milk
1½ level teaspoons baking powder	85g/3oz butter
½ teaspoon bicarbonate of soda	85g/3oz black treacle
	85g/3oz golden syrup
	115g/4oz Demerara sugar

Preheat the oven to 180°C/350°F/Gas 4 and lightly oil a 455g/1lb loaf tin. Line this with bakewell paper or lightly oiled greaseproof paper.

Sift the flour, spices, raising agents and salt into a mixing bowl. Beat together the egg and milk. Place the butter, treacle, syrup and sugar in a small saucepan and heat gently, stirring occasionally until the butter has melted. Pour the gooey contents of the saucepan into the flour, followed by the egg and milk, and beat vigorously with a wooden spoon until they are well mixed.

Pour the runny mixture into the loaf tin and bake for 1½ hours or until the gingerbread is well risen and feels firm to the touch. Leave to cool in its cake tin. Once it is tepid, turn it out on to a wire rack. Ideally the cold gingerbread should be wrapped up in foil and left to mature for a few days. I always find it impossible to resist eating after baking, but it does undoubtedly improve over 4 or 5 days, becoming increasingly sticky with a stronger ginger flavour.

Gingernuts

Otherwise known as ginger snaps or gingerbread biscuits, gingernuts are a spicy, crisp biscuit that the indulgent enjoy with a mid-morning cup of coffee or winter tea. As a child, I used to raid our rather ineffectual biscuit tin for old gingernuts as I loved eating them after they had turned soft and chewy. Aside from the ginger, you can add cinnamon or a pinch of ground allspice in place of the mixed spice. I have even come across recipes that included a tiny pinch of cayenne pepper. (Makes 18 biscuits)

115g/4oz self-raising flour
pinch of salt
½ teaspoon bicarbonate of
   soda
2 teaspoons ground ginger

½ teaspoon mixed spice
30g/1oz golden caster sugar
55g/2oz butter
55g/2oz golden syrup

Preheat the oven to 190°C/375°F/gas 4. Lightly oil 2 baking sheets and set aside.

Sift the flour, salt, bicarbonate of soda, spices and sugar into a large bowl. Melt the butter and golden syrup together in a saucepan over a low heat. Do not let it boil. Then, using a wooden spoon, stir into the spiced flour. As soon as it is mixed, discard the spoon and, using your hands, mix and mould the dough into a smooth sausage. Cut the sausage into 18 pieces and roll each piece into a small ball. Lightly flatten each 'nut' and arrange on the baking sheets, allowing plenty of room for each to spread a little as it cooks. Bake for about 15 minutes. The biscuits are ready when they are golden brown and covered in cracks. They will still be soft.

Remove from the oven and leave to cool and harden on the baking sheets for a few minutes. Then slip on to a cooling rack and leave until cold. Store in an airtight container to keep crisp, unless you like soft gingernuts.

See also
Parkin (page 211)

TROUT

River trout is a most delicious fish, highly esteemed by epicures. It is seldom met with of a large size, and those are most delicate in flavour which weigh from three quarters of a pound to one pound. The female fish is considered better than the male. It may be known by its body being deeper and its head smaller than the other. Trout may be dressed in various ways, amongst which boiling is last to be recommended, as it is then rather insipid in flavour. It is in season from May to September, and is in perfection in June.

Cassell's Dictionary of Cookery, 1899

For an island blessed with numerous brooks, rivers and lakes, it is strange to think that the majority of us only eat two varieties of freshwater fish, namely salmon and trout. Restaurants are of course partial to the odd pike or eel, but the pleasures of char, perch or grayling are confined to anglers. Perhaps the happy propensity of both salmon and trout to be farmed has led to their continued widespread popularity, since it allows them to be easily marketed by the supermarkets; yet I fear that as a nation we are deeply suspicious of fish and are unwilling to experiment with anything unfamiliar, particularly if it contains bones, thereby exposing us to social embarrassment.

Since the salmon has had more than its fair share of attention, I will dedicate this chapter to trout. In many ways it is the perfect modern fish with its lean, sweet-tasting, succulent flesh, perfectly adapted for everything from simple cures to the barbecue or frying pan. However, before I begin I feel that it is necessary to clarify a few points. There is no disputing the fact that a large number of us are culinary snobs and a great many of us have romanticized the idea that wild brown trout must by the very fact that it is both indigenous and wild be superior to farmed rainbow trout. No one I know has ever conducted a blind tasting to resolve this prejudice, so until someone does, perhaps it is better to consider each fish on its own merits. The wild brown trout varies considerably in flavour according to where it is caught, how it has dined and how quickly it is eaten. If it has a fault it is that it can suffer from a slightly muddy flavour. However, it can also suffer from having to 'hang about', often un-iced, until the angler is weary of his sport. Consequently, its flavour and texture can deteriorate before finally being cooked. The same problems can dog rainbow trout fished from the wild. Farmed rainbow trout, on the other hand, should be considered as a different fish. Their controlled diet means that fish from any one farm will taste the same. To my mind their delicate flavour is underrated but, as with all things in life, it is a matter of personal taste. They also benefit from being quickly cleaned, chilled and packaged ready for sale, usually within 24 hours of their having left their pond. It is therefore important to buy fish with a relatively long sell-by date, as this means they are still very fresh.

Brown trout, along with all other freshwater fish, were an important part of our national diet for many centuries, when religious laws enforced countless fish days to help mortify the flesh and reduce carnal passions. These were maintained under Protestant rule to support the fishermen. Ships and stalwart seafaring men were regarded as an essential part of our military defence. Naturally, freshwater fish were a welcome change from the endless dishes of salted or dried fish, particularly for those living far from the coast. So great was their importance that the majority of medieval estates established fish ponds and a system of fishing rights to their rivers to ensure a ready supply.

The end of compulsory fish days led Izaak Walton to write in his famous book *The Compleat Angler* in 1653 'that the casting off of Lent, and other fish days . . . hath doubtless been the chief cause of those many putrid, shaky, intermitting agues, unto which this nation of ours is now more subject, than those wiser countries that feed on herbs and salads and plenty of fish'. Nevertheless, the trout remained a popular delicacy and was eaten in all manner of forms from a simply fried midsummer breakfast to a chic highly flavoured stew.

Fish farms first appeared in the late nineteenth century in a bid to help restock our rivers and lakes. They bred both brown and the newly imported wild American rainbow trout for this purpose. However, it was not until some enterprising Danes arrived in Yorkshire in the 1930s that rainbow trout began to be farmed for the table. Its keen appetite, fast growth and easy-going attitude made it perfect for fish farming, unlike its brown cousins whose slower growth rate meant that they had to be nurtured for twice as long before sale. The trout was ready for the late twentieth-century mass market.

Practical guide

Most British cooks are familiar with two forms of trout: the farmed rainbow trout (*Oncorhynchus mykiss*) and the wild sea trout (*Salmo trutto*) which is sometimes called salmon trout. The latter is in fact an indigenous brown trout which has taken it into its head to live at sea. Its freshwater siblings or brown trout are rarely sold commercially, as anglers tend to return them to their watery home or distribute them among family and friends. For practical purposes the sea trout can be treated in exactly the same way as a salmon, so I will not deal with it here.

Freshwater trout, whether brown or rainbow, can be treated in the same way. If you are presented with an uncleaned trout, begin by cutting off its fins. You will then need to remove its scales by running the back of a knife at a slight angle along its skin from tail to head. As the scales will fly everywhere, work over the sink. Continue by slitting open the trout's tummy, from the vent to the gills, and pulling out its guts, making sure that any blood vessel running along its spine is also removed. Then, using a sharp pair of kitchen scissors, snip out its gills as these, along with any blood, can make the fish taste bitter. Rinse under the cold tap and pat dry unless you are preparing it 'blue', in which case you should merely wipe the trout clean. The blueness is attained by the charming practice of leaving the fish covered in its translucent slime, which turns blue-grey as the trout is briefly simmered in a court-bouillon. This dish can only be prepared immediately after the trout has been killed. Turn to Jane Grigson's *Fish Cookery* or *Good Things* if you are keen to try.

If you need to fillet the trout, cut off the head from behind the gills so that both fall off. Then, keeping your knife flat, cut along the backbone from the top of the fish down to its tail. You will need to hold the fish steady as you do this. The first fillet will come clean away as you cut, leaving the backbone still attached to the remaining fillet. Turn the fish over so that its backbone is lying on the board, and repeat the process. Pluck out the tiny pin bones with a pair of tweezers. To skin the fillets, place the first fillet flesh side up and slip your knife in at the tail end between the flesh and the skin. Keep the knife blade almost flat and hold the skin at the tail end as you slide the knife towards the head end of the fish, keeping it as close to the skin as you can. You will be left with a skinned fillet.

Rainbow trout are normally sold cleaned, either whole or as fillets. They usually weigh between 260g/9¼oz and 455g/1lb, although if left to their own devices they can, like their wily brown river cousins, grow very large. It is customary to leave the head attached, but diners have become so squeamish these days that you may feel happier decapitating your fish, rather than face the consequences.

Trout, like all fish, should be bought as fresh as possible. Check that its eyes and skin look bright, and that if its gills are still attached they are a healthy red. Avoid any dull, flabby fish, particularly if their eyes are sunken and bloodshot and their gills are tinged brown. Once home, transfer them from their packaging on to a clean plate, lightly cover and chill. They freeze well and can be bought frozen or fresh.

Smoked trout can be prepared in one of two ways – hot or cold smoked. Hot smoked trout is gutted, soaked in brine, and smoked whole, beginning at a cool 28°C/85°F and gradually increasing to about 80°C/175°F until the fish is cooked. The quality can vary enormously, but the best smoked trout are sold whole and suffer from none of the problems of ready-prepared fillets, such as slimy and tasteless flesh. Cold smoked trout looks and tastes very similar to smoked salmon, although it has a finer texture and lighter flavour. This is because it is cured in the same way by being split open and marinated in a salt cure before being smoked at a cool 28°C/85°F. It is normally sold ready-sliced. All forms of smoked trout should be kept refrigerated and eaten by the best-before date, as the smoking is too light to act as an indefinite preservative.

Taste notes

◊ Simple flavourings that enhance the delicate taste of trout work well, for example, butter, lemon, mace, nutmeg, cayenne and black pepper. Thyme, parsley, fennel and bay leaves all bring out its natural sweetness, as do Chambéry, cider and dry white or red wine.

◊ The contrasting sharpness of capers, anchovies or olives can also taste delicious combined with trout, although moderation is the key to success. These can be turned into gorgeous vinaigrettes or butters and served with grilled, fried or baked trout.

◊ A splash of pastis with some lemon juice makes an unusual but good flavouring for butter-fried trout.

◊ Fried trout can benefit from a textural contrast, for example, lightly dusted in oatmeal to achieve a crisp coating or accompanied with butter-fried blanched and split almonds or hazelnuts (see below, page 301).

◊ Cold trout, whether baked in paper or chargrilled, can be accompanied by mayonnaise, a piquant herb vinaigrette (which can include finely chopped walnuts) or a home-made horseradish sauce. The latter is also good eaten with smoked trout.

◊ Hot or cold smoked trout can be made into wonderful pastes or pâtés. Process the fillets with a little softened butter, lemon juice, cayenne pepper and seasoning, before finishing with some double cream. Alternatively flavour with home-made horseradish cream.

Cold smoked trout with potato cakes

Cold smoked trout is a delicious alternative to smoked salmon and should be treated in exactly the same way. These soft potato scones originated in Scotland and Ireland, but have recently been enjoying a revival in smart restaurants, usually accompanied by sour cream or crème fraîche and smoked fish or caviar. (Serves 4)

455g/1lb potatoes	½ lemon, juiced, added to
salt	taste
140g/5oz plain flour	freshly ground black pepper
40g/1½oz butter	285ml/½ pint sour cream
225g/8oz sliced cold smoked	4 tablespoons chives, roughly
trout	sliced

Preheat the oven to low, slipping in a baking sheet as you do so. Peel the potatoes and cut into large pieces. Place in a pan of cold salted water and bring to the boil. Continue to boil for 20–30 minutes or until the potatoes are tender. Drain and cover with a clean tea towel. Leave to steam dry for 5 minutes before returning to a clean bowl and mashing vigorously until smooth and fluffy. Sift the flour with a pinch of salt then gradually beat into the potatoes. They will form a malleable dough.

Preheat a lightly buttered non-stick frying pan or a well-seasoned griddle over a medium low heat. Tip the dough on to a well-floured surface and roll out to just under 5mm/¼ inch thickness. Stamp into scone-sized rounds and, using a palette knife, place in the frying pan or on the griddle. Cook for 4 minutes, then flip over and continue to cook for a further 3–4 minutes. Remove, butter and keep warm in the oven while you rework the potato dough. Continue cutting and cooking until the dough is finished. You should have about 12 cakes.

As soon as you have finished, divide the buttered potato cakes between 4 appetizer plates. Add the smoked trout and arrange attractively before seasoning with lemon juice and freshly ground black pepper. Finally top with a generous blob of sour cream and scatter with the chives. Serve immediately so that the potato cakes are still warm.

Fennel seed cured trout

The fashion for potting and pickling fish became widespread in the seventeenth century. Trout tastes surprisingly good lightly cured with sugar and salt like gravad lax. All manner of herbs and spices can be used, but I particularly like the delicate flavour of fennel seeds. Serve with finely sliced and buttered brown bread and lemon wedges. (Serves 6)

8 unskinned trout fillets	freshly ground black pepper
½ tablespoon fennel seeds	2 tablespoons brandy
1 lemon, finely grated	
2 tablespoons coarse sea salt	*Garnish*
2 tablespoons granulated	1½ lemons, cut into wedges
sugar	

Trim the fillets and, using a pair of tweezers, pull out any fine bones. Lightly run your fingers down the middle of each fillet to locate any that might be hiding.

Finely crush the fennel seeds, either in a pestle and mortar or under a rolling pin. Mix them together with the lemon zest, salt and sugar and season to taste with the pepper.

Place 4 fillets skin side down on a large sheet of clingfilm. Rub the flesh with half the brandy, then liberally cover with the spiced salt mixture. Rub the flesh of the remaining fillets with the rest of the brandy and sandwich flesh side down on to the spiced fish. Tightly wrap in the clingfilm and place in a shallow dish or baking tray. Cover with a weighted board, so that all 4 fish are evenly pressed. Refrigerate for 24 hours, turning them over after the first 12 hours.

Shortly before serving, unwrap the trout and slice as you would for smoked salmon, working your way up from the tail to the head.

Pan-fried trout

There is little debate that the best way to eat a trout is fried in lots of butter. However, as the trout benefits from slow frying, clarify the butter before cooking to prevent it from burning. (Serves 2)

55g/2oz butter
2 plump cleaned trout
salt and freshly ground black
    pepper
3 tablespoons plain flour

½ lemon, juiced
2 tablespoons finely chopped
    parsley
2 lemon wedges

Melt the butter in a small saucepan and allow to simmer very gently for 5 minutes, so that it throws up a pale froth. Line a fine sieve with a clean damp piece of muslin or a J-cloth and set over a small bowl. Slowly and carefully pour the butter through, leaving as much of the milky dregs in the saucepan as possible. These can then be discarded.

Lightly dust the trout with seasoned flour. Pour the butter into a large frying pan and place over a medium heat. As soon as it is hot, add the floured trout and fry gently but steadily for 5 minutes, then using a palette knife and spatula gently turn over each trout and continue to fry for a further 5 minutes. Their skin should be crisp and golden, the flesh moist and succulent.

Remove the fish to warm plates and add the lemon juice and parsley to the buttery juices. Let them bubble up, then pour over the fish and serve immediately with lemon wedges.

Note: There used to be a craze for garnishing such dishes with blanched split almonds or hazelnuts. If you enjoy the contrast between nut and trout, add the nuts to the buttery pan juices after the trout has been removed and fry gently until they turn golden brown. Continue as above by adding the lemon juice.

Trout in red wine

Here is a modern interpretation of a form of recipe that can be traced back to medieval cooking. Stewed trout was to remain popular well into the nineteenth century – Eliza Acton, for one, gives a couple of flavoursome recipes for trout cooked in veal stock, wine and herbs. (Serves 2)

3 tablespoons olive oil	2 sprigs parsley
1 fat shallot, finely diced	115ml/¼ pint Pinot Noir or
1 clove garlic, crushed	other red wine
salt and freshly ground black	6 black olives, stoned and
pepper	diced
2 tablespoons plain flour	15g/½ oz butter
2 plump trout, cleaned	2 tablespoons finely chopped
1 strip lemon peel	parsley
1 sprig thyme	

Heat the olive oil in a sauté pan over a moderate heat. Add the shallot and garlic and gently fry until soft. Season the flour and lightly dust the trout. Increase the heat slightly and add the fish to the softened shallot. Fry for a minute on each side until lightly coloured.

Meanwhile, tie the lemon zest together with the thyme and parsley sprigs. As soon as the fish is ready add the wine, faggot of herbs and olives. Bring to the boil then reduce the heat to a simmer and cover the pan. Cook for a further 10–12 minutes, then carefully remove the trout and keep warm while you finish the sauce. Remove the bundle of herbs. Whisk in the butter, followed by the chopped parsley, and adjust the seasoning to taste. Pour over the fish and serve immediately.

See also
Potted trout (page 185)

VENISON

And still at his sport spurred the castellan,
Hunting the barren hinds in holt and on heath.
So many had he slain, by the setting of the sun,
Of does and other deer, that it was downright wonderful.
Then at the finish the folk flocked in eagerly,
And quickly collected the killed deer in a heap.
Those highest in rank came up with hosts of attendants,
And, according to custom, had them cut open with finesse.

   Sir Gawain and the Green Knight (late fourteenth century)

The sight of deer, standing still in the early morning mist or jumping through the dappled light in the woods, brings to life the ancient legends of hunter and hunted, wooer and heart slain. Venison was the food of kings, restricted to those with aristocratic hunting privileges and only bestowed on others as a token of love, friendship or allegiance. A far cry from today, when tender cuts of venison grace the supermarket meat counters for all and sundry to buy. Yet 600 years of restricted availability have inevitably left their mark, making many irrationally shy of cooking such a meat, despite its excellence. Such reticence will no doubt gradually disappear as people become increasingly familiar with farmed venison.

The fear of toughness and an overpoweringly high flavour originated from a time when only wild venison was available and the cook had few ways of gauging the age of the beast or how well it had been hung. The resulting meat could be very tough and extremely high. Such niceties appear not to have bothered our ancestors, as Hannah Glasse rather graphically illustrates in her advice on how to make venison sweet when it stinks in *The Art of Cookery Made Plain and Easy* (1747):

If it stinks, or is musty, take some luke-warm water, and wash it clean; then take fresh milk and water luke-warm, and wash it again; then dry it in clean cloths very well, and rub it all over with beaten ginger, and hang it in an airy place. When you roast it, you need only wipe it with a clean cloth and paper it, as before-mention'd. Never do any thing else to venison, for all other things spoil your venison and take away the fine flavour, and this preserves it better than any thing you can do.

Modern farmed venison is far more to our taste, with its surprisingly mild, almost beef-like flavour and tender texture.

I have to admit that our manner of serving venison has always struck me as being peculiarly un-British. Perhaps the medieval penchant for high seasoning and sweet and sour sauces has survived because it was restricted to so few tables. Certainly the British aristocracy were deeply influenced by European culinary fashions and dined on food that was considered somewhat recherché by the rest of the country. Over the centuries venison has been enjoyed highly seasoned with ginger or cinnamon, cloves or rosemary, and partnered with piquant sauces, the most famous of which – *peverade* – was made with vinegar and pepper. Echoes of such combinations can still be found in modern recipes – peppered venison steaks, for example, or venison and spiced pear stew. Nevertheless, all such recipes are exceptionally good, and few can fail to enjoy a simple dish of roast venison or an elegant salad of smoked venison with fresh figs.

Practical guide

The majority of venison now sold is farmed. The British Deer Farmers Association has a quality assurance scheme called British Prime Venison, and any meat sold under this scheme is guaranteed to come from a deer that has been fed on natural foodstuffs with no growth promoters and is under 27 months old. It will have been shot without any stress before being hung and butchered in approved premises. In other words the meat will be tender due to its peaceful life, youth, death and hanging. Any one of these elements can cause wild deer to be tough, although careful hanging, marinating and larding can usually rectify such problems.

Three species of deer are eaten in Britain: red, fallow and roe. Red deer are the largest, while roe deer are about a quarter of their size. Fallow deer come half-way between the two. It is difficult to distinguish the different species by taste, but the smaller the deer the finer the texture of its meat.

All venison should be hung head down for 2–3 weeks after it has been eviscerated. It can then be butchered and used in the following manner: the shoulder is normally boned and diced for stewing and pies, or minced, along with any other scraps of meat, for sausages and pâtés. The saddle makes a good roast, as does the loin, which can also be sold as chops but is usually sold boned either whole or cut into medallions – these are sometimes sold as 'mini haunches'. The haunch (leg) is perfect for roasting, on or off the bone. Most prime cuts are sold ready barded in pretty white jackets of fat by the butcher or game dealer. Steaks are usually cut from the top of the leg. These days you can also buy ready-made venison sausages, venison burgers and even venison haggis.

Many of our culinary attitudes are based on having to cope with aged, tough game, so it is important to distinguish between cooking farmed and wild venison. The latter benefits from marinating and/or careful larding, since it is a lean dry meat and needs slow gentle cooking. The former can also be marinated or larded but more for the purpose of adding a greater depth of flavour to a dish.

If you are presented with some wild venison you should marinate it for between 6 and 12 hours, although large joints can be left (chilled) for up to 36 hours if wished. If the joint has already been larded, it will take less time to absorb the marinade. To do this, chill some thin strips of fat salt pork, then thread them on to a larding needle and pull through the meat. Try slowly roasting it by wrapping in buttered paper covered in huff paste. This is made by rubbing 140g/5oz of lard into 1.1kg/2½lb of plain flour with 30g/1oz of salt. 565ml/1 pint of cold water is then mixed in and the pastry should be rolled out to 5mm/¼ inch thickness. The paste and paper are then discarded before serving. Any excess meat can then be used in delicious little venison pies or pasties.

The increase in small independent smoking houses has led to a return of the old tradition of curing and smoking venison 'hams'. These are usually sold ready sliced in vacuum packs and have a piquant smoky flavour that will appeal to anyone who enjoys cured meats. They should be treated in the same way as Parma ham and served as a simple appetizer, in a plate of mixed meats or in a crusty sandwich.

Taste notes

◊ Traditionally roast venison is accompanied by a clear bright gravy, unthickened and made from the roasting juices, a little red wine or port and some melted jelly. Rowan jelly, redcurrant jelly or even red gooseberry jelly can also be served, along with fine chips and French beans. Dorothy Hartley recommends accompanying venison steaks or chops with a similar set of tracklements, adding only grilled mushrooms in place of the beans.

◊ Venison marinades often contain a dash of vinegar along with the wine and olive oil to help tenderize the meat. Then it is a matter of choosing compatible seasonings: orange and lemon zest, or juniper berries, cloves, black pepper, mace, allspice and dried ginger.

◊ Sweet spiced pickled melon was a popular accompaniment to venison dishes in the nineteenth century, just as pear has become fashionable in the twentieth century.

◊ Many older cookery books use hartshorn (harts' horn) to set jellies and revive a fainting fit. It was made from shredded antlers and was the main source of ammonia.

Smoked venison with fresh figs

An elegant and easy starter. Wild smoked Scottish venison is currently available from some supermarkets and delicatessens. (Serves 6)

½ tablespoon lemon juice
1½ tablespoons extra virgin
   olive oil
salt and freshly ground black
   pepper

6 ripe figs, trimmed and
   quartered
18 thin slices smoked venison
100g/3½oz ready-washed
   rocket

Whisk together the lemon juice and olive oil. Season to taste.

Arrange the figs between 6 appetizer plates. Weave the slices of smoked venison around them, then lightly dress the rocket with the lemon vinaigrette and add an airy pile to each plate. Serve immediately.

Venison pâté

An old-fashioned richly flavoured terrine perfect for a summer picnic. (Serves 8)

680g/1½lb minced venison
455g/1lb minced pork belly
115g/4oz unsmoked streaky
   bacon, finely diced
115ml/¼ pint Calvados
4 crushed juniper berries
freshly ground black pepper
freshly grated nutmeg
2 cloves garlic, crushed

a generous pinch fresh thyme
   leaves
3 tablespoons finely chopped
   parsley
1 lemon, finely grated
3 bay leaves
18 slices rindless, smoked
   streaky bacon, finely sliced
1 teaspoon salt

Place the minced venison and pork belly with the diced streaky bacon, Calvados, juniper berries, pepper, nutmeg, garlic, thyme, parsley and lemon zest in a large china bowl. Thoroughly mix together, then cover and chill for 24 hours.

Preheat the oven to 170°C/325°F/gas 3. Set 3 bay leaves along the centre of the bottom of a loaf tin. Take the bacon slices and stretch each one with the back of your knife before neatly lining the tin so that the end of each bacon slice flops over the rim of the tin. Set aside while you finish the pâté.

Beat the salt into the mixture and fry a small patty. Adjust the seasoning to taste, then carefully pack into the loaf tin, making sure that there are no air pockets. Fold over the bacon slices to seal in the mixture, then cover with foil, tucking it in around the top of the tin. Place in a roasting tray and fill this with boiling water. Place in the centre of the oven and bake for 1½ hours.

Test to see if it is done by inserting a thin skewer; if the juices run clear, the terrine is cooked. Remove from the oven and place the loaf tin on a clean plate or tray. Loosen the foil and cover with a weighted plate. Leave to cool. Once it is tepid and well pressed, remove from the loaf tin, wrap in foil and chill overnight. It is at its best eaten 2 days after cooking.

Serve sliced with crusty bread, unsalted butter and pickle as an informal lunch or with hot toast and tiny gherkins as a smart first course.

Peppered venison steak

The pepper brings out the natural sweetness of the venison in the most gorgeous way. Most supermarkets sell various cuts of venison steak, but the vacuum-packed packets of 'mini haunches' are particularly good as they can be treated like fillet steak. (Serves 6)

1½ tablespoons whole black peppercorns	200ml/7fl oz game or chicken stock (see page 339 or buy ready-made)
40g/1½oz plain flour	
salt	140ml/¼ pint red wine
3 tablespoons olive oil	2 tablespoons port
6 trimmed venison steaks, each about 170g/6oz	2 strips lemon peel, finely pared
2 tablespoons brandy	1 tablespoon redcurrant jelly
1 clove garlic, crushed	55g/2oz butter, diced

Preheat the oven to its lowest setting. Roughly crush the peppercorns and mix with the flour and a large pinch of salt.

Heat the oil in a non-stick frying pan over a medium heat. Lightly coat the venison steaks with the peppercorn mixture and fry briskly, colouring both sides. Cook for a total of 5 minutes for medium rare steaks, then pour over the brandy and set alight, standing well back. Once the alcohol has burnt off, transfer the steaks to the warm oven.

Add the garlic, fry for a minute, then stir in the game or chicken stock, red wine, port and lemon peel. Boil vigorously, scraping the pan as you do so, until the sauce has reduced slightly and is well flavoured. Stir in the redcurrant jelly and adjust the seasoning to taste. Remove from the heat and whisk in the butter, before returning the steaks to the sauce. Serve immediately.

Venison and spiced pear stew

Do not be discouraged by the long list of ingredients for this recipe – it is extremely easy to make and each stage can be prepared well in advance. The pears can be made several weeks ahead if wished. It makes a gorgeous, richly flavoured winter stew that is perfect eaten with butter-soaked jacket potatoes. (Serves 6)

3lb (1.5kg) venison haunch, trimmed of fat and cut into large dice

Marinade
1 bottle red wine
1 tablespoon wine vinegar
2 medium carrots, peeled and roughly sliced
1 large onion, roughly sliced
3 cloves garlic, roughly crushed
2 sticks celery, roughly sliced
6 black peppercorns
4 allspice berries
1 bay leaf
2 sprigs rosemary
2 sprigs parsley

Spiced pears
225g/8oz granulated sugar
285ml/½ pint white wine vinegar

3 allspice berries
2.5cm/1 inch cinnamon stick
4 peppercorns
2 dried red chillies
3 strips lemon peel, finely pared
6 small hard pears

Stew
6 tablespoons olive oil
225g/8oz shallots
2 cloves garlic, crushed
4 sticks celery, finely sliced
2 tablespoons flour
salt and freshly ground black pepper
3 strips lemon peel, finely pared
3–4 tablespoons redcurrant jelly
3 tablespoons finely chopped parsley

Mix the diced venison with all the marinade ingredients in a large china bowl, cover, and chill for a minimum of 8 hours.

Place the sugar, vinegar, spices, chillies and lemon peel in a small non-corrosive pan and dissolve the sugar over a low heat. Bring up to the boil then simmer for 10 minutes.

Peel, quarter and core the pears. Drop into the hot vinegar syrup. Simmer gently for 20 minutes until the pears are tender, then transfer to a clean covered container and chill once cool.

Drain the venison in a colander, saving both the marinade juices and the vegetables. You will have to carefully sort through the meat and remove all the vegetables or spices. Set these to drip dry in a sieve. Set aside the marinade juices.

Heat 2 tablespoons of oil in a frying pan and gently fry the whole shallots, garlic and celery until soft. Transfer to a clean saucepan. Add some more olive oil to the frying pan and increase the heat. Pat the venison dry, then fry in batches so that the meat colours quickly and evenly. Transfer it to the other pan as you go.

Finally add the drained marinade vegetables and spices to the frying pan and fry over a moderate heat until soft. Stir in the flour and continue to cook for a further 3 minutes before slowly stirring in the marinade liquid with 285ml/½ pint of water. Bring to the boil and cook vigorously until it has reduced by half and thickened slightly. Strain over the meat, adjust the seasoning to taste, then add the lemon peel and cover. Simmer gently for about an hour, adding more water if necessary. Once the meat is tender, stir in the redcurrant jelly to taste.

When you are ready to serve, reheat the pears in their syrup. Add the parsley to the stew and accompany with the pears, which should be removed from their syrup.

Roast venison

Ask the butcher to bone and dress the saddle for you, but save all bones and trimmings as these can be made into a delicious stock if you adapt the recipe for lamb stock on page 146. The butcher should then either lard the meat lengthways or wrap it in thin sheets of salt pork.
(Serves 4–6)

Marinade
140ml/¼ pint olive oil
3 strips lemon peel
1 lemon, juiced
6 sprigs thyme
6 crushed juniper berries
4 crushed black peppercorns

Roast
½ saddle venison,
   1.1kg–1.4kg/2½–3lb
   dressed weight

salt
3 tablespoons olive oil

Gravy
285ml/½ pint red wine
285ml/½ pint well-flavoured
   game stock (adapt lamb
   stock on page 146)
30g/1oz diced cold butter

Mix together the olive oil, lemon peel and juice, thyme, juniper berries and peppercorns in a large bowl. Add the venison and rub the mixture all over it, then cover and chill overnight.

Preheat the oven to 220°C/425°F/gas 8. Remove the venison from its marinade and pat dry with kitchen paper. Season it with salt and place in the roasting tray with the olive oil. Roast for 15 minutes, then reduce the temperature to 180°C/350°F/gas 4 and continue to cook for a further 45–50 minutes, basting regularly until the meat is cooked to your liking.

Transfer the venison to a clean plate and leave to rest in a warm place. Pour off any excess fat from the roasting tray, then set it on a moderate heat. Add the wine and vigorously scrape the bottom of the tray to remove any crusty sediments. Let the wine boil vigorously until it has reduced by two-thirds then add the stock and continue to simmer for a further 5 minutes. Whisk in the butter and strain before serving piping hot with the venison and some apple and rowanberry or redcurrant jelly.

WALNUTS

Harriet was very ready to speak of the share he (Mr Martin) had had in their moonlight walks and merry evening games; and dwelt a good deal upon his being so very good-humoured and obliging. 'He had gone three miles round one day, in order to bring her some walnuts, because she had said how fond she was of them and in every thing else he was so very obliging!'

Emma by Jane Austen (1816)

There are certain aspects of British gastronomy that are seldom written about, yet are nevertheless an essential part of our culinary culture. Take the walnut, for example, Britain's favourite whole nut; it barely gets a mention in most British cookery books, yet few could imagine Christmas without a bowl of walnuts. At the very least, they have to be stuffed into Christmas stockings along with the tangerines and toys. The custom of eating nuts at the end of a meal appears to stretch back to medieval times, when walnuts were eaten with hazelnuts and cobnuts to close the stomach. It has continued right up to the present day, much in the manner Tennyson describes, of 'after-dinner talk across the walnuts and wine'. There is something very relaxing about passing around a bowl of nuts with the nutcracker.

It is commonly believed that walnut trees were introduced into Britain from France during the fifteenth and sixteenth centuries. However, F. A. Roach, in his fascinating book *Cultivated Fruits of Britain*, suggests that they were already well established here in the late thirteenth century. Whatever the truth, the British have always imported large quantities of walnuts from abroad, saving much of their native (green) crop for pickling and catsup (ketchup). As Eliza Acton observed in *Modern Cookery for Private Families* in 1855, 'these highly-flavoured compounds are still much in favour with a certain class of housekeepers; but they belong exclusively to *English* cookery: they are altogether opposed to the practice of the French *cuisine*, as well as to that of other foreign countries.' No doubt such a peculiar habit was gained from necessity, as walnuts have a hard time ripening in northerly Britain. Green walnuts were usually plentiful, and pickles and catsup prevented excessive wastage of so valuable a crop.

Today, walnuts quietly slip into a wide variety of cakes, teabreads, ice creams and salads. There are few who do not appreciate their delicate flavour, and most would regard them as being more British than our native hazelnuts.

Practical guide

Traditionally, we have always picked walnuts in two stages, thinning out the crop while it is still green and tender in July and finally harvesting the ripe nuts in September or October. Green walnuts are ready when they can be easily pierced with a pin and there is no sign of a shell forming. Slice one open to check.

When walnuts are fully ripe they will fall from the tree. This normally breaks their thick green husk, revealing the now hard inner shell which will have ripened from white to brown. These are 'wet' walnuts and are extremely good eaten fresh. However, they will not keep in this state, so the remainder must be spread out and dried properly to prevent damp and mould permeating the shells and rotting the kernels. You will have to sacrifice a dry, airy room if you are lucky enough to have harvested home-grown walnuts.

Sadly, the majority of walnuts sold in this country are imported. These will all have been dried in special kilns to ensure that they do not rot. If you are buying walnuts loose, try shaking the shells – if the nut rattles it should be discarded, as the kernel will be dry and shrivelled inside. It is also worth remembering to buy walnuts in small quantities and store them in a cool place as their high oil content can quickly turn them rancid. Incidentally, the invention of the ratchet nut cracker has made shelling nuts a pleasure.

The majority of walnuts used for cooking come in neat little plastic bags, carefully cleaned and cut to specification. Although they do not have the same milky flavour as a fresh whole walnut, they are perfectly good for most recipes. However, if during the nut season you are serving walnuts in a salad or in any dish where you feel that they are on show, it is worth taking the trouble to shell fresh nuts. All ready prepared walnuts must be kept in a cool dark place to stay sweet and fresh. Discard if they have passed the best-before date.

Walnut oil has become a popular salad oil in the last few years – a strange thought for a British seventeenth-century cook, who would have considered it suitable only for mixing with delicate coloured paints. It has a relatively short shelf life, so should always be stored in a cool, dark place. Once the bottle has been opened, keep it in the fridge to prevent it turning rancid and remember to taste before using, just in case.

Taste notes

◊ Pickled walnuts are made from green walnuts that are soaked in brine for just under 2 weeks. The solution is changed every 4 days. The walnuts are then spread out on trays for about 12 hours or until they turn black. Finally they are placed in sterilized jars and covered with a hot spiced vinegar. Once cold, they are sealed and left to mature for a few months. They can then be added to richly flavoured beef stews or eaten with bread and cheese. Luckily you can also buy this curious British pickle in supermarkets.

◊ Walnut ketchup (catsup) is also made with green walnuts. These are roughly crushed or pounded before being placed in a large, non-corrosive bowl with salt, crushed garlic, shallots and vinegar. This is stirred every day for 10 days, before being strained into a saucepan. Salted anchovies and various spices are added and the mixture is simmered for 30 minutes. The result is bottled and left to mature. For the recipe turn to *The Constance Spry Cookery Book*. It is used both as a flavouring and as an accompanying table sauce.

◊ Shelled walnuts make a superb addition to a wide variety of moist tea-breads, iced layer cakes, ice-creams, toffees and fudges, as well as meringues, steamed puddings and biscuits.

◊ Some recipes recommend lightly roasting the walnut kernels for added flavour, although I find that this gives them a slightly bitter taste. If, however, you peel the kernels by covering them with boiling water, you will find all trace of bitterness removed. This is an extremely fiddly task which in my opinion is worth the effort only in extreme circumstances. Only soak a few at a time as they need to be warm to peel easily.

◊ Walnuts make interesting sauces, in particular horseradish and walnut or parsley and walnut pesto. Both are good eaten with salmon or grilled beef.

◊ Roughly chopped walnuts can be added to savoury stuffings, for example with breadcrumbs, lemon zest, parsley, butter, fried garlic and onions. Such stuffings can be used with roast pheasant, guinea fowl or chicken.

◊ Walnut oil makes a superb vinaigrette, particularly if combined with equal quantities of hazelnut and olive oil. It has a natural affinity with bitter winter endives, warm mushroom salads and wild rice salads.

Green bean and walnut salad

This simple dish makes a deliciously piquant accompaniment. Use fresh whole walnuts when available. (Serves 4)

Vinaigrette	Salad
2 tablespoons white wine vinegar	455g/1lb fine green beans
1 clove garlic, crushed	1 curly endive, trimmed and washed
3 tablespoons walnut oil	55g/2oz walnut halves, roughly broken
3 tablespoons hazelnut oil	
salt and freshly ground black pepper	

Whisk together the vinegar, garlic and 2 nut oils. Season to taste and set aside.

Top and tail the beans and if they are quite long cut into easy-to-eat lengths. Bring a large pan of water to the boil. Add a pinch of salt and the beans and cook briskly for about 5 minutes or until the beans are soft and tender as opposed to squeakily crunchy. The time will vary according to the thickness and variety of the bean. Drain immediately and leave to drip dry in a colander for a few minutes before tossing them warm in the vinaigrette. Place the endive leaves and walnut pieces in a large mixing bowl and add the cold dressed beans. Mix thoroughly and serve.

Walnut herb cream cheese with melba toast

Walnuts make a lovely addition to cream cheese. This elegant starter is served with melba toast, but you can always use it as a glorious sandwich filling. Use fresh whole walnuts when available. (Serves 4)

Walnut herb cheese
2 tablespoons finely chopped
    parsley
4 tablespoons finely chopped
    chives
½ tablespoon finely chopped
    tarragon
340g/12oz mascarpone cheese
8 tablespoons chopped
    walnuts
salt and freshly ground black
    pepper

Melba toast
10 medium thick slices of
    white bread

Salad
1 tablespoon champagne or
    white wine vinegar
3 tablespoons walnut oil
115g/4oz ready prepared
    mixed lettuces and herbs

Beat the herbs into the cheese with a wooden spoon. Stir in the chopped walnuts and season to taste. Chill until you are ready to serve.

Preheat the grill. Remove the crusts from the sliced bread. Lightly toast the bread on either side. Remove, cool and carefully cut through each slice so that you have 20 very thin slices of bread. Place these cut side up under the grill and toast until they begin to curl. Remove and set aside.

Whisk together the vinegar with the walnut oil. Season to taste.

When you are ready to serve, mould the cheese into 12 small lozenges by scooping it into a dessertspoon and shaping it with a second dessertspoon. Carefully drop each lozenge on to the serving plate and repeat until you have 3 on each plate.

Garnish each plate by lightly dressing the lettuce and herb leaves with the vinaigrette and arranging to one side of the cheese. Serve with the melba toast.

Walnut coffee cake

Layer cakes became popular at the turn of this century, imported from America, along with walnuts. There are countless variations, some with coffee icing, others with butter icing. This one is reminiscent of my childhood memories of the delicious Fuller's walnut cake, although I suspect that that had a plain butter cream filling.

85g/3oz walnut kernels + 8 good walnut halves (for decoration)
170g/6oz butter, softened
170g/6oz caster sugar
3 medium eggs
170g/6oz self-raising flour, sifted

Filling
2 teaspoons instant coffee
1 teaspoon hot water
85g/3oz butter, softened
55g/2oz icing sugar

Icing
a few drops of vanilla extract
2 tablespoons warm water
225g/8oz icing sugar

Preheat the oven to 170°C/325°F/gas 3, and lightly oil and flour an 18cm/7 inch cake tin.

Roughly chop the walnuts by hand, saving all their crumbs. They should be smaller than the ready-chopped walnuts. Beat the butter and sugar until pale and fluffy, then gradually beat in the first 2 eggs. Fold in a tablespoon of flour, then beat in the last egg. Tip in the flour and walnuts and lightly fold into the butter mixture. Spoon evenly into the cake tin and bake for 50 minutes. A cake is ready when it feels firm and springy to the touch. If you insert a skewer it should come out clean. Remove the cake and when it is cool enough to handle turn it out on to a cooling rack.

Meanwhile, dissolve the instant coffee with the hot water. Stir until there are no tiny granules. Beat together the softened butter, icing sugar and coffee and adjust the flavourings to taste. Set aside until needed.

Once the cake is completely cold, slice it in half. Neatly spread the coffee butter icing over one half and sandwich the halves together. Set the cake on an upturned plate ready for icing.

Beat the vanilla extract and water into the icing sugar until you have a thick paste, then, using a wet knife, carefully coat the entire cake, starting with the top and working down around the sides. Press the walnut halves around the rim and leave to set.

Honey walnut ice cream

The current fashion for serving simple ice creams, rippled with nuts, is perfectly illustrated by the following recipe. (Serves 4)

565ml/1 pint whipping cream	4 tablespoons whisky
6 large egg yolks	85g/3oz walnut kernels,
6 tablespoons honey, such as	roughly chopped
lime blossom	

Scald the cream and beat the egg yolks until they are pale. Slowly pour the hot cream in a thin stream on to the egg yolks, beating all the time. Pour the custard back into a heavy-bottomed saucepan and return to a low heat. Stir continuously with a wooden spoon until the custard thickens enough to leave a slight trail. You must not stop stirring or leave the custard unattended during this stage, as it can easily curdle. Immediately pour through a strainer into a clean bowl and, as you continue to stir, add the honey, followed by the whisky. Once the mixture is tepid, you can cover and chill.

Churn the honey custard according to your ice cream machine instructions until it reaches a soft set. Otherwise pour it into a shallow plastic container, cover and place in the fast-freeze compartment of your freezer. Every 30–40 minutes, mash up the ice crystals with a fork until the mixture has set into a smooth, soft set ice cream.

Roughly chop the walnut kernels and gently fold them into the ice cream. Cover and return to the freezer to firm up before serving. If serving the following day, allow the ice cream to soften by placing it in the fridge 20 minutes before serving.

Walnut bread

Walnuts taste delicious added to breads, scones and biscuits. Here is a classic bread recipe. (Makes two 455g/1lb loaves)

340g/12oz strong plain flour
340g/12oz wholemeal flour
2 teaspoons salt
1 sachet (6 or 7g/¼oz) easy-
    blend dried yeast
2 tablespoons walnut oil, plus
    extra for oiling
425ml/¾ pint tepid water
90g/3½oz walnut halves,
    roughly broken

Mix together the 2 flours, salt and dried yeast in a large bowl. Stir in the walnut oil and water and thoroughly mix until it forms a pliable dough. Turn this out and knead for 5 minutes or until it feels like satin. It should spring back if touched.

Spread out the dough and cover with some of the walnuts. Press these in and fold over the dough. Repeat until all the walnuts are incorporated, then gently knead the mixture to distribute them evenly. Place the dough in a large mixing bowl and lightly oil with some extra walnut oil. Cover and leave to rise in a warm place for an hour or until it has doubled its size.

Lightly oil 2 bread tins (if using) or a heavy baking sheet. Cut the dough in half. Either knead into a suitable shape for the bread tins or shape into 2 round loaves and place on the baking sheet. Brush with walnut oil and loosely cover with clingfilm. Leave for 1–1½ hours or until the dough is well risen.

Preheat the oven to 230°C/450°F/gas 8.

Once the dough is risen, remove the clingfilm and bake in the centre of the preheated oven for 25–30 minutes. The bread will turn light brown and rise a little more. Tap the base of the loaves as you turn them out – if they sound hollow the bread is cooked; if not, quickly return them to the oven for a further 5 minutes. Cool on a rack.

Note: Bread is very amenable – if your kitchen is cold, just allow it more time to rise. It can even be kneaded in the morning and left to rise slowly in the fridge for the day. Then continue as normal.

See also
Roast pears with Stilton and watercress (page 332)

WATERCRESS

Water-cress pottage is a good remedy to cleanse the blood in the spring, and helps head-aches, and consumes the gross humours winter hath left behind: those that would live in health may use it if they please, if they will not, I cannot help it. If any fancy not pottage, they may eat the herb as a salad.

Culpeper's Complete Herbal

The pretty leaves of watercress have cheered many a British table through the dark winter months when other salads were hard to come by. They have peeped out of rustic sandwiches, formed a decorative ruffle for roast pheasant and elegantly lightened countless salads. Yet many British cooks have almost forgotten the sheer delight of serving watercress in its own right. How many careless hands have quickly garnished a dish of grilled meat with watercress without so much as a thought for eating it? Who values it as highly as rocket in salads or considers its intrinsic value in complex sandwiches? Admittedly, watercress soup is still as popular as ever, but few modern cooks would dream of serving its refreshing leaves with a cooked breakfast. Surely it is time to rediscover this peculiarly British plant, with its contradictory hot yet cool-tasting succulent leaves?

The custom of garnishing certain game birds with watercress dates back to the eighteenth century, when pheasants were served on a bed of watercress. The distinctive flavour of the watercress perfectly complements the almost smoky flavour of many game birds, bringing out their inherent sweetness in a delicious manner. Some recipes dress the cress in a mustard vinaigrette, but I do not think this is necessary, as the bird's natural gravy wilts and seasons the watercress in an irresistible manner, especially when eaten with game chips.

The abundance of watercress through the winter months has inevitably ensured that it was eaten as a salad for centuries. Robert May in *The Accomplisht Cook* (1685), for example, combines watercress with sliced boiled parsnips, lettuce and alexander buds or with sliced oranges, lemons, alexander buds, raisins and pears, before dressing them with oil and vinegar. Once widely grown in kitchen gardens, alexanders now tend to grow wild in the south of England. Today, with its year-round availability, watercress can be eaten with all manner of foods from seared tuna fish to roasted pears. It should be chosen because its vibrant flavour will enhance the overall salad in a manner that lettuce alone cannot do.

The sandwich, as is well known, was invented in the eighteenth century by the Earl of Sandwich, who, fearing any interruption to his gambling, satiated his appetite by stuffing some beef between two slices of bread. Since then certain sandwiches have been labelled as being typically British, the most famous of which is cucumber. However, cress sandwiches come a close second (see below), despite the fact that they are rarely served these days, most people preferring to add all sorts of delicacies to them, such as prawn mayonnaise, avocado and bacon or curried egg mayonnaise.

Practical guide

Rorippa nasturtium aquaticum is the glorious Latin name of watercress. Its verdant leaves can be found growing wild in countless lowland streams, ditches and waterways. Only the Scottish Highlands and central Wales are deprived of this lush water plant. However, you would be ill advised to pick any from the wild, as unfortunately it is host to the rather nasty liver fluke larvae, which can be passed from cattle or sheep via the watercress to humans. Consequently, cookery books will always instruct copious washing of watercress. If for any insane reason you feel compelled to eat wild water-cress then you must boil it, as this will kill the fluke larvae.

Fortunately, watercress farms have thrived in Britain since the beginning of the nineteenth century. Rich in vitamin C and iron, it was, among other things, a popular remedy against scurvy. Man-made watercress beds are fed by clean spring water, uncontaminated by flukes or pollution, and the resulting watercress is truly delicious. Traditionally, watercress was con-sidered at its best from the autumn until early summer, although theoretically it can be harvested throughout the year, provided there is no frost. In reality, some watercress farmers have invested in Spanish watercress beds so that they can reliably supply the supermarkets during the coldest months of the year. Watercress rather sensibly retreats under water when frost sets in.

Watercress is usually sold either by the bunch or ready prepared (in other words washed and trimmed) in pillow packets. In either case make sure that the leaves are not wilting or yellow. Bronzed or sunburnt leaves indicate a finer, stronger flavour, as they come from a slightly older growth. Sometimes watercress is sold while flowering; although the tiny white flowers make an attractive addition to salads, it does indicate that the plant is in the process of bolting and consequently may taste somewhat bitter.

Ready-prepared packets can be stored unopened in the salad drawer of the fridge for a couple of days. Once opened, they must be used within a day as they quickly wilt. Bunches of watercress are initially sold to the greengrocer packed with chipped ice in specially designed waxed cardboard boxes. It is well worth buying one of these boxes if you need a large quantity of cress.

Store the box in the fridge, making sure it has a drip tray for the slowly melting ice. It will last for several days. Individual bunches are more temperamental. I have not yet read two cookery writers who agree on how to keep them. To summarize such contrary advice, you can place them stem down, head down or completely immersed in water, in or out of the fridge! Some maintain that they lose their texture in the fridge, others that they turn slimy out of the fridge. I usually store my watercress in the following manner: trim the stalks, then wrap in very wet kitchen paper and place in a plastic bag. Inflate this with air like a balloon and seal before storing in the fridge salad drawer.

Bunched watercress must be thoroughly washed before use. Submerge in plenty of cold water and gently swish to remove any tiny particles of dirt. Drain and repeat before drying. Use a salad spinner if possible, as the fleshy leaves bruise easily.

Taste notes

◊ To serve watercress as a vegetable, blanch and squeeze dry, then unscrumple and reheat gently in olive oil when ready to eat. In other words treat like spinach (see page 117). It can also be blanched and dried before being dressed cold as a salad or relish. Try tossing in a sesame oil, soy and garlic dressing or a sherry vinegar, olive oil and shallot vinaigrette.

◊ Watercress can be used as a herb in just the same way as parsley. It is very good mixed with finely chopped tarragon, parsley and chives, but can also take the stronger flavours of other seasonings such as paprika, cayenne pepper, finely chopped anchovies, capers or lemon zest.

◊ It works well in a wide variety of sauces from a simple stock-based cream sauce to mayonnaise. The former can accompany fish, chicken, veal or pork. The latter – green mayonnaise – is made by pouring boiling water over watercress, parsley and tarragon leaves. These are then cooled under cold water, dried and finely chopped before being added to the egg yolks. Continue as if making normal mayonnaise.

◊ Cress sandwiches are made by spreading good bread with the best butter you can buy. The clean dry watercress sprigs are then dusted with some fine sea salt and pressed in generous quantities into the buttered bread before being covered and cut into the required shapes. The crusts are not trimmed, as this spoils the flamboyant look of the watercress. They can be served with fresh shrimp sandwiches for tea or as an accompaniment to a good tomato soup.

◊ Watercress butter can also be used as a sandwich filling with, for example, lobster, or, if you wished to be recherché, as a canapé spread on to hot toast and topped with caviar. Season with a squeeze of lemon juice. Otherwise it can be served as savoury butter for grilled meat, in particular steak, veal and all manner of fish.

◊ There must be an infinite number of salad combinations using watercress. Some of the popular British accompaniments are pears, blue cheese and walnuts; oranges, red onion and black olives; prawn, avocado and lettuce; beetroot; or salsify. Its peppery flavour works well with a wide variety of fish, as well as with bacon, cold chicken and hard-boiled eggs. It is also good with many lettuces, radishes and certain endives.

◊ Any salad containing watercress should be dressed at the very last moment, as it quickly turns soggy. A wide variety of vinaigrettes can be used, as it can withstand robust flavouring. Try, for example, a good balsamic vinaigrette or a lemon and walnut oil dressing.

◊ Other good watercress combinations are watercress and crab or leek tarts, baked watercress eggs (oeufs en cocotte) and herb-filled omelettes. It makes an excellent accompaniment to cheese and biscuits. Choose the lighter-flavoured cheeses such as Wensleydale or a mild Cheddar.

Luxurious watercress soup

Watercress has been added to soups and broths since at least the seventeenth century, although how much this was for pleasurable as opposed to medicinal purposes is hard to ascertain, since early recipes are few and far between. However, there is no doubt that watercress has become an extremely popular twentieth-century British soup. The most puritanical of recipes are made with only potatoes, watercress and water, but I prefer a more sybaritic version made with leeks, potatoes and lashings of cream. It can be served hot or chilled. (Serves 4)

4 tablespoons olive oil
2 cloves garlic, crushed
2 large potatoes, peeled and diced
595g/1lb 5oz leeks
salt and freshly ground black pepper

170g/6oz ready prepared watercress
285ml/½ pint single cream

Garnish
6 watercress sprigs

Heat the oil in a large saucepan and gently fry the garlic for a few seconds before stirring in the diced potatoes. Make sure they are well coated with oil before cooking over a low heat for 5 minutes, stirring regularly until they begin to soften.

Meanwhile trim the leeks and remove their tough outer leaves. Discard the dark green tops and finely slice the white and pale green stems. Wash thoroughly in several changes of water and drain well. Add to the potatoes and continue to fry for a further 5 minutes or until soft.

Add 710ml/1¼ pints of hot water and season to taste. Bring to the boil, then simmer over a moderate heat for 25 minutes or until the vegetables are very soft. While the soup is cooking, wash the watercress and pick off all the leaves. Discard the stems (they are always impossible to liquidize), then add the leaves to the soft vegetables. Allow to cook for a further 2 minutes, then immediately liquidize and pour into a clean container. This will keep the soup a pretty fresh green.

If you are serving the soup cold you can add the cream at this stage; otherwise reheat when needed before adding the cream. Do not let the single cream come to the boil or it will split. Adjust the seasoning and serve. Garnish the individual bowls of soup with the watercress sprigs.

Seared tuna and watercress salad

The cool pepperiness of watercress makes it a useful addition to a wide variety of composite salads. Here is a typically modern British salad, combining influences from the East and the West. (Serves 4)

2 tablespoons rice vinegar
6 tablespoons extra virgin
   olive oil
1 clove garlic, finely diced
1 small fresh chilli, finely
   diced
½ small red onion, finely diced
2 tomatoes, peeled and finely
   diced
1 avocado, peeled and finely
   diced

1 tablespoon finely chopped
   coriander
salt and freshly ground black
   pepper
4 tuna steaks, each weighing
   about 140g/5oz
1 tablespoon vegetable oil
1 bunch watercress or a
   75g/3oz ready-prepared
   packet

Shortly before you are ready to serve, whisk together the vinegar and olive oil and mix in the finely diced garlic, chilli, onion, tomato, avocado and coriander. Season to taste.

Preheat a ribbed cast-iron oven-top grill pan or a non-stick frying pan until it is very hot. Brush the fish steaks with the oil and season on each side. Quickly sear each side until lightly coloured, but the centre is still rosy. The time this takes will depend on the thickness of your steaks, but remember that tuna, more than any other fish, continues to cook after it has been removed from the heat. As a rough guide, allow 2 minutes for each side.

Place the hot tuna in a large salad bowl and break into large chunks. Pour over a third of the avocado dressing. Mix it in and leave to marinate while you prepare the watercress.

Wash and sort through the watercress before drying. Transfer to a large mixing bowl and mix in the remaining avocado dressing. Gently add the tuna with its juices and arrange in as pretty and airy a manner as possible on 4 appetizer plates. Serve immediately with lots of crusty bread.

Roast quail with watercress

The refreshing taste of watercress has long been used to accompany the lighter types of game such as pheasant, partridge or quail. It works particularly well combined with the heat of paprika and the fresh taste of lemon. Here is a modern version of a traditional dish. The delicate flavour of quail benefits from a light marinade. (Serves 4)

8 quail, whole or boned	salt and freshly ground black
4 tablespoons olive oil	pepper
3 cloves garlic, crushed	55g/2oz softened butter
1 lemon, finely grated and	140g/5oz ready prepared
juiced	watercress
2 teaspoons paprika	

Trim the quail by cutting off their wing tips. Place in a shallow bowl with the olive oil, garlic, lemon zest and juice and mix thoroughly. Allow to marinate for 30 minutes.

Meanwhile beat the paprika, salt and pepper into the butter and set aside. Wash and, if necessary, trim the watercress before drying.

Preheat the oven to its highest setting. Remove the quail from their marinade and lightly season. Roast for 10–15 minutes. They should be faintly pink and juicy when ready. After the first 5 minutes liberally coat them in the paprika butter. Baste once again after a further 5 minutes.

As soon as they are ready, arrange the watercress on a warm serving platter (or individual plates) and sit the cooked quail on top. Spoon over the aromatic, buttery juices and serve immediately.

Roast pears with Stilton and watercress

A classic modern British salad that can be served as either a starter or a savoury. It is particularly good eaten with crusty walnut bread. (Serves 4)

Roast pears
½ tablespoon walnut oil
200g/7oz ripe Stilton
4 ripe pears, for example,
　　Passa Crassana or Rocha
1 tablespoon lemon juice

Salad
1 curly endive
1 bunch watercress or a
　　75g/3oz ready-prepared
　　packet

55g/2oz walnut halves,
　　roughly broken
1 tablespoon champagne or
　　white wine vinegar
3 tablespoons walnut oil
salt and freshly ground black
　　pepper

Pre-heat the oven to 220°C/425°F/gas 7 and brush a baking dish with walnut oil. Mash the cheese with a fork and season to taste with freshly ground black pepper.

Carefully core the first pear using an apple corer. Then peel and cut in half lengthways before tossing in the lemon juice. Repeat with the remaining pears. Arrange them in a baking dish, cut side up, and stuff their cavities with the mashed cheese.

Place in the oven and bake for 20 minutes or until the pears are lightly cooked and covered in bubbling golden cheese. Meanwhile, clean the endive and watercress. Roughly tear the endive leaves and trim the watercress stalks, and place in a bowl with the walnut kernels. Whisk together the vinegar and walnut oil and season to taste. As soon as the pears are ready, dress the leaves and divide between 4 plates. As you plate the pear halves, scrape up all the lovely crusty melted cheese and serve immediately.

See also
Avocado, bacon and shrimp salad (page 261)
Leek and watercress roulade (page 166)

APPENDIX

Note: If a recipe states 'Take 225g/8oz pastry', it means the amount of pastry obtained by using 225g/8oz flour.

Shortcrust pastry

Shortcrust pastry is very easy to make and freezes well. (Makes 225g/8oz pastry)

225g/8oz plain flour	115g/4oz cold unsalted butter
½ teaspoon salt	cold water

Quick method
Place the flour and salt in a food processor and give a quick whiz to mix and lighten. Cut the butter into small cubes and add to the flour. Start the processor, stopping frequently to check the consistency of the butter and flour. Stop as soon as the butter and flour have turned into fine crumbs. If you over-process they will become a paste, which will make your pastry very short.

Transfer the mixture to a mixing bowl and cautiously add a little cold water. Mix with a fork, adding a little more water, if necessary, until the crumbs begin to form themselves into larger balls of dough. At this stage place the dough on a scantily floured surface and lightly knead by hand. Wrap in clingfilm, greaseproof paper or foil and refrigerate for 30 minutes. Roll when needed.

Manual method
Sift the flour and salt into a large mixing bowl. Cut the butter into very small dice and add. Using your fingertips, lightly rub the butter into the flour until it forms fine breadcrumbs. Then add the cold water and continue as above.

Suet pastry

Suet pastry should be made just before it is needed, never in advance, as water and heat trigger the raising agents in the flour. (Makes 225g/8oz pastry)

225g/8oz self-raising flour	85g/3oz shredded suet
½ level teaspoon salt	140ml/¼ pint cold water
55g/2oz diced butter, chilled	

Check that your saucepan can hold the pudding basin with a tight-fitting lid. Then pour enough water into the saucepan to reach half-way up the empty basin. Remove and bring the water to the boil. Carefully butter or oil the pudding basin so that it will not stick on being turned out.

Sift the flour and salt into a mixing bowl. Rub the butter into the flour until it forms fine breadcrumbs, then mix in the suet before stirring in the water with a fork. Turn the dough out onto a scantily floured work surface and lightly knead until the mixture becomes smooth and supple.

Remove a quarter of the dough for the lid. Roll this out to about 5mm/¼ inch thickness and press the rim of the basin lightly into it. Cut around the inside of this indentation and set aside, covered by a tea towel.

Shape the remaining dough into a circle large enough to line the pudding basin. Sprinkle with flour and fold in half, and then half again, so that the pastry forms a triangle. Lift this over the basin and gently press against the sides, so that it acts as a neat lining. You may need to cut away the odd extra fold – if so just reseal by firmly pressing the dough together.

Fill the basin up to 1–2.5cm/½–1 inch of the rim with whatever filling you choose and then flip over the excess pastry. Brush this with water and then cover with the lid and press firmly to seal. Place a fitted circle of buttered greaseproof paper on top.

To cover the basin, take a square of foil and fold a pleat down the centre so that the pudding can rise. Place over the basin and press down the sides. Then take a good length of string and loop it over so that double the length can go round the pudding basin, just beneath the rim. Thread the string through its own loop, pull back as tightly as you can, and bring the string round to the opposite side. Tie in a firm knot.

Steamed puddings are extremely difficult to remove from a bubbling hot pan. One solution is to make two long strips of foil, folded over several times for extra strength. Place these in a cross, sit the basin on the cross, and then pull up the foil ribbons over the top and twist together to form a handle.

At this point lower the pudding into the pan of boiling water and cover.

Keep the water at a gentle boil throughout the cooking time. You will need to check the water level regularly and replenish with boiling water. It must never run dry or the pudding will burn and the basin may crack when the water is added. Cook an 850ml/1½ pint pudding for 2 hours if your savoury filling has already been partially cooked.

When you are ready to turn the pudding out, remove from the water and allow to sit for a couple of minutes before removing the foil and greaseproof paper. Place a warm serving plate over the top and invert the two together, giving a few gentle shakes until you feel the pudding slip out.

Puff pastry

Whenever I make puff pastry I always wonder why I don't do it more often. The reason is simple; it requires a certain amount of planning as it needs time to chill between each rolling. However, it is well worth the effort. (Makes 225g/8oz)

225g/8oz plain flour	225g/8oz unsalted butter
½ teaspoon salt	140ml/¼ pint cold water

Sift the flour and salt into a large mixing bowl and rub in 30g/1oz cold butter. This can be quickly processed in a food processor. Mix in by hand about 140ml/¼ pint of cold water and then gently knead into a dough on a lightly floured work surface. Wrap in clingfilm and refrigerate for 30 minutes. Remember to leave out the remaining 200g/7oz butter, so that it can soften.

Flatten the butter into a 2.5cm/1 inch thick rectangle. Roll out the dough on a floured surface into a rectangle that is 3 times the length of the butter and about 2.5cm/1 inch wider than the width of the butter. Place the butter in the centre of the dough and then fold over each dough flap, so that the butter is completely covered. Using the rolling pin, lightly press down on each edge so that the butter is sealed in. Give the dough a half-turn clockwise.

Using short sharp strokes, roll out the dough so that it returns to its previous length (3 times that of the butter) but retains the same thickness. Then fold over the 2 ends as though they were covering the butter, press the edges with the rolling pin and give a further half-turn clockwise. If the butter is breaking through the pastry or the pastry is becoming warm, stop, wrap and refrigerate for a further 30 minutes. If not, you can repeat the rolling process one more time before resting the dough. Make a note of which way the pastry is facing before chilling, as you will need to continue with the clockwise half-turns.

After resting the pastry, replace on the floured surface in the position that you left off and continue with a further 2 rolls and half-turns. Refrigerate for another 30 minutes and then continue with 2 more rolls and half-turns. Wrap and refrigerate until needed or divide into 2 and freeze.

Chicken stock

A darker, richer flavoured chicken stock can be achieved by roasting the bones and vegetables before simmering as described for the lamb stock on page 146.

2 raw chicken carcasses
½ bottle white wine
2 leeks, coarsely chopped
2 outer sticks celery
2 large carrots, coarsely
chopped

4 shallots, peeled and coarsely
chopped
2 cloves garlic
1 bouquet garni (parsley,
thyme, bay leaf, clove)
4 black peppercorns

Put all the ingredients in a large saucepan and cover with cold water. Bring to the boil, and as soon as any scum appears, skim off and reduce the temperature. Simmer over a low heat for a good 4 hours, skimming occasionally if necessary. Ideally, the stock should throw up gentle bubbles; if it boils too vigorously it will make a cloudy stock, as tiny globules of fat and food particles will become suspended in the liquid. Gentle cooking allows the fat to float to the top and the food particles to sink to the bottom.

Once the stock tastes good, remove from the heat and strain into a large bowl. Leave to cool in the coldest place you can find. Once it is cold, you will be able to skim off any excess fat from its surface. Then pour into clean containers, leaving any sediment in the bottom of the bowl. Cover and chill or freeze.

Vegetable stock

This is a delicious recipe that can be used as a replacement for chicken or fish stock. (Makes 2 litres/3½ pints)

2 litres/3½ pints water
2 litres/3½ pints dry white
  wine
4 ripe tomatoes
2 leeks, coarsely chopped
2 large carrots, coarsely
  chopped
1 celeriac root, peeled and
  coarsely chopped

2 large onions, coarsely
  chopped
1 head garlic, cut into 2
1 bouquet garni (parsley,
  thyme, bay leaf)
6 black peppercorns
2 cloves
a tiny pinch of salt

Put all the ingredients in a large saucepan. Bring to the boil. Skim off any scum, then gently simmer uncovered for 3 hours, stirring from time to time.

Strain the stock through a sieve. The liquid should have reduced by half. Add salt to taste.

USEFUL SOURCES

If you are trying to locate indigenous food, it is worth contacting one of the following offices. They can direct you to their local producers, whether it be an eel smoker or a lavender grower. For particularly difficult problems, contact Food from Britain, as this is the umbrella organization.

Food from Britain
123 Buckingham Palace Road
London SW1W 9SA
Telephone: 0171 233 5111

A Taste of the South East
Brinsbury College
North Heath
Pulborough
West Sussex RH20 1DL
Telephone: 01798 874250
Covers Surrey and Sussex

A Taste of Ulster
Room 550
Dundonald House
Upper Newtownards Road
Belfast BT4 3SB
Northern Ireland
Telephone: 01232 524162

Hampshire Fare
PO Box 211
Winchester
Hampshire SO23 8WB
Telephone: 01962 845999

Kentish Fare
Kent County Council
Springfield
Maidstone
Kent ME14 2LL
Telephone: 01622 671411

Middle England Fine Foods
NFU Offices
22 Springfields
Camel Gate
Spalding
Lincolnshire PE12 6ET
Telephone: 01775 712141
Covers Derbyshire, Leicestershire, Lincolnshire, Northamptonshire and Nottinghamshire

North West Fine Foods
Old Council Offices
High Street
Garstang
Preston
Lancashire PR3 1FU
Telephone: 01995 600073
Covers Cheshire, Cumbria, Greater Manchester, Lancashire and Merseyside

Scottish Enterprise
Food Team
120 Bothwell Street
Glasgow G2 7JP
Scotland
Telephone: 0141 248 2700

Taste of the West
Agriculture House
Pynes Hill
Rydon Lane
Exeter
Devon EX2 5ST
Telephone: 01392 440745
Covers Cornwall, Devon, Dorset, Gloucestershire, Somerset and Wiltshire

Tastes of Anglia
Charity Farmhouse
Otley
Ipswich
Suffolk IP6 9EY
Telephone: 01473 785883
Covers Bedfordshire, Cambridgeshire, Essex, Hertfordshire, Norfolk and Suffolk

Welsh Food Promotions
The Food Hall
Royal Welsh Show Ground
Llanelwedd
Builth Wells
Powys LD2 3SY
Wales
Telephone: 01982 552952

Yorkshire Pantry
Economic Development Centre
North Yorkshire County Council
Northallerton
Yorkshire DL7 8AH
Telephone: 01609 780780

SELECT BIBLIOGRAPHY

Eliza Acton, *Modern Cookery for Private Families* (1855), Southover Press, 1993.

Isabella Beeton, *Beeton's Book of Household Management* (1861), Chancellor Press, 1994.

Frances Bissell, *A Cook's Calendar*, Papermac, 1985.

Maggie Black, *A Taste of History*, British Museum Press, 1993.

Joanna Blythman, *The Food We Eat*, Michael Joseph, 1996.

Lizzie Boyd, *British Cookery*, Helm, 1988.

Catherine Brown, *Broths to Bannocks*, John Murray, 1993.

Catherine Brown, *Scottish Cookery*, Chambers, 1985.

Edward Bunyard, *The Anatomy of Dessert*, Chatto & Windus, 1929.

Robert Carrier, *The Robert Carrier Cookery Course*, Sphere Books, 1976.

Cassell's Dictionary of Cookery, Cassell & Company Ltd, 1899.

Terence and Caroline Conran, *The Cook Book*, Mitchell Beazley, 1982.

Margaret Costa, *Four Seasons Cookery Book*, Grub Street, 1996.

Elizabeth David, *An Omelette and a Glass of Wine*, Penguin, 1986.

Elizabeth David, *Spices, Salt and Aromatics in the English Kitchen*, Penguin, 1970.

Elizabeth David, *Summer Cooking* (1955), Penguin, 1965.

Alan Davidson, *North Atlantic Seafood* (1979), Penguin, 1980.

J.C. Drummond and Anne Wilbraham, *The Englishman's Food* (1939), Pimlico, 1994.

Farmhouse Fare, Hulton Press, 1950.

Theodora FitzGibbon, *A Taste of Wales*, J.M. Dent & Sons Ltd, 1971.

Hannah Glasse, *The Art of Cookery Made Plain and Easy* (1747), Prospect Books, 1983.

Good Housekeeping Complete Book of Preserving, Ebury Press, 1991.

Jane Grigson, *English Food*, Penguin, 1981.

Jane Grigson, *Fish Cookery*, Penguin, 1975.

Jane Grigson, *Good Things*, Penguin, 1977.

Jane Grigson, *Jane Grigson's Fruit Book*, Michael Joseph, 1982.

Jane Grigson, *Jane Grigson's Vegetable Book* (1978), Penguin, 1980.

Dorothy Hartley, *Food in England* (1954), MacDonald, 1964.

Joy Larkcom, *Oriental Vegetables*, John Murray, 1991.

Joy Larkcom, *Vegetables for Small Gardens*, Hamlyn, 1995.

Mrs C.F. Leyel and Miss Olga Hartley, *The Gentle Art of Cookery* (1929), Graham Watson, 1947.

Caroline Liddell and Robin Weir, *Ices*, Grub Street, 1995.

Lady Llanover, *The First Principles of Good Cookery* (1867), Brefi Press, 1991.

Richard Mabey, *Food for Free*, HarperCollins, 1992.

Robert May, *The Accomplisht Cook* (1685), Prospect Books, 1994.

F. Marian McNeill, *The Scots Kitchen* (1929), Mercat Press, 1993.

Jekka McVicar, *Jekka's Complete Herb Book*, Kyle Cathie, 1994.

Joan Morgan and Alison Richards, *The Book of Apples*, Ebury Press, 1993.

Mary Norwak, *English Puddings Sweet & Savoury*, Grub Street, 1996.

Sarah Paston-Williams, *The Art of Dining*, National Trust, 1993.

Molly Perham, *Yorkshire Country Recipes*, Ravette Books, 1988.

Roger Phillips, *Wild Food*, Pan Books, 1983.

Reader's Digest, *The Cookery Year*, 1981.

F.A. Roach, *Cultivated Fruits of Britain Their Origin and History*, Basil Blackwell, 1986.

Elizabeth Rundell, *Modern Domestic Cookery*, 1853.

Roseanne Sanders, *The English Apple*, Phaidon Press, 1988.

The Scottish Women's Rural Institutes Cookery Book, 1946.

Eliza Smith, *The Compleat Housewife* (1758), Studio Editions, 1994.

Constance Spry and Rosemary Hume, *The Constance Spry Cookery Book*, Weidenfeld & Nicolson, 1994.

Richard Stein, *English Seafood Cookery*, Penguin, 1988.

Katie Stewart, *The Times Cookery Book*, Pan Books, 1972.

Thomas Tusser 1557 Floruit His Good Points of Husbandry, Country Life, 1931.

Florence White, *Flowers as Food*, Jonathan Cape, 1934.

Florence White, *Good Things in England* (1932), Jonathan Cape, 1951.

C. Anne Wilson, *Food and Drink in Britain*, Constable, 1973.

INDEX